Explanation Patterns

Understanding Mechanically and Creatively

ROGER C. SCHANK

Yale University

LEA LAWRENCE ERLBAUM ASSOCIATES, PUBLISHERS
1986   Hillsdale, New Jersey   London

Lawrence Erlbaum Associates, Inc., Publishers
365 Broadway
Hillsdale, New Jersey 07642

Library of Congress Cataloging in Publication Data

Schank, Roger C., 1946–
   Explanation patterns.

   Bibliography: p.
   1. Artificial intelligence. 2. Cognition. I. Title.
Q335.S3863 1986   006.3   86–19872
ISBN 0–89859–768–4

Printed in the United States of America
10 9 8 7 6 5 4 3 2

Contents

Preface

In the age of the computer, conjecture about things mechanical has naturally led to the question of whether machines can think. As the emphasis on Artificial Intelligence (AI) has grown rapidly, questions about machine intelligence have begun to have a certain urgency. There is, at the same time, an opposite, almost whimsical type of question that arises when one begins to consider whether machines can think, namely, *Can people think?*

People seem willing enough to grant machines the possibility of doing calculations of tremendous complexity with utmost ease. They seem willing to believe that machines will be able to talk, walk, hear, and evaluate, but when it comes to the possibility that machines might be creative, on their own, most people deny the possibility? Why? What magic power do we believe people to possess that we also believe machines to be inherently incapable of possessing?

This is why the question of whether machines can think is actually one of whether people can think, or, to put this another way, if the present pursuit of algorithms that describe the process of thinking in sufficient detail actually enables a machine to emulate that process, we can expect, based on past reactions to machine intelligence, that people will begin to worry about the nature of their own humanness. If a machine can do something "human," then that "something" has been reduced to a mere mechanical process that no longer seems worth doing.

The question we are concerned with in this book is: If we can find a set of processes that machines can slavishly follow, and if by so doing, these machines can come up with creative thoughts, what would that tell us about human beings? If the machine's procedure was adapted from a human procedure, that is, if all the machine was doing was what we know people are doing, would we abandon our inherent skepticism about the abilities of machines, or would we demystify our inherent admiration for things human?

In a sense, these are the issues I deal with in this book. I say "in a sense" because this book is no way a philosophical treatise. Rather it is an exercise in Artificial Intelligence and in Cognitive Science. It is an attempt to come to understand one of the most complex problems of mind by examining some of the mechanisms of mind: to define the apparatus that underlies our ability to think. In other words, this book is about people. But, it is not only about people, it is about simulating people doing what they consider to be their most human-specific act, *being creative.* Thus, it is also a book about machines and machine-capabilities.

Why discuss creativity at all? Why, in an era of great difficulty in getting machines to do the simplest understanding tasks, should one even begin to consider creativity, certainly one of the most complex issues of all? My premise is that the simplest mental tasks and the most complex of mental tasks are all interrelated. Understanding the simplest sentence is a creative act. Seen as a simple process involving merely the syntactic parsing of a sentence, it is hard to see where the creativity might lie. But, understanding a sentence also involves relating what you have understood to what you already knew, and that task involves memory search. Memory search, as I attempted to show in Schank (1982) involves learning since memory is never quite the same as it was the last time it was used and will not be the same after the new sentence is processed. And, learning involves creativity since it isn't always so clear what should be learned. All these things are really part of the same process. Thus it follows that AI will never exist in any important way until machines are capable of some basic creativity.

This premise has been at the base of most of the work being done at the Yale AI laboratory in recent years. I wish to thank my graduate students who have helped me formulate these ideas by serving as a sounding board, by writing programs based on these ideas, by revising some of these ideas with their own better worked out ones, and by reading and commenting on the manuscript. I also wish to thank the Advanced Research Projects Agency of the Department of Defense, the Air Force Office of Scientific Research, the Office of Naval Research, and the National Science Foundation for its support of this work.

To Joshua
who is more creative
than today's computers

1 The Explanation Game

THE TURING TEST

The question of whether machines can think is perhaps a bit tired at this point in the history of computing, but the question of what would be required in order to make machines think is just beginning to be explored. Of course, each question relates to the other, so, in order to begin the process of building a thinking machine, we must consider not only if such a project is possible, but also what elements of the human thinking process are inextricably bound up with our sense of what we mean when we talk about a thinking machine. To build a machine with Artificial Intelligence, we must come to understand, in a profound way, what it means to have intelligence. For years, researchers in AI could content themselves with adding yet another cute feature to their programs, allowing machines to do new things, one by one. But, it is becoming increasingly clear that to really make intelligent machines, as opposed to machines that exhibit one or two aspects of intelligence, one must attack the basic issues of the nature of human thought and intelligence head on.

There have, of course, been many discussions of machine thought, by far the most famous of these by the British mathematician, Alan Turing (Turing, 1963), when computers were in their infancy. Turing proposed a test, which he called the Imitation Game, that has become a common but often misunderstood way of judging the ability of a machine to understand. Turing's major argument was that the question of whether a machine can think is meaningless. He suggested the following alternative: If a person failed to distinguish between a man imitating a woman (via teletype) and a computer imitating a man imitating a woman, then the machine succeeded in the Imitation Game. Turing argued that success in this game was, in the long run, inevitable.

What Turing actually said, and what has been made of it, have not always been the same thing. He did not say that machines are thinking if they played the Imitation Game successfully. He merely said that successful imitation was the real issue for computer scientists. In the subsequent history of Artificial Intelligence, two general lines of argument on this issue have developed. One has been that machines will never duplicate human thought processes; the other is that no matter how well machines imitate human behavior, they cannot be said to truly understand in the same way as a human being. To put this another way, the claims made are first, **that the Turing test will never be passed;** and second, that **even if it is passed, it does not prove that machines understand.** Of course, Turing himself disagreed with the first claim; he regarded the second one as meaningless.

It is now more than thirty years since Turing's paper. With the exception of Kenneth Colby (Colby, 1975), a psychiatrist who found that other psychiatrists could not tell his computer version of a paranoid from the real thing, no researcher has claimed that he has created a program that would pass the Turing test. And, no matter how many times people have affirmed that Turing was correct in his assessment of the validity of the question, it has failed to go away. Further, there is little reason to believe that it will go away. No achievement in building intelligent software can dispel it because there are always those who believe that there is something more to the nature of intelligence than any amount of software displays.

Critics of Artificial Intelligence seem always to be able to "move the line" that must be crossed. "It would be intelligent if it did X" is nearly always followed by "No, that was wrong; it would be intelligent if it did Y" when X has been achieved. But the problem of the ultimate possibility of an intelligence that is different from our own and possibly even superior to our own, embodied in something not made of flesh and blood, will not be determined by critics with arbitrary standards. It is time to look again at the twin questions of the criteria for the ultimate *thinking ability of computer programs* and the nature of what is meant by understanding.

ON MEN AND WOMEN

One of the interesting, if not serendipitous, facets of Turing's Imitation Game is that, in its initial conception, the problem is to find the difference between a man and a woman via teletype. The seeming implicit assumption is that there are differences between men and women that are discernable by teletype. On the other hand, given that the problem is merely to get the computer to do as well at the Imitation Game as the man did, and assuming that there is no difference between men and women that would be recognizable via teletype, the task of the machine is to duplicate a human in its answers. Thus, Turing's test doesn't actually depend upon men and women being discernably different. But, the nature of what it means to understand may best be illustrated by that distinction.

To see what I mean, let us consider the question of whether men can really understand women, (or alternatively, whether women can really understand men). It is common enough in everyday experience for men and women to both claim that they really do not understand their opposite number. What can they mean by this? And, most importantly, how is what they mean by it related to the problem of determining whether computers can understand?

When the claim is made that men and women are really quite different (mentally, not physically), what is presumably meant is that they have different beliefs, different methods of processing information, different styles of reasoning, different value systems, and so on. (It is not my point here to comment on the validity of these assertions. I am simply attempting to use the principle of these assertions in my argument. These same assertions might be made about different ethnic groups, cultures, nations and so on; I am simply using Turing's domain.)

The claim that I assume is not being made by such assertions is that men and women have different physical instantiations of their mental processes. (Of course, it is possible that men and women do have brains that differ physically in important respects, but that would be irrelevant for this argument.) So, what is it that makes men and women feel they have difficulty understanding each other? Empathy. Understanding involves empathy. It is easier to understand someone who has had similar experiences—and who, because of those experiences, has developed similar values, beliefs, memory structures, rules-of-thumb, goals, and ideologies—than to understand someone with very different types of experiences.

Understanding consists of processing incoming experiences in terms of the cognitive apparatus one has available. This cognitive apparatus has a physical instantiation (the brain, or the hardware of the computer) and a mental instantiation (the mind, or the software of the computer). When an episode is being processed, a person brings to bear the totality of his cognitive apparatus to attempt to understand it. What this means in practice is that people understand things in terms of their particular memories and experiences. People who have different goals, beliefs, expectations and general life styles will understand identical episodes quite differently.

Therefore, no two people understand in exactly the same way or with exactly the same result. The more different people are from one another, the more their perception of their experiences will differ. On the other hand, when people share certain dimensions of experience, they will tend to perceive similar experiences in similar ways. Thus, men tend to understand certain classes of experiences in ways that are different from women.

It is unlikely that an experience that in no way bears upon one's sex will be understood differently by men and women. Recall that the assumption here is that the baseline cognitive apparatus is the same regardless of sex. Any experience that does relate to the sex of the observer in some way will be processed differently. This can involve obvious issues, such as the observance of an argument between a man and a woman. There, we would expect a man to observe the episode from the point of view of the man and a woman to observe it from the point of view of the woman. In addition, such identification with different characters in a situation can extend to observations of situations where the feuding characters are of the same sex, but one displays attributes more traditionally male and the other displays traditional female behavior. Identification, and thus perception, can thus be altered by one's understanding of the goals, beliefs, or attitudes underlying or perceived to underlie the behavior of the characters in an episode one is observing.

Thus, for example, one's perception of the validity and purpose behind a war can be altered by whether one is the mother of a son who is about to be drafted or whether one previously fought in a war and found it an ennobling experience. In general, one's sense of what is important in life affects every aspect of one's understanding of events.

The claim then, is that men and women, as examples of one division of human beings, do not, and really cannot, understand each other. The same argument can be put forward, with more or less success, depending upon the issue under consideration, with respect to Arabs and Israelis or intellectuals and blue collar workers. In each of these cases, differing values can cause differing perceptions of the world.

COMPUTERS AND PEOPLE

Now let us return to the question of whether computers can understand. What exactly does it mean to claim that an entity—either a person or a machine—has understood? On the surface, it appears that there are two different kinds of understanding to which people commonly refer. We talk about understanding another human being, or animal, and we talk about understanding what someone has told us or what we have seen or read. This suggests that there are actually two different issues to confront when we talk about computers understanding people. One is to determine whether computers will ever really understand people in the deep sense of being able to identify with them or empathize with them. The other is whether computers will be able to comprehend a news story, interact in a conversation or process a visual scene. This latter sense of understanding comprises the arena in which AI researchers choose to do battle. Often the critics of AI (e.g. Weizenbaum, 1976; Dreyfuss, 1972) choose to do battle in the former.

In fact, these two seemingly disparate types of understanding are really not so different. They are both aspects of the same continuum. Examining both of them allows us to see what the ultimate difficulty in AI is likely to be and what problems AI researchers will have to solve in order to create machines that understand.

Weizenbaum claims (Weizenbaum, 1976) that a computer will never be able to understand a shy young man's desperate longing for love, expressed in his dinner invitation to the woman who is the potential object of his affection, because a computer lacks experience in human affairs of the heart. In some sense this seems right. We cannot imagine that machines will ever achieve that sort of empathy because we realize how difficult it is for people who have not been in a similar situation to achieve that level of understanding. In other words, Weizenbaum's statement is, in some sense, equivalent to saying that no person can understand another person without having experienced feelings and events similar to those one is attempting to understand. Where does this leave the poor computer? Where does this leave a child? Where does this leave a happily married man who met his wife when they were both small children and married her when they graduated high school, before he ever had to cope with asking her out to dinner?

Weizenbaum is correct as far as he goes, but he misses a key point. Understanding is not an all-or-none affair. People achieve degrees of understanding in different situations, depending upon their level of familiarity with those situations. Is it reasonable to expect a level of empathy from a machine that is greater than the level of empathy we expect from human beings?

The important point for researchers in AI, psychology, or philosophy, is not whether machines will ever equal humans in their understanding capabilities. The important scientific questions are about people, not computers. What processes does a person go through when he is attempting to understand? How does our recognition that understanding involves empathy and the ability to relate and draw upon common experiences help us to better understand the nature of mental processes? It is this issue that is of primary importance.

So, there are really three main questions:

How can we understand enough about the nature of what it means to understand so that we can make the issue of comprehension, by people or computers, more concrete?

How can we get a better grasp on exactly how particular experiences affect the understanding process?

What abilities must a machine have before it could possibly be considered to be intelligent?

This book is about the second and third of these questions, but this chapter is about the first. Understanding involves a multiplicity of types and levels of understanding; and different people understand things differently. These statements are obvious and seemingly well-known. But in reality, AI research, as well as criticism of that research and expectations about the progress of that research, has proceeded as if those facts were hardly even viable possibilities. Explaining how a better understanding of what is involved in being intelligent can change our view of what AI is, and perhaps even what psychology should be, is the goal of this book.

THE NATURE OF UNDERSTANDING

The easiest way to understand the nature of understanding is to think of it in terms of a spectrum. At the far end of the spectrum we have what I call COMPLETE EMPATHY. This is the kind of understanding that might obtain between twins, very close brothers, very old friends, and other such combinations of very similar people.

At the opposite end of the spectrum we have the most minimal form of understanding, which I call MAKING SENSE. This is the point where events that occur in the world can be interpreted by the understander in terms of a coherent (although probably incomplete) picture of how those events came to pass.

Now let us step back for a moment. Before we complete this spectrum, it would be worthwhile to discuss both what the spectrum actually represents and what the relevance of current AI research is to this spectrum.

There is a point on this spectrum that describes how an **understander** copes with events outside his control. The end points of this spectrum can be loosely described as, on the one hand, the understander saying to himself, yes, I see what is going on here, it makes some sense to me, and, on the other hand, his saying, of course, that's exactly what I would have done, I know precisely how you feel.

In our recent research (for example, Schank & Riesbeck, 1981; Schank, 1982) we have been concerned with the nature of understanding because we are trying to get computers to read and process stories. In the course of that research, we have considered various human situations that we wished to model. We built various **knowledge structures,** that attempt to characterize the knowledge people have of various situations. The restaurant script, for example (Schank & Abelson, 1977), was used in an attempt to **understand** restaurant stories, and it was that script which prompted Weizenbaum's criticism about understanding *love in a restaurant*. Since that earlier research we have come to realize that these knowledge structures function best if they are dynamic. That is, they must be able to change as a result of new experiences. In other words, we expect that as knowledge is used, it changes. Or, to put this another way, as we undergo experiences we learn from them.

At the core of such an hypothesis is the notion that in attempting to understand we are attempting to relate our new experiences to our prior experiences by utilizing knowledge structures that contain those previous experiences. Consider, for example, the following situation. Imagine that you are hungry and that someone suggests a marvelous restaurant to you called Burger King. You happily go to this restaurant, armed as you always are, with a set of expectations about what will happen there. Specifically, you expect that you will: **ENTER; BE SEATED; GET & READ MENU; ORDER; BE SERVED; EAT; PAY;** and **EXIT.** The items written in bold face are called *scenes* and can be best understood as bundles of expectations themselves that concern the particulars of how those scenes will actually take place. The assertion put forth in Schank (1982) is that such scenes are derived from experience and are subject to constant change by experience.

You were told that you were going to a restaurant, so you brought out your Memory Organization Package (or MOP) for restaurants (M-RESTAURANT) that told you what scenes to expect. What you find in Burger King, however, is a different sort of thing altogether. The order of scenes is ENTER; ORDER (without a menu exactly); PAY; SERVE (but it doesn't look much like the other SERVE); BE SEATED (but on your own); EAT; LEAVE. So what is a processor to do?

The obvious thought is that you have been fooled. This is not a restaurant at all. Or maybe this is just a weird restaurant. Without other evidence, it is hard to know what to do. What a processor can do is mark the expectation failures. That is, we expected that scenes would come in a certain order, and we expected that scenes would proceed in a certain manner, but they didn't. What we do in this case is to index the exceptions so that we will be able to recognize them when they occur again.

Now suppose that after you complain to your friend about Burger King, he suggests that you try another restaurant, called McDonald's, instead. You are confronted with a new situation which you must attempt to "understand." And it is reasonable to say that you have understood McDonald's if you recall the Burger King experience (in other words, are reminded of Burger King) and use it to help create expectations about what will happen next. The key point, however, is what happens to your memory as a result of these two experiences.

You have now encountered two exceptions to a MOP that were themselves quite similar. It is reasonable, therefore, to create a new MOP that has expectations in it that correspond to these new experiences. We might call that new MOP, M-FAST-FOOD. We can index this MOP as an exception to M-RESTAURANT so that it will be available to change and grow as new experiences relevant to it occur.

The important point here then is that when we are reminded of some event or experience in the course of undergoing a different experience, this reminding behavior is not random. We are reminded of this experience because the structures we are using to process this new experience are the same structures we are using to organize memory. Thus, we cannot help but pass through the old memories while processing a new input. There are an extremely large number of such high level memory structures. Finding the right one of these (that is, the one that is most specific to the experience at hand) is one of the things that we mean by understanding.

In other words, an important part of what we mean by understanding is the accessing of extant knowledge structures in which to place our new experiences. We feel that we have understood when we know where a new input *belongs* in memory. Sometimes understanding is more profound than that, however. The creation of new knowledge structures in memory is also part of understanding. Such structures are created in terms of old ones. The more these new structures differ from the old, the more complicated understanding can be.

In this view then, understanding is finding the closest higher level structure available to explain an input and creating a new memory structure for that input that is *in terms of* the old closely related higher level structure. Understanding is a process that has its basis in memory then, particularly memory for closely related experiences accessible through reminding and expressible through analogy. Further, the depth of understanding will increase if there are many available relevant personal experiences in terms of which inputs can be processed. Lastly, understanding means finding some memory, any memory at all sometimes, that will help one cope with an experience that initially seems novel. We want to feel that we have understood, and we feel that way to the extent that we can believe that what we have just seen really is like something else we have seen previously.

With this definition of the nature of understanding then, let us now return to our understanding spectrum.

THE SPECTRUM OF UNDERSTANDING

COMPLETE EMPATHY exists when individuals have many shared experiences that have in turn created very similar memory structures. The consequence of this is that, given a set of similar goals and beliefs, new episodes would be processed in the same way. The above caveat is very important. Similar experiences, but different goals and beliefs, would still result in differing perceptions of the events, or to put it another way, in a lack of COMPLETE EMPATHY in understanding of each other's actions.

The point to be made about the understanding spectrum then, is: **The more that goals, beliefs, and prior experiences and memories are shared, the more complete the level of understanding that can take place.** On the opposite end of the spectrum, MAKING SENSE involves finding out what events took place and relating them to a perception of the world that may be quite different from that in the mind of the actor in those events.

Let us now consider what may well be a midpoint on the understanding spectrum. We discussed earlier the problem of men and women understanding each other, in general. The point there was that despite a cognitive apparatus that was identical, something was preventing complete understanding. This mid-point I label COGNITIVE UNDERSTANDING. By this I mean that although a man may be able to build an accurate model of a given woman, he may still not really understand what her motivations, fears, and needs are. That is, he lacks COMPLETE EMPATHY with her, but he still understands a great deal about her. To claim that he doesn't understand her can only mean understanding in its deepest sense. Certainly by any measure of understanding less than COMPLETE EMPATHY he could rightly claim to understand what she does and not be accused by Weizenbaum of failing the understanding test.

Thus, there are obviously many different kinds of understanding. Where do computers fit in? The claim I want to make is that, given a spectrum as we have described:

MAKING SENSE—COGNITIVE UNDERSTANDING—COMPLETE EMPATHY

today's work on computer understanding can only reasonably claim the left half of the spectrum as its proper domain. It is a legitimate argument that computers will never understand, if what is meant by that is that they would be unlikely to understand much at the right hand side of the spectrum. Computers are not likely to feel the same way as people do, are not likely to have the same goals as people do, and will never, in fact, be people. Given that most people fail to understand each other at points on the right hand side of this spectrum, it seems no great loss to admit to the likely failure of computers to achieve this level of understanding. Computers are unlikely to do better than women at understanding men or vice versa.

On the other hand, computers can and will share some experiences with people. They may be able to read newspapers and build models of behavior almost as well as people do. And, perhaps most important (with respect to what follows in this book, in any case), computers should be capable of explaining unforeseen events in terms of their own experiences, even to the point of being creative in their interpretation of new events. In order for them to do this, we will have to learn a great deal more about what it means to understand.

In reading a news story about terrorism, just because the terrorist and I share the feature of being human (and even perhaps the same age and sex), it does not follow that I will understand the story better than a computer. It seems safe to say that I can understand such stories better than a computer can, as of now at least, but this is due to my experience with such stories and my general level of interest in human affairs, both political and sociological. If a computer were to attain a similar level of background knowledge and interest, it too would be able to understand such stories.

The real question is: Is it possible, and if so, exactly how would one go about, getting a machine to have such knowledge, cause the interaction of new knowledge with old knowledge to generate the need to know more, and use that need to know to guide its processing of news stories?

This is only one kind of processing, however, and is thus really an example of only one kind of understanding. Another kind of understanding is shown by what we have already done with respect to computers and newspapers. Cullingford (1978) in SAM, DeJong (1979) in FRUMP, Lebowitz (1980) in IPP, and Lytinen (1984) in MOPTRANS, all demonstrated computer programs that could process news stories at various levels. SAM summarized, answered questions, and translated a variety of fairly simple news stories. FRUMP did a more superficial analysis of a wider range of stories, providing summaries of the key points. IPP did an in-depth analysis of stories in one domain (terrorism), attempting to modify its memory and make generalizations from what it read. MOPTRANS also processed terrorism stories with an eye towards translating them from any of three or four languages into any other of those languages.

Did these programs understand? Certainly they performed some tasks that humans perform when they are said to be understanding. At the level of understanding measured by unsophisticated language comprehension tests, they understood in the sense that they could answer the who, what, where, and when questions. Is this understanding? Or, to really understand do we have to be much more sophisticated in our analysis of a story?

One things seems clear: understanding is not a yes or no, all or none affair. Granting that there are many levels to understanding, the key question for AI is not whether the levels we have already achieved can be construed to be examples of understanding, but rather how we can achieve the levels of understanding that are still eluding us. MAKING SENSE has been achieved by computers in certain domains. On the other side of the spectrum, it may well be the case that computers cannot, in principle, completely understand people, any more than men can completely understand women or vice versa. COMPLETE EMPATHY is just an end point on the continuum. There is a lot of space in between the end points. The real issue is not whether computers can understand, but how to make them understand better. To do this, we must get a better picture of what it means to understand.

How different are these three points on the spectrum in terms of what processes would be necessary in order to construct machines that met those criteria? What does a machine do in order to achieve the ability to MAKE SENSE, and what would it have to do in order to COGNITIVELY UNDERSTAND or show COMPLETE EMPATHY?

THE REVISED TURING TEST

Turing's Imitation Game has not left everyone in AI thrilled by the prospects of having to meet its criteria as a measure of success. Colby (1973) argued that his paranoid simulation program did indeed pass Turing's test. He found that psychiatrists who were presented with output from Colby's PARRY program and output in a similar form from an actual human patient, were unable to effectively distinguish between them. This *passing of the Turing test* failed to convince AI people that Colby's program *understood* or *thought,* nor should it have done so. Despite whatever validity Colby's program might have as a model of paranoia, it would seem that the failure of experts to distinguish between imitations and the real thing should not be taken as much more than a statement of the competence of the experts. In fact, in the case of the psychiatrists, the Imitation Game was a particularly poor test since a psychiatrist's choices upon facing a non-normal patient are not that extensive. PARRY was not brain-damaged or schizophrenic, so "paranoid" was, given the presence of a few paranoid signs, a reasonable diagnosis. What Colby seems to have done is effectively simulated various aspects of the output of a paranoid, which may or may not reflect accurate processes underlying the production of that output. The issue then, is one of the distinction between good output and good simulation.

Ideally, the test of an effective understanding system, if I may use that word, is not the realism of the output it produces, as Turing would have it, but rather the validity of the method by which that output is produced.

Unfortunately, we cannot create a test that depends upon the evaluation of methods for two reasons, one practical and one philosophical. The practical reason is that it is difficult to cut open either the machine or the human to see what is going on inside. Examination of hardware doesn't tell us much anyway. From a software point of view, people are extremely hard to test in a controlled experiment, given the wide range of their possible experiences prior to that experiment. Programs, on the other hand, are hard to evaluate with respect to establishing exactly what claims they are making.

The philosophical point is that we do not examine the innards of people in order to establish that they are understanding. It might seem that we grant them an ability to understand based on their humanity. But, it often happens, in schools, offices, and other places that do such evaluations, that we do assess a human's ability to understand. It seems sensible therefore, that the methods that are good for the human are also good for the computer.

To see what I mean here, let's consider the spectrum of understanding again. For the sake of argument, assume that it is possible, in theory, to produce a program that meets the output requirements of each of the three levels of understanding noted earlier. To make this argument more concrete, I list here some possible outputs for each of these points on the spectrum:

MAKING SENSE

input: news from the UPI wire

output: a summary of a newspaper story—a translation of a speech into another language

COGNITIVE UNDERSTANDING

input: a set of stories about airplane crashes, complete with data about the airplanes and the circumstances

output: a conclusion about what may have caused the crash derived from a theory of the physics involved and an understanding of the design of airplanes, used in conjunction with algorithms that can do creative explanation

COMPLETE EMPATHY

input: I was very upset by your actions last night.

output: I thought you might have been, it was a lot like the way you treated me last week.

input: But I meant you no harm.

output: Do you remember the way your father used to treat you on holidays when he made you call all your relatives? He meant no harm either.

input: I see what you mean.

output: I thought you might; there's no friend like an old friend.

Assuming that these input/output pairs are not entirely fanciful, I would now like to draw some conclusions about them that are reflective of my view of what a reasonable test should comprise. My conclusions are effectively summarized with the following words:

ACCURACY; SURPRISE; EMOTION

The claim I am making is, to the extent that output is an effective way of characterizing degree of understanding (although that is to a very limited extent indeed, it may well be our only choice), we can judge the significance of that output in terms of its place on the understanding spectrum with respect to the following features:

The extent that that output accurately accomplishes a task that a competent human could do.

The extent that that output characterizes an especially original or important result that most humans cannot easily accomplish.

The extent that that output effectively seems to replicate a real live human being with whom someone is familiar.

The above three standards reflect the essence of the three points on the understanding spectrum that I have been discussing.

Turing's Imitation Game then, can be seen, as a result of further insights into AI since the time that Turing first concerned himself with these issues, to be somewhat outdated. Merely fooling people is not the true task in AI. Rather we must, in addressing fundamental questions about the nature of intelligence, devise a set of requirements that any intelligent entity ought to be able to meet. And, if we are talking about intelligent beings with linguistic capabilities, any test we devise can have an added level of complexity. That is, the true value of language in an intelligence-testing framework is that we can transcend the limitations of only being able to get solutions to problems or answers to questions. Linguistically equipped intelligent beings can explain their own actions.

THE EXPLANATION TEST

In the end, any system, human or mechanical, is judged on its output. We do not take apart a human to look at his insides in an effort to establish that his understanding mechanisms are of the right sort. Nor is it clear what the right sort of mechanisms are. We are faced with a dilemma then. We cannot use output to tell us if a system really understands. On the other hand, output is all we can reasonably expect to get.

To resolve this dilemma we must address the question of self-awareness. The issue of consciousness is a vast one and I do not mean to address it here. Rather, I wish to claim that the fundamental difference between a system that can produce reasonable output and one that meets the criterion that is implicit in the term *understanding system* is that *an understanding system should be able to explain its own actions.*

One might ask: *explain its own actions to whom?* There are two answers to this question, each of them quite important in their own way. The first answer is, of course, **to those who inquire about how the system works.** The second answer is, **to itself.** It is this latter answer that represents the essence of the understanding process, although, quite naturally, it is the latter answer which is also the most difficult to assess.

A system that not only does interesting things, but can explain why it did them can be said to understand at any point on the understanding spectrum where that explanation is sufficient. In other words, being able to say what sequences of actions were followed in a chain of reasoning passes the explanation test at the level of **making sense.** SHRDLU (Winograd, 1972), MYCIN (Shortliffe et al., 1973) and other programs in AI therefore, can be said to understand at the level of making sense since they can explain why they did what they did to the extent of being able to describe the steps that they went through in performing their respective tasks.

SHRDLU manipulated blocks in a *blocks world* by responding to English commands. One of the most impressive aspects of that program was that when asked why the program had performed any given action, the program could respond with a causal sequence of actions. It could say that it had done X to do Y in order to do Z and so on. At the end of its chain of reasoning, it had only the initial command given by the user. In that case, it would respond, I did that because you asked me to. This latter response became well-known and was pschologically very appealing. (For example, Restak (1979) used the phrase "Because you asked me to" as the title of a chapter in a popular book on the brain. That chapter was on various aspects of AI and only touched upon Winograd's work.) Although it was not put this way at the time, one of the reasons that Winograd's program was much appreciated was because it *understood* at the MAKING SENSE level on the understanding spectrum. It understood its world of blocks as well as a human would. Now, it would not have passed Turing's test, because it understood nothing but blocks. But, I claim, it should be recognized as having passed the Explanation Test at the level of MAKING SENSE.

Each point on the understanding spectrum has essentially the same requirements in the Explanation Test. For COGNITIVE UNDERSTAND-ING, the program must be able to explain why it came to the conclusions it did, what hypotheses it rejected and why, how previous experiences influenced it to come up with its hypotheses and so on. We do not let a human being come up with innovative ideas, generalizations, correlations and so on, unless he can explain himself. Creative scientists are supposed to be able to tell us what they do—not what they do while they are being creative, but what the reasoning is behind what they have discovered. We may not expect Einstein to know how he came up with his creative ideas, but we certainly expect him to be able to explain the physics behind them. We will put up with unexplained brilliance for a while, but eventually we object, we believe that we are somehow being fooled. We cannot put up with a scientist who says: $E = MC^2$, *I don't know what that means, but I am sure it is true.* There is no reason why we should let a machine off more easily. The machine must be able to answer the question, *How do you know?* to the satisfaction of an examiner in a school who would expect no less from his students on a similar accomplishment in a similar domain.

The last point we have presented on our spectrum, that of COMPLETE EMPATHY, has no easier test. Any system purporting to satisfy this level of understanding must satisfy its examiner in the same way that a human would satisfy him in a similar situation. I am claiming that this is not likely in its fullest sense, and that this improbability is what all the uproar is about with respect to the assessment of the possibilities for Artificial Intelligence by laymen. No machine will have undergone enough experiences, and reacted to them in the same was as you did, to satisfy you that it *really understands* you. One is extremely lucky if one meets one person in one's lifetime who satisfies that criterion.

The second aspect of explanation is much more complex. What would it mean for a system to explain something to itself, and why does that matter? The argument put forward in this book is that what is important about understanding is how it changes over time. A machine that understands at the level of making sense fails to convince us that it really has understood because it continues to understand in the same way every time. The computer programs that we built at Yale during the 1970's, all had the feature, as do most AI programs, of behaving exactly the same way every time.

But, people, especially intelligent people, do not behave this way. They adapt to new circumstances by changing their behavior. How do they do this? The argument put forward in this book is that the method that they use for this adaptation is also based upon explanation, but explanation to oneself. Explaining something to yourself means, in essence, attempting to correct an initial misunderstanding by finding relevant experiences in one's memory that might account for the incomprehensible event. The result of such explanation can be a new understanding of old information as well. In other words, explanation, learning, and also creativity, are inextricably bound together.

To explain something to yourself at the making sense level, one need only find a relevant knowledge structure in which to place a new input. Seeing a new event as an instance of an old event constitutes understanding at a very simple level. But, trying to find the theory that explains a group of events can be a much more complicated and more profound type of understanding. Explaining a group of events to yourself can thus mean coming up with a theory of those events. Thus, cognitive understanding really requires a good grasp of what would constitute a reasonable explanation for something in general.

From the perspective of a test of a computer's understanding ability then, this spectrum allows us to set some criteria that will allow us to examine whether an understanding system is understanding by looking at that systems's powers of explanation. But, more important is a system's ability of self-explanation. That is, one cannot easily examine how a system changes itself as a result of its experiences, one can just observe it over time. But the claim is that the concept of explanation is key in bothe cases. Explaining the world, to others and to oneself, is, in essence, the heart of understanding.

QUESTIONS AND EXPLANATIONS

It was suggested by Riesbeck (personal communication) that one way to make the distinction between passing the Explanation Test at each level is to use the example of a joke. A computer understander that simply understood the joke, in that it could explain what had happened, would be understanding at the level of MAKING SENSE. A program that actually found the joke funny, to the extent that it could explain what expectations had been violated, what other jokes it knew that were like it that it was reminded of, and so on, would be understanding at the level of COGNI-TIVE UNDERSTANDING. Finally, a program that belly laughed because of how that joke related to its own particular experiences and really expressed a point of view about life that the program was only now realizing, would have understood at the level of COMPLETE EMPATHY. In all of these cases, perhaps the most important aspect of understanding is left untestable, however. Was the program changed in some way by the joke? This is not an irrelevant question for a person, nor should it be for a machine, though it might a bit difficult to answer in either case.

What will it take to get a machine to the level where it satisfies people that it understands at the level of COGNITIVE UNDERSTANDING? Or, to put this question another way, what is it that people do with each other that makes us believe that they are understanding at that level? The answer can, I believe be reduced to two words: **questions** and **explanations.**

People generate questions about those things that they did not fully understand. Sometimes those questions cause people to find explanations, sometimes novel and sometimes mundane, for the odd, unexpected, situations that they encounter. Sometimes those questions remain, to be answered at a later date, or to be combined with new explanations as the seeds of more creative explanations.

This book is about what it would take to achieve COGNITIVE UNDER-STANDING. But it is not a philosophical work. I am interested in how to push the level of intelligence that computers have already achieved to the next step. I am also interested in exactly what it is that people must be doing when they do intelligent things.

Because of that, this book is about questions and explanations. It is a book about people and machines. It addresses the questions of how humans formulate questions and how humans formulate explanations. The idea here is that if we can find out what it is that humans do when they are thinking and learning, then maybe we can model our machines on them.

The real intent of Artificial Intelligence, is, I claim, to find out what intelligence is all about. We tend to say that a person is intelligent to the extent that he is insightful, creative, and in general, able to relate apparently unrelated pieces of information to come up with a new way of looking at things. We tend to claim that a person is unintelligent to the extent that his behavior is thoroughly predictable with reference to what we know that he knows. Thus, when a person does things the way he was told to do them, never questioning and thus never creating new methods, we tend to see him as unintelligent.

I mention this here because I see the Explanation Test as a kind of intelligence test. We are not asking the computer to simply replicate intelligent behavior because we have no knowledge of which aspects of such behavior are more intelligent than others. Is composing a sonnet a more or less an intelligent act than playing chess? There is no way to answer this objectively because it isn't the acts themselves that are at issue here, but rather the quality of those acts. Turing could not differentiate between these feats because he did not have the experience of trying to build programs to do each task. But now, as a result of years of AI research, such a question is easier to answer.

We can make a program write bad sonnets or play poor chess fairly easily. Neither of these feats seem much of a mark of intelligence. Indeed, working on either of them would not be considered AI any more, although such work was done by AI researchers not so long ago. Today, work on computer poetry or computer chess falls within the domain of AI only to the extent that it mimics the complex cognitive processes associated with the creativity inherent in both acts. Thus, if the computer poetry program started with a set of feelings and was able, by relating such feelings to its personal experiences, to create poetry, particularly poetry of some new type, we would be legitimately impressed. Similarly, if our computer chess program was capable of improving its playing ability by inventing a new strategy or employing an old one that it recalled having seen in a match it knew about, that would be an AI-type feat.

We have come to understand in AI that it isn't the tasks themselves that are interesting. What matters is how they are done. Thus, I claim, the only way to know if our machines are intelligent is to make them do what we would expect a human to do in a similar situation. We must expect them to be able to explain how they did it. Furthermore, those explanations should have some connection with how the task in question actually was performed. Often this is a difficult task for people to perform. We do not always know where our creative powers come from or how they were employed in any given instance. But, we can attempt to give rational explanations. We should demand no less from machines.

HOW THE EXPLANATION TEST WORKS

It should be clear that there is no passing or failing of the explanation test as such. The reason for this is that the test refers to a continuum of understanding and thus it is possible to pass the test at one point and fail it at a point immediately to its right.

The test itself is simple. It revolves around the completion of a specific task. A mental task is given to a machine on the one hand, and a person on the other, as in Turing's Imitation Game. The interviewer is asked to question the machine or person about how each came up with the behavior that it or he did. If the interviewer judges one subject's answers to be more insightful and explanatory than the other's, then that subject is judged to have passed the Explanation Test. If that subject happens to be the machine, then the machine can be said to be understanding at the level of explanation that the task itself was rated. In other words the degree of passing is related to the complexity of the task.

As long as people give better explanations than machines for given tasks, then we can say they understand better than machines. When machines outstrip people in their explanatory ability, however, machines will be safely claimed to be better understanders, and hence more intelligent, than people in that area of knowledge. To give a simple example, machines can already out-computer humans. What they cannot do is explain the computation processes that they use because they do not understand them any better than a hand-held calculator can be said to understand its operations. Thus, while we might prefer to use a computer for our calculations, until we prefer to use a computer over a mathematician to explain the nature of the operations in mathematics, machines will not be able to pass the Explanation Test for mathematics. Here too, however, the different points on the spectrum are operating. We may be able to enable the machine to accurately explain what it does mathematically and thus achieve the MAKING SENSE level of explanation in mathematics. But, we would have to get a machine to understand why it did what it did to come up with some new mathematical idea in order to claim the COGNITIVE UNDERSTANDING level.

The Explanation Test then, is not really a question of imitation. Our question is not so much whether a person could fool us into believing that he is a machine or whether a machine could fool us into believing that it is a person. Rather, we are interested in finding out whether anybody or anything that we talk to can be coherent in its understanding and explanation; can be creative and self-referential in its understanding and explanation; can be truly insightful in its understanding and explanation; and can be thinking about things on its own.

To understand is to satisfy some basic desire to make sense of what one is processing, to learn from what one has processed, and to formulate new desires about what one wants to learn. Our question is how people do this and how machines might do this.

CHANGING MACHINES

The issue then is change. Intelligent beings change themselves as a result of experience. They accomplish this change through the process of attempting to explain what they do not understand. In other words, they change when a given change facilitates understanding. How can we get computers to change themselves over time? How can machines adapt to new experiences that they cannot initially understand? The answer I provide in this book can be expressed in three words: **Explanation, Questions,** and **Creativity.** The task is to get computers to explain things to themselves, to ask question about their experiences so as to cause those explanations to be forthcoming, and to be creative in coming up with explanations that have not been previously available.

During the course of processing a new event, information from old events is called into play. We understand new events by using our prior experiences. We interpret the new in terms of the old. To do this, we must be able to retrieve old events by matching aspects of new events to indices that enable old events to be retrieved.

When this retrieval occurs successfully, we think nothing of it at all and simply go on with our processing. In those cases we are understanding in terms of fairly standard and nonspecific old memories, ones that cause no particular notice because they are so ordinary.

On other occasions, we take immediate note of the old episode that we have suddenly found in our consciousness. We say that we have been "reminded" of this old event and often we tell others about that event if there is someone to tell, or we ponder the old event for a while. The difference between these two circumstances is representative of the difference between processing that enables learning and processing that does not. And, most importantly for our purposes here, the difference reflects when explanation is necessary and when it is not.

A key element in reminding is explanation. The most important thing we can find out about human memory is what the indices to specific memories are like. The basis from which those indices often seem to be constructed are explanations that have been developed to differentiate one experience from another. In other words, if indexing in memory is the key problem in AI, then explanation is an important part of the solution. When we explain things to ourselves, other things come to mind. Creative thought to a large extent depends upon our ability to explain things.

Let me illustrate the explanation/reminding problem with a true story:

I was having dinner with a friend of mine who eats only kosher food. He ordered a pasta dish made with cream sauce and mushrooms on the grounds that even though he was not in a kosher restaurant, the ingredients were all kosher, so it would be all right to eat it. When the dish arrived, it had small red bits of things in it which looked suspisciously like meat. Since he could not eat it if it were meat (and probably could not eat the entire dish because of the meat), I asked him if he wanted me to taste the red things to see what they were. He laughed, said no, and then told me a story of which he had just been reminded. He said he had a cousin who decided to become more orthodox in his religious practices. The more he studied, the more he found out about orthodox Jewish rules. These included the fact that it was only all right for a man to have sex with his wife during two weeks out of every month. At this point he stopped studying. He told my friend that there were some

things he just didn't want to know. My friend said that this applied exactly to the current case. He just didn't want to find out that he couldn't eat the dish. He decided to not eat the red things, but to eat the rest as he just didn't want to know.

The concept of memory organization that we are talking about here is very well illustrated by this example. Once one has concocted an explanation of an event (in this case, my friend explained his own behavior with "there are just some things I don't want to know"), memories get activated. Because explanations themselves are such strong indices, other memories, especially ones in similar contexts (in this case, Jewish religious prohibitions) become activated whenever an explanation is concocted. Their value? Well, sometimes it is to illustrate a point by telling a story. But they have a much more significant use. They allow us to check the validity of the explanations themselves. And, they often force us to think of new explanations when old ones seem to no longer suffice.

If we constantly predict something will happen and it never does, or the opposite always happens, we feel inclined to change our predictions. We need to remember events that show our predictive rules to be in error. Now, this doesn't mean that we always do remember them. People are very good at forgetting bad things that happen to them, thus enabling them not to have to revise their expectation rules. But, when they feel that their expectations really were wrong, they attempt to recall past errors to help them formulate new expectations.

In order to do this, it is necessary to explain what went wrong initially and, to do that, one needs evidence. Since prior evidence must be around for consideration when a new expectation is to be formed, it is important that events that did not conform to that expectation were stored in terms of the failed expectation. Thus, one kind of index is a failed expectation itself. Events are stored in terms of the expectations that they violated.

Because humans are intelligent enough to wonder about why something has gone wrong when it goes wrong, it is important for them to attempt an initial characterization of what exactly the problem was. Thus, they construct initial explanations, which serve as indices as well. The reason is clear enough. If explanations were not available, they would be lost. That is, what we were trying to learn at any given point would be immediately lost as soon as we stopped considering it for a moment. To avoid this, memory keeps available tentative explanations. Where to store them? With the expectations that failed, naturally.

EXPLANATION IS UNDERSTANDING

A first assumption in this book, then (first stated in Schank, 1982), is that when our expectations are found to be in error we must attempt to explain why. Failures lead to attempts to explain failures. We want to avoid making the same mistake twice. How? By understanding what principles underlie the expectations that we had in the first place. We must understand them so we can fix them.

In the remindings that we examined, one thing that we found (Schank, 1982) was that each pair of events that we connected by a reminding had in common not only an identical expectation failure, but an identical explanation of that failure as well.

Explanation is critical to the understanding process. As understanders, we want to know what others around us are doing, and will do. Furthermore, we want to know why others do what they do. Thus, people are constantly seeking explanations for the behavior of others. One of the simplest kinds of explanations is a script (Schank & Abelson, 1977). We believe that we understand why a person is doing what he is doing if we can point to a script that he is following. Knowing that someone is doing a particular action because it is part of the behavior prescribed by a commonly adhered to set of rules makes us feel comfortable that we have explained his behavior. We can, of course, look for explanations that are more profound than saying "he is doing that because he (or someone in his situation) always does that." We usually feel that we have understood without going that deep, however. And, it is this script-type of understanding that we are referring to when we talk about Making Sense. But, when script-based understanding is not enough, when we really want to understand something in a deep way, the explanation process must come into play. It is the creation of new explanations that produces Cognitive Understanding.

At the root of our understanding ability is our ability to seek and create explanations. What we are trying to do when we seek an explanation for an actor's behavior, is to find a set of beliefs that the actor could hold with which the actions that he took would be consistent. So, what is understanding then? In this view, understanding can be seen to be no more than, and no less than, explanation.

We have, in AI, gotten used to speaking of "computer understanding," meaning by that term that an input sentence has been combined with a memory structure of some sort. To put this graphically, we have believed that:

AN INPUT SENTENCE

+

A MEMORY STRUCTURE THAT INDICATES WHERE TO PLACE THAT SENTENCE

results in

AN UNDERSTOOD SENTENCE

In other words, the process of understanding, for computers in the early stages of AI research, was embodied in the notion that understanding something means putting it in its proper context, or Making Sense of it.

The major problem with this point of view is that, on occasion, the proper context either does not previously exist, or, it is difficult to determine exactly what that context is. Graphically:

AN INPUT SENTENCE

but

NO MEMORY STRUCTURE IS PREPARED TO ACCOMMODATE THAT SENTENCE

results in

A SENTENCE THAT NEEDS EXPLANATION

The premise here is that, in principle, what we are doing when we understand is explaining what we have heard. Most of the time those explanations are very mundane, so we don't *feel* as if we are explaining anything. Rather, we are simply placing the new information in a previously extant structure. In other words, we don't have to explain why someone is reading a menu in a restaurant since we know exactly when and where such actions take place. Explanations are necessary when an action fails to come in the way we expected, or cannot be placed into an existing structure.

But, the point is that we are always needing to explain every action we encounter. We *feel* that we are explaining when we are doing something other than accessing an everyday, run-of-the-mill, structure, or when, while using such a structure, we have still found ourselves incapable of deciding exactly what to do. Thus, explaining and understanding are the same thing, one is just more conscious a process than the other. And, explanation must be a more conscious process, because it occurs when something has gone wrong and needs to be fixed.

WHERE WE ARE GOING

In the remainder of this book, I attempt to show how the explanation process works. To do this, I develop the concept of an explanation pattern. Simply put, an explanation pattern is an ossified explanation, like a script in character, but more adaptable. The premise is that, since creating new explanations is of such importance in human cognition, it is fairly unlikely that such a task should prove to be extremely complex in nature. The explanation pattern is, in essence, a trite explanation, one that has been used before, and can be adapted during the process of explanation, for use in new circumstances.

This process of adaptation of old standard explanations for use in new areas allows for creativity. The argument, is then, that in order to find an explanation, what is required is to find an applicable old pattern, determine to what extent it differs from the current situation and begin to adapt it to fit that situation.

The issue, in the end, is one of change. When a standard memory structure is used to understand something, the net effect of understanding, in terms of its impact on memory, is nothing. You may have understood what you needed to, but as long as all processing conformed to the expectations that were available, and the standard methods were used, little will be learned from the experience.

However, in cases where a new explanation is conconcted, even though it will often just be an adaptation of an old explanation pattern, something is learned. A new pattern will be added to memory. Planning, even what seems to be the creation of brand new plans, is really no more than the adaptation of old plans to new circumstances. Learning takes place by the adaptation of old structures in memory to new circumstances.

In Schank (1982), I discussed a case of reminding where someone heard a story and got reminded of a joke about how mathematicians solve new problems by first solving an old problem and then adapting the solution to the new situation. In fact, this behavior is not confined to mathematicians. Computer programmers write programs by adapting old programs to the new problem, for example. Writers and artists adapt the old into the new in their creative acts. Creativity is often an adaptation of the old into the new.

What has creativity to do with explanation? Everything. When we come up with a new explanation we are being creative. The claim I want to make is that the creativity embodied in coming up with a new explanation is at once the essence of what it means to think, and the heart of what we mean by understanding. Such creativity is not magical, rather it is mechanistic in principle, and possible for computers to replicate. Computers can begin to achieve Cognitive Understanding. To do so requires an understanding of how humans explain, question, and create.

2 What Needs To Be Explained

What actually needs to be explained? We do not, after all, seem to be walking around all day looking to make explanations. We go about our daily business, attempting to achieve various goals, long term and short term, of grand importance, and of trivial consequence. When is it, exactly, that we find ourselves seeking explanations?

Certainly it seems obvious that we seek to explain what we do not understand. But, there is a sense in which we understand very little most of the time. We do not have complete models of the people with whom we interact. We do not have a fully-developed model of the physical world from which we can make accurate physical predictions. And, we most definitely have an incomplete model of how or why the social institutions that control our lives behave the way they do. In fact, the problem of the prediction of social and physical forces constitutes entire fields of academic inquiry. It seems fairly obvious that no one person would seek to, or ought to seek to, explain everything that he does not understand. This, of course, brings us back full circle to the original question, namely: *what do we seek to explain?*

The answer, naturally, must involve *goals*. We do not seek to fully understand the factors that determine foreign currency fluctuations, for example, unless some important aspect of our lives *needs* this explanation. So, it is not just a question of goals, it is primarily a question of priorities of goals for a given individual. In other words, one cannot be intensely involved in attempting to understand everything to the greatest level of detail possible. One makes choices in this regard, and those choices depend upon the intensity of the need that a given goal has been created to satisfy.

Implicit in all this then, is a *spectrum of need.* This *spectrum of need* relates strongly to the problem of understanding in general, so it is important that we spend some time on it here, before proceeding in our discussion of explanation.

THE SPECTRUM OF NEED

Since understanding is not an *all or none affair,* it follows that explanation cannot be *all or none* either. If explanation is used for remedying understanding failures, then for explanation to occur at the right times, it would follow that what constitutes a failure to understand must be a question of degree. That is, we do not simply understand or not. Rather, we accept our limited degree of understanding based upon the need behind the goal that was being pursued. We are unsatisfied by an incomplete understanding when the goals that are being blocked by a failure in understanding are very important to us. On the other hand, when we are asked to make an explanation in an area that is not of great importance to us, although we can construct one easily enough, its lack of precision will not bother us at all. Explanations matter when the goals behind them matter.

To get a better idea of what I mean here, consider the following exchanges:

Why do you think bank robberies are occurring more frequently?

1. Society's posing a challenge for the robbers to deal with all the publicity and all the guards.
2. The punishment isn't great enough for bank robbery.
3. It's a good way to find sustenance if you're having trouble making life on the outside.
4. The state of the economy.
5. It's probably because people aren't receiving long enough jail sentences.
6. People need the money, now more than ever. They have no other way of getting it, and a bank is the best opportunity because it's the largest return for the least effort.
7. The court system is all backed up. The prison systems are too backed up. Chances are they'll get off with a very light prison sentence if they get caught at all. There's a big risk involved, but they have a good chance of just getting away with it and getting the money.

(These responses to the above question are from a radio program called *60 Seconds* that is run on WHCN, a radio station in Hartford, Connecticut. They are interviews conducted with random people concerning a question of the day. The interviews quoted above as well as others used in this book, were all conducted during the 1981–1982 time period.)

As will be clear when other interviews such as these are presented, people are, in general, not very coherent when responding to a question of this type. What makes this set of responses interesting, is, in this case, the high likelihood that prior to hearing the question, the respondents had no idea that the premise of the question was the case. That is, 1981 wasn't an especially important period with respect to bank robbery in Connecticut. Nevertheless, the respondents were capable of composing an explanation, on the spot, of a circumstance that they were told, in essence, needed an explanation.

So, perhaps the first thing one must understand about explanation is that people are very good at coming up with what they consider to be plausible ones. But, from this realization, something very important follows: **If one can easily construct an explanation, it is likely that very little will be learned from the process.** To see what I mean here, let's consider some of the responses above.

Most of the responses are reaffirmations of already extant beliefs. In other words, the process of constructing an explanation involved attempting to find a knowledge structure in which the new information could easily reside. In essence, this conforms to the standard view of understanding that we have been espousing for some time, (see Schank & Abelson, 1977, and Schank, 1982), namely, that understanding means finding an extant knowledge structure in memory and placing the information being processed within that structure. Explanations then, in this view, can be had at a cheap price. One need only see a given input as yet another example of structure X, where structure X represents a belief in memory that has already been determined to be true and in which the placement of a new input dooms it to a lack of further processing.

Of course, these are not quite the kind of explanations that we had in mind when we set out to discuss explanation. Why not? What makes these explanations different? The answer of course is *learning.* Some explanations are intended to *explain away* a phenomenon by showing it to be another example of something that is already well-understood. The explanations that we are interested in, in this book, have quite a different character however. Explanations that are critical to learning are those explanations that are intended to *add knowledge* by the process of explanation.

In general, we can distinguish three types of explanation at this level. The first kind of explanation, which we referred to while discussing the explanation test, is made for the sake of others, to tell them what you already know. Since such explanations are almost always present in the mind of the explainer before the explanation is given, these are **canned explanations.**

That is, they exist in full form in the mind of the explainer, ready to go when needed. (Of course, sometimes someone is called upon to explain something to another person that he has not already explained to himself. In that case, the explainer uses either of the next two types of explanation.) The second kind of explanation is the kind being done in these interviews. It is what I call **explaining-away explanation.** Its intent is to cause an understanding system to not have to change as a result of understanding a new input. But, it is the third kind that is critical to the learning process, and it is thus the third kind in which we are interested. We call these explanations **additive explanations.**

An explanation is additive when it is the case that after the explanation is finished, the explainer now knows something that he didn't know before. The question still before us then, is: *when is an additive explanation called for?*

Let's put this another way: were additive explanations called for in the above interchange about bank robberies? It should be obvious that the answer is that that is precisely what was being asked for in principle. When someone asks for an explanation of something they usually want to learn something from the explanation. Often, this is misinterpreted by the hearer as a request for the explicit statement of a knowledge structure or belief that the hearer has in his repetoire under the perhaps mistaken impression that the questioner has somehow managed to not have heard this usually rather banal belief. That is, *explaining away* is a relative process. Something is not being explained away if the explanation really is new to the person who asked the question.

We can assume then, that the person who requests an explanation is always asking for an additive explanation. So, how does an explainer decide whether to honor this request? Or, to put this another way, why would one decide to attempt to construct an additive explanation?

The answer is, as we have said, a function of goals. What was interesting about the responses in the bank robbery question was, among other things, how little actual relevance these purported additional bank robberies made in the lives of the respondents. The real issue is whether the explanations might have been more likely to have been additive if the explanations being constructed were more directly related to the goals, and the need behind those goals, of the respondants.

So, we must return to what we have labeled *the spectrum of need.* The premise of this spectrum is that an explanation is likely to be additive to the extent that the need behind the explanation is great. In other words, if something important rests on the creation of an explanation, it is more likely that an understander will make the effort necessary to create an additive explanation. When no real need is driving an explanation, it is likely that explanations that are created will have as their primary intention, to *explain away* the phenomenon. The spectrum that we are discussing then, relates two variables, **need** and **type of explanation.** The premise is that the explanation sought varies with the need that underlies the process. In situations where a failure of some kind has occurred, the creation of additive explanations is sought after, with a variety of techniques being employed for this purpose.

NEED:	external	respond	empathize	remedy failure
EXPL:	explain away	canned	analogical	additive

For now, we discuss, only briefly, four points on this spectrum, which relates need and explanation. The relationship expressed by the spectrum is simple enough: given a certain amount of need, certain types of explanation will suffice. The premise is also that the spectrum increases with difficulty from left to right. In other words, behind every explanation type there are a set of techniques for producing that type of explanation. And, those techniques get more complicated as we go from left to right on the spectrum. In other words, we don't try to hard to understand deeply unless there is a strong need to understand. Consequently, any discussion must involve the different techniques that are employed under different circumstances. And, one would assume, that these techniques, as they go from left to right on the spectrum, require more work of the understander who employs them.

The premise is then, that as needs get more and more internally motivated, that is, as needs go from those of others to those that drive and organize one's own memory, explanations become more critical to the system. In other words, we are satisfied with explanations that simply cause the problem to go away when the problem wasn't ours in the first place. As the problem becomes more one of our own, we need more and more complex explanations. Thus, the explanation types must correspond to explanation techniques, and, these should range in complexity from left to right on the spectrum.

The first technique corresponds to the intent of *explaining away* when the need to explain is derived solely from someone else's needs for which there is little or no empathy (as in an exam perhaps, or a sidewalk interview as above). Explaining away means attempting to find a belief for which the episode given as data can be seen as an instance. The technique employed in the explanation process is the **search for a justifying belief.** I will call this technique **JB-SEARCH.** IN JB-SEARCH, the problem is to uncover the premise under which a given action or group of actions is being performed. In other words, what is being asked for is a reason for a set of actions that were not your own.

The first technique within JB-SEARCH therefore, is to attempt to make those actions your own. That is, one poses to oneself the question: *Assuming I had done such a thing, what might have motivated me to do it?* To answer this question, one must find a belief, in one's set of beliefs, that would justify the action in question. If one can find such a belief, then that is the explanation. If one cannot, then one must transform the question again, this time into: *What conditions would have to be present for an action such as this to occur,* or alternatively, *what conditions might have prevented such an action from occuring?* This is the second technique within JB-SEARCH, namely finding or creating a set of conditions under which an action can be seen to naturally occur even though it may not be justifiable.

Thus, **explaining away means finding a hypothetical world in which a given action or set of actions** *makes sense.* Then, the actions, and their explanations, can be filed away with **no real effective change to the understanding system itself.**

The reason that explaining away is a simple thing to do, is that JB-SEARCH is really the most ordinary of understanding processes. In the normal course of understanding we find knowledge structures that place an event in context. *Why did the waitress bring the check?* Because the restaurant script says for her to do that at that point. In other words, finding a knowledge structure explains an action.

JB-SEARCH is simply the attempt to find a relevant knowledge structure that will make a given event explainable. The sense of explainable here is: explainable by virtue of having found a relevant knowledge structure. If this seems a bit circular, that's because it is. We feel satisfied with such circular explanations that explain away the phenomenon when our need isn't very great. *Why is X doing that in situation Y? Because that is what X's do when Y occurs.* Not very profound, but quite acceptable to most people most of the time.

A second explanation technique, corresponding to the second point on the spectrum above, is that of **explanation-pattern search,** or **XP-Search** for short. Canned explanations are those that have been created before and are simply retrieved as needed. Usually they have been used many times before. One reason why we are so unimpressed with them as a way of demonstrating a computer's thinking ability is that they often don't even seem impressive as a demonstration of human thinking ability. Any computer can be given an explanation that it does not understand and repeat it when called upon to do so. Similarly, any person can produce the explanations of others, when needed, to explain a subject that he himself may never have thought about. All kinds of indoctrination, from the obvious to the subtle, work in this way.

XP-Search is the attempt to find a good canned explanation and produce it at the right time. The search for such explanation patterns (XPs) would not occupy our time at all if it were not for the fact that the misuse of these patterns can result in very creative explanations. Or to put this another way, when the need is more than just a need to respond, this simple XP-Search technique can yield quite powerful results. We shall see how this works in subsequent chapters and so have no more to say about it here.

A third technique in explanation, corresponding to the third point of the spectrum shown above, is what we might call **empathetic-analogical explanations.** These occur quite frequently in natural conversation. One person expresses a problem or concern of his, perhaps by telling an amusing story that happened to him or to a friend. The second person responds with a story that he was reminded of. People tell a joke after hearing one, or make a complaint after hearing one, and so on. What is occuring there is a kind of explanation, although it may not seem so consciously.

The technique involved in this kind of explanation is the search for a relevant story. We have discussed this technique at length in Schank (1982). Simply summarized, the technique consists of extracting an index from an input story or situation, usually by finding the expectation failure that underlies the basic problem in the story. At this point the expectation failure is explained by attempting to relate another story that has the same index and finding the generalization that holds between the two.

Thus, explanation here is a *one-shot affair.* That is, one is not attempting to be scientific in any way. One is merely trying to find a memory that is close enough in kind to the one being discussed so as to enable two things to occur. First, the aim is to continue the conversation. Second, the aim is to combine the two experiences so as to profit in some way from their combination. This is, then, a form of additive explanation. albeit a very simple one. Ideally, both understanding systems (those of the two people involved in the conversation, that is) now have a new rule, based in two experiences, that will allow them to create better predictions in the future when events with a similar index re-occur. We have called this kind of explanation, and the technique employed in creating those explanations, **explanation by reminding.** To keep to the same style I have been using, I call this technique **REMINDAND-SEARCH** or **REM-SEARCH** for short. That is, the technique of REM-SEARCH is an attempt to find one, and only one, analogous episode from which a generalization can be drawn.

The last technique, represented by the right hand side of the spectrum, strikes at the heart of what I have been calling additive explanation. The need that underlies it is far stronger than the needs that we have been discussing. To start JB-SEARCH, one's need had to be no more than an interest in answering someone else's question. For XP-SEARCH, one's need can be either external or internal, but we have discussed only external needs so far. For REM-SEARCH to start, the need had to be no more than an empathy for the speaker and a desire to continue the conversation. But, here, the need is to accurately predict, and, I argue, accurate prediction is at the very center of the process of understanding and therefore of explanation.

How does the need to make an accurate prediction arise? It comes from what we do when we attempt to understand. The assertion here is that, with respect to additive explanations at least, it is the predictive nature of understanding that drives the process. We attempt to predict how things will turn out. When they do not turn out the way we expected, and when the need to predict accurately is strong enough, then we must explain what went wrong. There are three subclasses of additive explanations that are important to discuss corresponding to the need to predict outcomes of events (predictive explanation); the behavior of others (intent explanation); and the need to understand events that have already occurred (pattern-based explanation).

ADDITIVE EXPLANATION: PREDICTIVE EXPLANATION

We are constantly seeking to predict outcomes. The most common case is that of gambling. Sometimes gambling is done with a coherent theory behind it, and sometimes it is done quite randomly, but in either case a bet signifies an attempt to predict an outcome. Of course, gambling is only an exaggeration of the general phenomenon of business decisions. When a shoestore decides to locate in a new shopping mall, or when a restaurant decides to add some more expensive wines to its wine list, these are also attempts to predict outcomes. When an individual buys a house for himself and his family he is attempting to predict outcomes. Even when he decides upon the proper school for his child he is attempting to predict outcomes.

Essentially, the prediction of outcomes involves the creation of a theory, and the decision to allow one's fortunes to rise or fall on the quality of one's powers of prediction. Because the prediction of outcomes is so significant a part of what we do in our daily lives, a very important aspect of our ability to make explanations is embodied in our attempts to figure out why a given prediction went wrong.

People are, in essence, *theory creators.* These theories may not be very elaborate or especially scientific. People create theories about how certain events will turn out, and if they are wrong, they attempt to modify those theories by incorporating the new data into the old theory. Of course, people are not all that logical, so they easily forget old data, or conveniently rework the evidence to fit the theory. They are by no means perfect theory-makers. But, they do try to make theories, about what horse will win, about what stock will go up, about what philosophy of child-raising works best, about who provides the best education, and so on. When these theories fail, it is reasonable that the person who created the theory would attempt to explain why. Such attempts, if they are motivated by a real need to create an accurate theory, result in additive explanations.

Additive explanations have an essentially hopeful quality to them. An expectation has failed, but the belief is that there will be another opportunity where a revised theory will allow for a better prediction to be made. The claim then, is that learning is essentially a process of additive explanation. Thus, to understand learning we must understand how additive explanations get made. And, since additive explanations can, at times, be quite novel, to understand creativity we must also focus on additive explanation.

One type of additive explanation is that which can remedy faulty predictions, or account for unexpected results. This kind of explanation is called **PREDICTIVE EXPLANATION.**

Perhaps the best domain in which to consider the question of predictive explanation is that of sports. People who are interested in sports tend to attempt to predict what team, person, or animal, is going to win a given event. Their involvement with that prediction may be heavily emotional, as with a rabid fan of a particular team; it may be financial, as with a bettor on a horse race or a football game; or it may be simply theoretical, as with an analyst who believes that he understands the factors involved and can therefore determine the outcome.

In all of these cases, a successful prediction is used to justify the belief that gave rise to the prediction. Thus, someone might believe that:

New York will beat Boston   because
              New York is a better place than Boston;

Mama's Joy will win the race   because
              early bursts of speed on a dry race track contribute to an easy victory;
                        and
                        Mama's Joy usually shows early bursts of speed and the track is dry

The Mets will win tonight   because
              nobody can beat Dwight Gooden when he pitches
                        and
                        Gooden is pitching for the Mets tonight

and so on. In the end, it is usually the case that very little is learned from success. The belief that generated the prediction is seen as being accurate and will be called upon again, with an even greater credibility.

With respect to learning, and therefore with respect to additive explanation, it is failure that is of interest. When a prediction turns out to be wrong, an understanding system must adjust. In short, the belief that generated the prediction is called into question. But, of course, people do not abandon their beliefs on the basis of one failure. The confirmed New York sports fan does not now begin to believe that Boston is really a more noble place in which to live. The horse race fan does not easily abandon his belief about early speed on a dry track. And, *Dwight Gooden is still a great pitcher, but he has to lose sometimes doesn't he?*

Our question is this: **What does an understanding system do when its predictions fail?** Obviously, it attempts to explain failures. The issue for us is what techniques are available to someone whose predictions have failed. Actually, the most commonly employed technique is no technique at all. Quite frequently, the explanation for a poorly predicted outcome is to note that an exception has occurred, and then to proceed to ignore it. Of course, one cannot ignore it totally. If Dwight Gooden never wins another game, or if Boston always beats New York, it would seem rather stupid to fail to take note of those facts. So, an understanding system must note an exception (i.e., remember it), but it need not do much more than that.

For the purposes of this discussion, we assume that it is the goal of an understander, when he tries to explain why a given prediction has failed, to come up with an additive explanation, so that he will not make exactly the same mistake again. Below are three techniques of predictive explanation:

1. **Similar Case Retrieval**

2. **Domain-Free Pattern Application**

3. **Library Catalogs**

Technique 1: Similar Case Retrieval

We have, of course, seen this technique before. It is what we earlier called REM-SEARCH, and is, as we said in Schank (1982) a very common method of explanation. As applied here, the idea is simple enough. When a prediction fails, one attempts to discover another case that was similar to it. When New York loses to Boston, you attempt to recall another time when New York lost to Boston, or lost to another team it should have beaten, or lost when you didn't think that it would. Having been reminded of this one other circumstance, the idea is to find some common ground that they share. Maybe the weather was bad in both games, or a key player was injured, or you were wearing a certain hat that you now decide never to wear again.

Explanations constructed by using REM-SEARCH tend to not be very scientific, given that they are constructed by the comparison of only two data items. The difficult part in constructing explanations in this manner is in the retrieval of the second episode. In order to do this, one must be able to classify the current episode in such a way as to conform to previous classifications that would have been constructed for the prior episodes. In other words, one would have had to have taken note of the fact that it was raining during the last game, and, one would have had to have used that note as an index under which to classify that game. Thus, deciding what features are critical, such that one can utilize those features for later recall, is the key part of REM-SEARCH. Or, to put this another way, the hard part of REM-SEARCH occurs long before it is actually employed.

Explanations derived by the use of REM-SEARCH tend, therefore, to be easy to construct, assuming the initial indexing was done reasonably well. They result in slightly amended rules, that, in the case of predictive explanation, do not last for a long time. That is, while the explanations are intended to be additive, the phenomena to be explained tend to be so complex that the new addition to the original rule can be rather inconsequential. So, if we discover, for example, that Dwight Gooden lost to the same team twice, but hardly ever lost to anybody else, we can, if we are the manager, decide not to use him the next time that that team comes to town. However, the correlation of those two facts can easily be irrelevant, and assuming that we are not in charge, but merely want to predict an outcome, when that team does come to town and Gooden pitches, is it reasonable to assume that he will lose?

The conclusion from this has to be that although REM-SEARCH is a technique that is much-employed for constructing explanations that are predictive, its results are not especially insightful a great deal of the time, and, its results may often be that what is added to an understanding system is a belief that is, in fact, quite wrong.

Technique 2: Domain-Free Pattern Application

There is no reason why explanations have to be derived solely from experiences entirely germane to the problem at hand. Often we find ourselves drawing analogies from one domain of knowledge to help us in understanding an entirely different domain. It may be that the reason that Gooden lost a game might be the same as the reason behind a recent drop in stock market prices. Of course, this seems a bit silly, but one is always reading about how the Democrats win elections when the American League team wins the World Series or some such nonsense.

But, there is a difference between random correlations of facts and genuine explanations derived from different domains. It is quite possible to better understand one's error in predicting a horse race correctly by considering one's behavior in attempting to make accurate predictions in the stock market. Although these two things may have little in common, the person who is doing the predicting may make similar errors in each domain. Further, it may well be the case that the explainer has already found an explanation for his problems in the stock market (maybe he is too impulsive or he always believes what he reads in the papers and finds that when he acts on that information it is too late).

It is not inappropriate for an explainer to consider this information in his analysis of his mistakes at the prediction of horse races. In order to do this, he must relax the constraints on his indexing in memory so as to allow *stock market information and explanations* to appear while he is thinking about horse racing. Relaxing these constraints will allow him to recognize that if he has been following the advice of the handicappers in the newspapers, that that advice may be too late also, but in a different sense of the term. The advice may not be too late to predict the race, but it may cause the price that the winning horse pays to go down because too many people have followed the handicapper's advice.

In order to come up with explanations drawn from analogous domains, the technique used is that which I earlier called **EXPLANATION-PATTERN SEARCH** or **XP-SEARCH.** The premise of XP-SEARCH is that once an explanation has been found for a given situation in memory, it can be used again and again by changing it in certain ways so as to make it appropriate to the situation at hand. To put this another way, it is possible to understand something that you do not understand, by trying to see that thing as an instance of something you *do* understand.

The trick in XP-SEARCH is knowing where to look for appropriate old patterns. When Dwight Gooden loses, it is easy enough to attempt to explain his loss by seeing him as an instance of Dwight Gooden in a previous loss. (That is, we explain it by REM-SEARCH for cases where Gooden has lost before.) It is also easy to see the loss as an instance of a great young pitcher losing, thus calling to mind other losses by other great pitchers. The trick is to begin to stretch the analogy so that we see this loss in terms of losses by great quarterbacks, great hockey stars, overwhelming favorites in horse races, overwhelming favorites in presidential elections, and so on. The task is to enable oneself to continually change the parameters of the original problem, so as to allow other, non-obviously related episodes, to come to mind to serve as candidate explanations.

Quite a bit of this book is about the use of explanation patterns, so we need not go into more detail here. Suffice it to say, for now, that the power of the use of explanation patterns is in their ease of obtaining original explanations without doing the work of starting from scratch each time.

Technique 3: Library Catalogs

XP-SEARCH is additive in that the use of old patterns, when applied to new situations, results in new patterns that can be applied still further. By contrast, Library Cataloging is a more scientific method. The intent of this method of remedying failures in predicting outcomes is to store all the failures together so that they can be compared to each other. Thus, it is possible to collect together all of one's errant predictions in the hope of being able to glean from them the true explanation of the method behind it all.

There are a number of difficulties in doing this, however. First, this cannot easily be done in one's head. Try as you may, it is very difficult indeed to remember every single race that you ever bet on, if you are betting on horses, and to further catalog those by wins and losses and explanations for each. The natural indexing system in human memories allows for the classification of individual experiences by unique qualities that characterize them. However, what is needed here is a much finer level of detail than this system allows. Human memory tends to place things that are similar in one package, with things that are unique in the experiencing of the event to distinguish them. However, if what is unique about an episode is its *pattern-based* analysis, this relies upon features that human memory often fails to distinguish. In other words, if the distinctive feature in an experience was part of the experiencing of the episode itself, then it may be possible to recall it using that distinctive feature. Usually this feature is a failure of some kind of expectation however, and since all losses in a horse race have basically the same experiental expectation-failure, it can be very hard to distinguish them.

An alternative to doing the kind of analysis needed for a more rational explanation of one's mistaken premises is to collect one's experiences on paper of course. And, this is precisely what scientists and others who are attempting to be careful in their analyses do when they attempt to make explanations of observed phenomena. This book is most definitely not about scientific explanation, however. Much has been written about that subject and I have nothing to add to it here. Since such explanations are not used to index human memory or to reorganize episodes in order to better learn from them, scientific explanation is not the natural province of this work.

But, more importantly, it may also be the case that scientific explanation is, in essence antithetical to the kind of explanation that the mind naturally does. The reason for this stems from the problems inherent in the initial classification of a set of data. When the mind encounters an event, it cannot, of course, know exactly how to classify it. What seems obviously to be an example of X may also many years later turn out to be an excellent example of Y, but at the time perhaps Y was unknown. The kind of scientific analysis that depends upon unique classifications of events, putting an event in a given file cabinet with a given label, for example, tends to prevent that event from being seen as anything other than the event it was originally perceived to be. Of course, the scientist himself can reclassify it if he stumbles upon it later, but then, that is the point. Humans are quite good at reclassifying, whereas classification systems are not. That is, the human leaning system depends upon a very flexible classification system.

In some sense, then, library cataloging will only be useful when the flexible indexing problem is solved. There may come a time, of course, when computers get very good at making scientific explanations of collections of observed data. However, that time will not naturally arrive prior to the solution of the kinds of problems of explanation that I have in mind here because indexing and explanation are, in principle, the same problem.

Let's now return, having discussed some techniques of predictive explanation, to the second type of additive explanation, namely **intent explanation.**

ADDITIVE EXPLANATION: INTENT EXPLANATION

We seek to understand why others behave the way they do. These *others* can be our friends, our boss, political leaders, or the institutions with which we must deal. Here again, we create expectations about the kinds of behaviors we are likely to see with respect to those with whom we interact. We know the usual attitudes and behaviors of Aunt Mary, we have a theory of what Ronald Reagan's position is likely to be on a given issue, and we have sense of what IBM might do next in the computer market. People and institutions tend to act the way they have been acting and we, as understanders and observers of this scene govern our expectations accordingly.

When someone does something we did not anticipate, either because we simply did not predict it or because we predicted something different, we need to explain it. Most of the time this explanation process is quite simple. We cannot anticipate every move of everyone we know and of every institution that is part of our lives. We would do nothing else if we tried to consciously predict everyone's actions. Consequently, we are frequently in the situation of having to explain things after the fact. When someone does something, we ask ourselves if this is something that we would originally have expected them to do. When we hear that John was angry so he went for a ride to cool off, if this is something he always does, we have very little to explain or be concerned with. If this is something he has never done, or if it is something he has done before with disastrous effect, we might indeed worry. Knowing what to concern ourselves with and what to ignore, is part of understanding a given individual.

Consequently, we seek to understand the reasons behind various decisions that are made by others. When we understand them to be completely predictable in principle, that is, when we realize that we could have predicted them if we had only thought about it, we can go on to other concerns. We need not revise our theory of that person or that institution. But, when we cannot quickly explain someone's action, when the answer is not found to be present in our memories, then we must construct an explanation. We must attempt to find out why our theory was inadequate or incomplete.

This kind of explanation is called **INTENT EXPLANATION.** It is an attempt to create theories about the reasoning patterns that drive the decision-making processes of the people and institutions that concern us. Such explanations are additive because they are driven by great need, and because they result in new rules that allow us to better cope with other individuals and institutions.

But why does it matter? Why must we know what our friends and neighbors might do next? Roughly, the answer to these questions can be summed up with the following words: **empathy, imitation,** and **opportunity/ preservation.** We seek to have an accurate model of the people in the world around us, to the extent that their actions relate to our goals. These three goals motivate a great deal of our understanding. And, consequently, when that understanding fails, we seek to update our knowledge in these areas.

Empathy

Explanations constructed under empathetic concerns tend to be rather personal in nature. That is, when other people who we care about do something that we cannot understand, we attempt to explain it. What does it mean to fail to understand something in this sense? Understanding the actions of a person that we care about means identifying the beliefs under which they were operating. Essentially, the hypothesis is that an action fits, ordinarily, into the following paradigm:

belief
|
goal
|
plan
|
action

This is the vocabulary of Schank and Abelson (1977), but I am using the term *belief* in a broader sense than the term *theme* that was used in that work. To make the above diagram a little more concrete, we might have, as an example, the action *John hit Mary* and the following underlying structure:

BELIEFS
Children should be taught what behavior is unacceptable.
Mary is the child of John.
Parents are responsible for their children's upbringing.
Pain teaches avoidance of the behavior that led to the pain.

|

GOAL
Teach Mary Not to Repeat Her Action

|

PLAN
Cause Pain to Mary

|

ACTION
John hit Mary

The premise here is that it should be possible, using an analysis of this sort, to isolate any understanding problem so as to be better able to explain it. Thus, when *John hits Mary,* and one says *I don't understand, I need an explanation,* the explanation will focus, in general, upon the beliefs inherent in the action, although they can focus anywhere on the above diagram. In other words, possible explanations focus on each and every item shown above, some more reasonable than others. Below, next to each item in the above diagram, I have given an explanation of *John hitting Mary* that might have been made with that particular belief or plan in mind. In other words, if someone asked, *why did John hit Mary,* the claim is that any of the answers shown below would be acceptable in principle, although, some are clearly better than others:

BELIEFS
Children should be taught what behavior is unacceptable.
John believes that children must learn what thay should and shouldn't do.
Mary is the child of John.
John is Mary's father.
Parents are responsible for their children's upbringing.
John believes that he must teach his children about behavior.
Pain teaches avoidance of the behavior that led to the pain.
John believes in negative reinforcement, and he thinks pain is a good negative reinforcer.
|
GOAL
Punish Mary

John wanted to punish Mary.
|
PLAN
Cause Pain to Mary
John believes that pain is a punishment.
|
ACTION
John hit Mary
John believes that hitting is a way to cause pain.

The sentences written in bold face in the above diagram are all explanations of John's behavior. Some of them seem like good explanations, and some of them seem stupid or obvious. But, in fact, such judgments are entirely in the eye of the beholder. The explanations that seem best to us as explanations are those that refer to a belief that we do not actually agree with. So for example, when an explanation focused upon something that we not only agree with, but believe that everyone agrees with, it seems silly. That is why *John believes that hitting is a way to cause pain* seems absurd as an explanation. Similarly, *John believes that he must teach his children about behavior* seems silly too, but in that case we can imagine that there might be people who believe that all matters of children's upbringing ought best be left to servants. Issues such as whether hitting children is a good idea, that is, issues that matter in our culture, usually also seem silly as explanations, but the reason here is different. Here we want a deeper explanation. We *know* that John must believe that. We can figure that out for ourselves. We want to know *why* he believes that, what his evidence is, and so on.

Thus, explanation revolves, in principle, around the notion that understanding may have failed because an inference wasn't made that would serve to fill in the **belief-goal-plan-action** chain. But, in actual use, explanation is really about expanding upon a belief that one cannot easily infer, or the beliefs that underlie a belief that is being called into question with respect to its accuracy. This having been said, we can return to the issue of empathy.

When someone whom we care for does something that we cannot understand, we demand that he explain himself, or, if that is not possible, we create our own explanation of his behavior. To not be able to understand, in this context, means that we cannot imagine what the belief is that might be held, or if we can, we cannot imagine why he would hold such a belief. Explanation, then, in this context, means finding a belief, or a belief that is behind a belief.

Usually there is no *right* explanation in these cases. What we are really saying to ourselves in these situations, is that *we* would not have acted that way ourselves, so the person whom we care about must hold some belief we don't ourselves hold. In finding out what this belief is, we either just want to know what it is, or influence a change if we believe that the belief in question is wrong. The technique involved in finding such beliefs is not all that difficult in general, as can be seen by examining some more of the WHCN data:

If you could live anywhere, where would it be?

1. Right here in Connecticut 'cause I like having all four seasons.
2. Boulder, Colorado. That's where my man is.
3. I want to live in a sand trap at the third hold of golf acres.
4. I'd live in New England because it has everything in it. It has all the culture, tradition, history.
5. A tropical island with a mountain for skiing and a beach for swimming.
6. I'd like to live in an enchanted castle with goblets of wine, joints of beef and wenches at hand.
7. Essex, Connecticut. I could dock my yacht there.
8. Hawaii. It's still in the U.S. and I wouldn't want to go out of the U.S. I'd like to stay here.
9. Bristol, Connecticut. That's where I live right now and I love it.
10. New York City. Its got a lot of class.
11. Estonia, but I can't because it got taken over by the Russians.
12. I think I'd like to live in Disneyland so I would never have to face reality.

Assume that these people are friends of yours and they have just answered your question. It is easy to see that the beliefs inherent in these answers are readily inferrable. Each of these people is telling you something about himself, about his priorities in life, about his value system, and about how he makes decisions. Since most of these people do not live where they said they would like to live, they are also telling you something about how they make decisions and why. Reason-based explanations, when they are empathetically motivated, focus on beliefs, and especially upon beliefs about how one makes decisions in life. In attempting to construct **empathetic-belief/intent explanations,** we are looking to build a world model that will enable us to better understand our friends so that we can anticipate their actions, decide if we want to be friends with those people in the first place, and help out those people whom we believe to have mistaken beliefs to prevent their making a mistake that could cause them pain.

With that in mind, let's look at some of the answers above. Consider, for example, the first one (#1). This person believes that *weather* is a major factor in deciding where you live. So does the person who said he wanted to live in Hawaii (#9). The woman in #2 believes that *love* ought to be the determining factor, but she can't believe this too strongly or else she'd be there. The people who gave answers #3, #5, and #7 believe that recreation is a very high priority, although here again, not the highest. The person who gave answer #11 presumably believes being with with your own people is the highest priority, but not at the price of the loss of one's freedom.

How do we determine that these beliefs are the ones that these people hold? To construct explanations of this sort, a relatively simple technique is used. Normally, we make inferences during the course of understanding. Inferences of various sorts have been discussed at length in various works including Rieger (1975), Cullingford (1978), and Wilensky (1978). The technique used here is also one of inference. It combines assumptions and actions into a formula that prioritizes what the subject must believe with respect to which actions and which goals take priority over one another. We will call this technique **belief-inference.**

Belief inference requires that one match goals with actions. Thus, if someone claims to have goal A, but performs an action which is normally in service of goal B, then it follows that this person either has the belief that goal B is *more important than* goal A, *more noble than* goal A, *more attainable than* goal A, or something of that sort. The task in belief inference is to determine the relationship (in italics). For example, the woman who would rather be in Colorado is saying that being in Connecticut is *more something than* being in Colorado. The task in belief inference is to figure out what the *something* is. We have some hints, of course. We know that goal A is driven by the belief that a woman should live with the man she loves. We must determine what would impede her from moving to Colorado. Perhaps her job is in Connecticut. In that case, she must believe that *a career takes precedence over love in important life decisions.* Perhaps her parents have forbidden her to go. In that case, she must believe that *loyalty to her parents is more important than loyalty to her boyfriend.* In any case, our worry is not with her. Belief inference is possible if one knows what the goals are exactly. Determining the beliefs that a given person holds will, of course, help to predict their future actions, and that is what additive explanation is all about.

Imitation

The premise behind the explanation of actions under the goal of imitation is simple enough. If someone seems to be doing well in things that matter to both him and you, it is not unreasonable to consider an explanation for his success so that he can be imitated. It is the old question: *What does he have that I don't have?* Explanations gathered here do not tend to focus on beliefs as much as they do on plans. The assumption is, after all, that the imitator and the imitatee share preconceptions about what is important, i.e., they share beliefs and goals, but not necessarily plans or the ability to carry out those plans.

Plans are learned by imitation. The way people actually plan is, I believe, considerably different than the kinds of plans to be found in the AI literature. It is unreasonable to assume that people construct new plans when faced with new problems. Rather, as with other kinds of memories of this sort, people have a vast assortment of possible plans at their disposal, all stored in memory in terms of the past experience of using those plans. That is, rather than having a set of abstract rules about what one should do in various situations, people know what they <u>have</u> done, and what others have done, and, **they copy past plans.** Or, to put this another way, they **get reminded of past plans.** After a plan has been called to mind, it is highly likely that the plan, which was used in a different situation from the one now being considered, will have to adapted in some way. So, the basic planning algorithm is:

GET REMINDED OF PRIOR PLAN

ADAPT PLAN FROM REMINDING TO FIT NEW SITUATION

To see what I mean here, let's yet again look at the WHCN tapes:

What do you think of our increased assistance in El Salvador?

1. I'm against it. I don't want to see us get involved anymore. I think we have to start taking care of things at home first.
2. It makes me fairly nervous. I look at it as a sort of Viet Nam. I think it's great for the U.S. when a country does indeed need help, but I also think we should be very careful about how spend our money, the way the economy is here in the states ourselves.
3. What happened in Viet Nam should have taught the American people a lesson.
4. I'm fearful that it might lead to a situation similar to what we faced in Viet Nam 15 years ago, and therefore I would examine carefully anything we did before we got ourselves stuck into a situation we can't get ourselves out of.

These people aren't planning exactly; what they are doing is reacting to plans, or trying to determine an underlying plan. Yet, it is rather striking that they are *all* reminded of Viet Nam. (There were two more, very simple, answers in the set that essentially said *stay out* without giving a reason.)

Why does this reminding occur? Basically what we are saying here is that one reason why we seek explanations for the reasons that underlie people's actions is that we want to be able to copy the plans that that person had if we see that they have worked. The other side of that coin is that we want to avoid imitating bad plans of others when those plans have failed. We do not need a scientific explanation as to what caused the success or failure. We are happy to store away entire plans together with their results and the conditions under which one might use those plans. Then, when we must make a decision involving planning, whether we are choosing a plan for ourselves, or evaluating the plans of others, we make these decisions by referring back to prior relevant plans.

It was, in a sense, impossible for an American to fail to be reminded of Viet Nam in this instance. These people did not consider, in any great detail, how the situations in Viet Nam and El Salvador might differ. They simply **got reminded, evaluated the consequences** that resulted from a similar plan last time, and **made a decision.**

So, the claim about imitation is this. Very low level explanations are acceptable when the explanation sought is the reason for the success or failure of an action. In-depth analyses are not routinely made. Rather, prior plans (one's own or those of others) are stored away for future evaluation and possible use. This technique of explanation I call **explanation by plan-copying.** It is a very weak form of explanation in the sense that it isn't very explanatory. But, my claim is, it _is_ what people do. And, it is quite additive in that it results in new plans being available to an understanding system.

Opportunity/Preservation

The last type of intent explanation is goal-based. One reason that we need to explain the actions of others is to attempt to predict the future. Predicting the future is, of course, a hazardous occupation, but to some extent we all engage in it. By attempting to assess what might happen, we can avoid danger, and, we can take advantage of possible opportunities. With respect to understanding or explaining the actions of others, the idea is that if we can determine what beliefs are generating current goals, then we may be able to figure out what goals will be generated in the future.

Let's return to the WHCN tapes again:

If you had it to do over, would you vote for Ronald Reagan or Jimmy Carter? (asked in 1981 after Reagan had been President for a short time)

1. I'd vote for Ronald Reagan five more times if I could. I think he's the best President I've seen. He's really going to help out the middle class.

2. Definitely Ronald Reagan. I think he's trying his hardest to help the country and I think he's boosted morale an awful lot and we need a hero and I think we have one now.
3. Jimmy Carter or anybody else except Ronald Reagan because his plans to cut taxes and a lot of other things are gonna affect me and they're gonna affect my roommate and it's really hitting home.
4. I think I'd vote for Ronald Reagan because I like what he's doing with our defense budget and after what happened in Iran, Jimmy Carter looked pretty bad. He made us look pretty bad.

Of course, voting in an election is an attempt to predict the future. What one does when one votes is to attempt to make opportunity/preservation explanations with respect to what a candidate has said or done so as to be able to predict what he will do. One continues to do this after someone has been elected as well. Simply put, we attempt to figure out what given persons will do in the future by explaining what they have done in the past. If we explain the Iran crisis by *Jimmy Carter was weak,* then we are also predicting what will happen in another situation that would require presidential strength. It is not known what action or statement Ronald Reagan made that caused person #1 above to explain it by saying that *Reagan really wants to help the middle class.* But the fact that person #1 did come up with that explanation explains why he voted for him. Similarly, (from the point of view of explanation if not of belief), person #3 has explained Reagan's plan to cut taxes as demonstrating that Reagan's intent is to hurt the middle class.

The point is that we are always in the situation of attempting to determine the belief that underlies the actions taken by an individual whose actions might affect us. We watch that person's actions because we want to take advantage of opportunities and avoid risks.

ADDITIVE EXPLANATION: PATTERN-BASED EXPLANATION

Sometimes we encounter events that we cannot have anticipated, that we never thought about one way or another, but which once seen, seem quite odd. Here we have no theory that has been directly violated. Also, we are not monitoring the behavior of particular individuals or institutions so as to better predict their next move.

In the previously discussed types of explanation, we were essentially concerned with what might be called, *top-down explanation.* That is, we had a model of the world that made a prediction that was wrong (predictive explanation) or that would have made a prediction that was wrong (intent explanation) had it been invoked. In both cases we are trying to update and modify our theories of the world to enable more accurate predictions in the future.

But, there is a kind of *bottom-up explanation* as well. After all, we cannot have predictions for every event that ever occurs. In the normal course of understanding, we often have to approach things in a bottom-up fashion. When we encounter a new event, we attempt to place it within a structure. In other words, as long as we have seen, and understood, something like that event before, we can deal with the event by treating it as an instance of an earlier event of a similar kind. The role of memory structures is to provide contexts for events.

The problem arises when we don't have an available memory structure to provide the context for an event. We feel the need to explain an event when we can't *figure out* exactly what the chain of states and actions that led up to that event might have been. Or, in other words, when we search for an available memory structure in which to place an event, and we come up empty, we feel that the new event must be explained. Explanations such as these are additive in that they result in brand new memory structures, which can be quite useful in the future. Developing a new memory structure seems on the surface to be a rather complex process. But, as we shall see, it can be far simpler than is obvious at first glance. We call this type of explanation **PATTERN-BASED EXPLANATION.**

One of the reasons why pattern-based explanation is of interest is that it relates very strongly to our ability to be creative. In attempting to understand why something has happened that we had no reason to expect would happen, we can often stumble upon new ideas. This takes place in the following way. First, we find ourselves wondering why something has occurred. We look for a set of beliefs or rules that would explain this event. But, it often happens that we don't have such rules. (If we did, there is a good chance that we would have been able to predict this event in the first place.) So, the next step is to attempt to find rules from some other domain that might fit the case at hand. As often happens, when a new question occurs in a domain to which it has not previously been applied, interesting things occur.

For example, imagine that over a period of three months, six major plane crashes occur. People who travel by plane tend to worry about such things. They are, quite naturally, afraid that they will be on the next one that crashes. They also try to explain the crashes. Now, of course, there is a strong desire that the answer be that the crashes were random, with no underlying knowledge to be gained from examining them. That is, since explanations are often hard to find, saying that there is no explanation often suffices.

A pattern-based explanation would be one that would link these unforseen and inherently unpredictable events into a whole whereby a prediction could be made. Paranoid explanations abound with this kind of explanation. Since it is quite difficult to ascertain the *correct* explanation in general in this kind of explanation, it is also difficult to prove that it isn't a plot of the *commies* (especially when they shot one of them down) or of the *Arab terrorists* (especially when they admitted to hijacking one of them).

Scientific explanations are harder to come by in these situations, but, quite naturally, people do look for them. But, these scientific explanations are really only quasi-scientific. They find the commonalities in a few of the crashes and chalk the others up to chance. So, if two of the planes had mechanical trouble, good explanations of this type might be that *mechanics don't care about their work anymore* or *the planes are getting old.* And, who knows, these may be quite accurate in those cases.

These generalizations from only a few instances, far from being a bad thing, are actually quite significant with respect to the issue of creativity. Creativity requires the ability to make an explanation, especially a pattern-based explanation, where we are seeking new knowledge rather than correcting misinformation. Often, **creative explanations are copied from one domain to another** with creative results. So, for example, the explanation that *the planes are crashing from too much radiation in the air caused by nuclear testing,* copied from an old standard explanation about why the weather is weird in any given month, although on the face of it quite silly, might give food for thought with respect to finding a real explanation. Or, to put this another way, sometimes just attempting to refute an *off-the-wall* explanation causes one to re-examine certain assumptions, and brings up enough new items for consideration, that quite creative explanations can result. This kind of explanation is quite important, and we shall have more to say about it later.

To take another example, an article appeared in the newspaper not too long ago claiming that one out of every 100 American nuclear families was worth over one million dollars. Now such a fact might seem surprising and, if it did, understanding it would require explaining it. In essence, to understand such a sentence we must begin to consider why it might be true. Are Americans richer than people in France for example? If so why? Are the people who are millionaires all old, in which case maybe they accumulated this wealth by saving, or are they young, in which case perhaps they got rich by inheritance. Are these wealthy families all wealthy because there are so many new high-tech companies in the U.S., or is it that one can make that much money from a retail store?

The point is that we look for answers. We look for answers in the newspaper article we are reading, and a good article will try to anticipate your questions and answer them in the article. (This one did, the claim being that most of these people were over 60 years old and had owned a small business.) Reading requires formulating questions that will enable the explanation process to begin. The explanation process in this case, seeks patterns; patterns that are then added to our repetoire of patterns, allowing us to call upon them in the future.

When we fail to understand something, we have failed in our attempt to find a relevant pattern to apply. In that case, we must create a new pattern. Pattern-based explanation means discovering, or creating, the relevant pattern that will render a new piece of data comprehensible.

Our aim is to study the relationship between explanations, learning, and creativity. We seek to determine how the generation of explanations changes the internal structure of an understanding system. In general this means that explanations cause learning to take place. But, sometimes, this learning is of a more profound sort, such that a system is coming up with genuinely new ideas, some of which can seem quite creative. The assertion here is that there are algorithms by which such creativity occurs, that it is possible to find them, and that it is possible for machines to employ them. At the heart of this creative behavior is pattern-based explanation, but it will take a few chapters to explain why.

SUMMARY

Since this has been a fairly wide-ranging chapter, perhaps a summary is in order. What needs to be explained? Explanations are driven by needs. There is a **spectrum of need** that relates needs to explanations. When the need is external, explanations are constructed with the intent of explaining away a phenomenon, and these are of little interest. However, when explanations are additive to a system, they are of value. Explaining away involves a search for justifying beliefs (**JB–SEARCH**). **At the mid-point of the need spectrum, there is a technique called REM–SEARCH,** which involves a search for **empathetic/analogical explanations** by the use of **one-shot remindings.** The end point on the spectrum of need is the need to be able to predict what is going to happen in the world and thus, explaining predictions that failed is the most important issue for explanation.

Within the realm of explaining failed predictions, there are three types of additive explanations that help us to make better predictions: **predictive explanation, intent explanation,** and **pattern-based explanation.** There are three useful techniques within the area of the predictive explanation: Similar Case Retrieval; Domain-Free Pattern Application; and Library Catalogs. REM–SEARCH is used within Similar Case Retrieval but does not result in very profound learning. XP–SEARCH, involving domain-free pattern application is possibly quite useful for learning, but library cataloging is beyond most people's ability to do in their heads.

The essential part of intent explanation is its reliance on the attempt to determine the beliefs and goals inherent in an observed action. Understanding means filling in a **belief-to-action chain,** and, for intent explanation, explanation means filling in holes in that chain.

Pattern-based explanation is critical to creativity because of its reliance on one-shot generalization and on copying old explanations and applying them to new domains.

Now, with all this in mind, let's begin to look at explanation in more detail.

3 Explanation Goals

One of the most important things to understand about explanation is that people know quite readily if an explanation that has been supplied to them is sensible or not. When the newspaper asserts that so many Americans are millionaires because so many own small businesses and save their money regularly so that they are millionaires by age sixty, we find ourselves holding an opinion as to whether that is a good explanation. We may not have an alternative explanation, but we know what we don't like. The same is true of the explanations that we come up with on our own. To understand at the simplest level, we must assess whether the hypotheses that we have formed as to what is going on are valid. We must know if the patterns into which we have tried to fit the data work well or not. In short, we must be able to formulate tentative explanations and reject them if they seem to be fallacious.

It seems obvious that creativity depends upon our ability to speculate about explanations. It may be less obvious, but it is nonetheless true that basic, everyday understanding depends upon our ability to speculate about our own explanations. People endlessly pose questions to themselves, and they propose answers to these questions. The explanations that they propose to themselves, or that others suggest to them, are quickly accepted or rejected. We know an explanation when we see one, whether it comes from our own head or is told to us by someone else, and we find ourselves quite capable of deciding if an explanation that is proposed actually is an explanation.

It is important, in any discussion of explanation, to recognize that a significant part of the explanation process must be our ability to recognize an explanation when we see one. But, in order to look into the issue of how we know if an explanation that we are given actually is an explanation, it is important to first consider what types of explanations there are. That is, we must know if the explanation that we are considering, if it is one that someone else has supplied to us, is the kind of explanation we were looking for.

To do this, we must have some idea of what we were looking for. In other words, accepting an explanation as an explanation depends heavily upon the goals one had in the first place. A proposed explanation is an explanation if it relates to one's implicit goals. Thus, if one has the goal of being a millionaire one would require a different explanation of our sentence about American millionaires than if one were a communist who was intent on proving the inadequacy of capitalism. Explanation depends upon goals.

What constitutes an acceptable explanation? How do you know when you have one? One thing seems clear. People know when something has been explained to their satisfaction. One minute they are confused and the next they feel satisfied that the mystery has been cleared up. This fact leaves us in a bit of a quandry. How is it that we can have no idea what is going on and still feel certain, minutes later, that now we do? It must be the case that we have a standard set of expectations about what constitutes an explanation. We must be able to "know one when we see one."

To get an idea what I am talking about here, consider the following sketch, taken from a Monty Python Movie entitled *The Meaning of Life:*

In this scene, two men dressed in a tiger suit are encountered by British soldiers in the jungle in the early twentieth century. They demand to know why the men are dressed as they are, and the men give one explanation after another trying to satisfy them. (The wording here is not exactly as it was in the movie):

Why are you dressed up in a tiger suit?

We are on a mission for British Intelligence. There is a pro-Czarist Ashanti Chief. . . .

We are doing it for an advertisement for Tiger-brand coffee.

Somebody important did it fifty years ago and we are re-creating the incident.

God told us to do it.

We are completely mad.

We are inmates of a Bengali psychiatric institution and we escaped by making this outfit out of cereal packages.

It is because we are thinking of training as taxidermists and we wanted to see things from the animal's point of view.

We found the tiger suit in Cairo and are transporting it to Dar-es-Salaam.

This scene is interesting because it demonstrates clearly what one aspect of the explanation process is about. First, we must determine the anomaly to be explained. The British soldiers find being dressed up in a tiger suit in the jungle to be anomalous. But they clearly find it anomalous in a particular way.

Anomaly means an inability to find a knowledge structure that naturally would contain the action being processed. Thus, the anomaly here is that they can't figure out what plan being dressed in a tiger suit is a part of. The soldiers could have guessed that this was part of a plan for catching tigers and then could make a judgment about whether this was a reasonable plan. **If one cannot find any plan to fit another person's action into, one assumes that there is an unknown plan or that the actors involved are behaving irrationally.** So the responses here refer to those assumptions implicitly. The original question to the men in the suit is really something like: *What is the plan that you have in mind here, or are you simply crazy?* Their answers can be re-considered in this light:

Why are you dressed up in a tiger suit?

IS THERE A REASONABLE PLAN UNDERLYING THIS SEEM-INGLY IRRATIONAL ACTION OR ARE YOU SIMPLY DOING SOMETHING CRAZY?

We are on a mission for British Intelligence. There is a pro-Czarist Ashanti Chief. . . .

WE AREN'T REALLY CRAZY. WE ARE SPIES. SPIES SOME-TIMES HAVE TO ACT CRAZY AS A SUBTERFUGE FOR WHAT THEY ARE ACTUALLY DOING.

We are doing it for an advertisement for Tiger-brand coffee.

WE AREN'T CRAZY, WE ARE ACTORS. WE ARE PRETEND-ING TO BE SOMETHING WE ARE NOT FOR THE SAKE OF MAKING A POINT. THE POINT IS SELLING SOMETHING.

Somebody important did it fifty years ago and we are re-creating the incident.

WE AREN'T CRAZY, WE ARE ACTORS. WE ARE PRETEND-ING TO BE SOMETHING WE ARE NOT FOR THE SAKE OF MAKING A POINT. THE POINT IS AN HISTORICAL TRIBUTE.

God told us to do it.

WE ARE NOT RESPONSIBLE FOR OUR ACTIONS. SOME-ONE TOLD US TO DO IT. WE DID IT BECAUSE THAT SOMEONE WAS GOD, SO YOU CAN'T ARGUE WITH THAT.

We are completely mad.

WE ARE CRAZY.

We are inmates of a Bengali psychiatric institution and we escaped by making this outfit of cereal packages.

WE ARE CRAZY, BUT WHAT WE ARE DOING ISN'T CRAZY BECAUSE IT IS A SUBTERFUGE FOR AN UNDERSTAND-ABLE PURPOSE.

It is because we are thinking of training as taxidermists and we wanted to see things from the animal's point of view.

WE AREN'T CRAZY, WE ARE TRYING TO GET A NEW POINT OF VIEW ON SOMETHING IMPORTANT TO US.

We found the tiger suit in Cairo and are transporting it to Dar-es-Salaam.

WE AREN'T CRAZY, WE ARE DOING SOMETHING SEN-SIBLE. WE ARE DOING IT IN A CRAZY WAY HOWEVER.

What constitutes an explanation here? If the assertion that underlies the anomaly to be explained is that the actor is crazy, then the explanation must address that assertion. Thus, we have a very simple rule: **Behind every anomaly is an underlying assertion. We feel that we have found an explanation (or recognized one) when the assertion that underlies the anomaly has been addressed by the explanation.**

FINDING AN EXPLANATION

To see what I mean by an underlying assertion for an anomaly, let's look at some examples of anomalies. The following examples include various anomalies that must be resolved in order to feel that one has understood what is going on. Initially, I present these examples without their explanations so as to get a better feel for the acceptability requirements for an explanation. I then briefly present some explanation methods that might be tried for these examples, just to give a feel for how a potential explanation can be considered with respect to how it addresses the underlying assertion of the anomaly.

EXAMPLE 1
In a store in Vermont, there is a sign saying that they will close tomorrow for inventory. This seems anomalous as it is the middle of their busy season.

EXAMPLE 2
At a hotel they ask my name as well as my room number when I request a wake-up call. This seems unusual.

EXAMPLE 3
A organization has made an appointment for me that they are apologetic about. It turns out that the man is not with that organization. Why did they make the appointment and why are they apologetic?

EXAMPLE 4
FROM The New York Times:
After dashing down the long flight of stairs to the subway, a woman just missed her train and was exasperated. A guard informed her that she shouldn't worry as he felt a local coming soon.

EXAMPLE 5
FROM The Washington Times:
Whenever Dan Rather does a broadcast from a studio other than the one in New York City, his gray hairs seem to disappear.

In example 1, the anomaly is that ordinally businesses want to make money and this one's behavior seems to be counterproductive. Now the question is: what kind of explanation will make us come away feeling satisfied, that is, feeling as if something (though not necessarily something cosmic) had been learned and that we now understand?

The available data here is sparse. But, suppose I told you that this store was part of a national chain. That information helps because it changes one of the available data items. One data item was the maker of this bizarre decision. Now we find that the maker was someone other than who we thought it was. The decision is still odd, but now we believe that other factors may have entered into the decision process.

If something that needs to be explained can be seen as being different from what was originally assumed to be the case, then maybe that different thing can be more easily explained. Or, perhaps it needs no explanation at all. So, one step in trying to make an explanation is to try and change the variables, one at a time, to see if some hypothetical event emerges that is easily explainable. We shall see, later on, that this technique is rather ubiquitous in explanation. If you cannot explain the matter at hand, you can change what needs to be explained into something you can explain. That is, essentially one tries to transform the situation into one that is more understandable and use what one has understood previously to explain the new situation. This technique is reminiscent of means-ends analysis as embodied in the old GPS approach of Newell and Simon (1972). The idea there was to reduce the differences between a problem that you had and one you knew how to solve. The same basic idea applies to explanation, but, as we shall see, with some very different consequences. The technique that is applicable here is what we called XP-SEARCH in Chapter 2, where the constraints on the problem are relaxed so that old applicable patterns can be applied.

Explanation of 1: The store was part of a national chain that was headquartered in Ohio where it was most certainly not the busy season. All the stores did their inventory at the same time.

Why this had to be the case I never found out. I created my own explanation that it had to do with taxes. Thus the basic principle behind the anomaly was unchanged. This business did indeed care about business, but there were other considerations involved. Nothing crucial is learned when the explanation simply involves picking up new facts that are wholly relevant to the specific problem at hand. If we can't generalize from an explanation, then the problem being explained had better have been intrinsically important. If it is not, then nothing is gained from the explanation.

Now let us consider example 2. One possibility here is that the hotel asked my name simply as a way of making sure that they did not wake up the wrong person. What we have here is a script violation, however. That is, when a script is violated, it is usually for a reason. (Although one explanation might be that their script was different than mine.) Scripts tend to be rather sacrosanct. People do things in a given way because they have always done them that way. In any case, I pondered why they had done that, but as it wasn't that fascinating a problem, I soon forgot about it.

Explanation of 2: I assumed that it was just a check to make sure I was the right person. Later when my wife told me she had called and they said I hadn't yet registered, I realized they probably had no record of anyone being in that room.

Here we have a case of a new fact constituting an explanation of an event that had been almost forgotten. Obviously it had not been completely forgotten since I was capable of retrieving the relevant information and connecting it up.

The question here is how I knew that this new information constituted an explanation of the early minor mystery. One method of explanation is the **COORDINATION OF ANOMALIES.** Actually, this is not exactly a method of explanation in that the explanations produced by it, are often not very good explanations. As we discussed in Chapter 2, Library Cataloging, while a desirable goal as a method of explanation, fails to work in the human mind because of its incredible demands upon memory. What humans do therefore, is generalize from one or two cases.

The coordination of anomalies approach is simply to take two things that are anomalous, in the same domain of knowledge, and assume that they are related, without any hard evidence. These two events were certainly candidates for application of that rule. But, it was also important that the EXPLANATION TYPE (we shall get to this idea shortly) be correct. For a script to be violated, it is usually the case that some other aspect of the script had to be violated first. In other words, there isn't a *free for all airplane seating* unless some problem occured that causes the *airplane seating script* to go awry. The same is true of hotels. It is clear then that the explanation type that I sought was from a SCRIPT VIOLATION RULE, which says to look for an explanation for a script violation in some other preceding condition in the script. In other words, something must have fouled up somewhere, and I was looking out for it.

Now consider 3 (the organization's appointment example). Why would this organization be apologetic to me? The first part of this reasoning chain is simple: they must have done something bad to me. That is why people apologize. And, why would this organization have done something bad to me, since my visit there was entirely one of good will? This is also easy to answer: someone must have made them do it.

Thus, here we have two rules of explanation. The first is what I shall call the STATE-EVENT CORRESPONDENCE rule. When there is an extant state (apologetic in this case), look for an event that matches to it (something to apologize for). This is an obvious and simple rule. For example, if the dog is cowering in the corner, he must have done something bad and his owner may be prompted to look around for what.

The second rule is one of a category of rules that relate to people's behavior. A very common rule of this sort is QUID PRO QUO. If you want to know why someone has done something, one possibility is that he has done it as what he perceives as an equal response to something you did earlier to him. That rule might be considered and rejected in this case. The rule that wins is the DELTA AGENCY rule, also known as SOMEONE MADE ME DO IT. If you cannot find an equivalent action that caused the event that needs explaining, then one choice is to find an actor who made the other actor do what he did. In a big organization, this might be someone further up in the hierarchy.

With all that having been said, it should now be clear that the explanation process is set up by these rules in this case. Thus, I was set up to look for an event that would be unpleasant for me. Also, I was set up to look for a reason for that event that had something to do with the fact that this man had some power over the people I was meeting.

Explanation of 3: Both turned out to be true. This man was someone who clearly knew very little about what he was talking about and was quite annoying. He turned out to be a personal friend of the head of the organization.

Now consider example 4. Here we have an example of a phenomenon that seems quite out of the ordinary. We need an explanation because most people do not have the belief that you can feel a train coming, particularly a given type of train. What will satisfy us as an explanation?

Earlier, we listed some questions that we claimed are ordinarily asked about actions of individuals and that, among other things, help us find anomalous behavior. In this case, we have an instance of a **belief-based anomaly.** That is, clearly this guard has a belief that we do not share. The explanation is either that there is a fact missing from our belief systems or that his belief system is peculiar in some way. Thus, the explanation we seek is either a fact about trains that makes them *feelable* or a fact about this person that enables him to feel things that others cannot. Failing that, we seek a fact about this person that makes it clear exactly what kind of craziness he has. (However, given that this story appeared in a human interest section of the New York Times, it seems obvious that this latter type of explanation will not be what is forthcoming.)

Explanation of 4: The guard stated that *"You can always tell which train is coming by the strength of the breeze down the platform. The local gives off a weak breeze, the express a strong one."*

As we stated above, a new fact will always serve as an explanation. However, in this case the new fact is not enough. We are forced to make sure that this new fact makes sense. We must ask ourselves why a train would give off a breeze. Answering this requires knowing something about the effects of objects that are going through enclosed spaces and the effects of the variable speed of those objects. In other words, an understander, in order to believe the statement of the guard would have to know, or be able or figure out, that express trains travel faster than locals in the New York Subway System.

Now let's consider example 5. What can cause a man's gray hairs to disappear? The simplest kind of explanation is done by use of the CAUSE AND EFFECT rule. We have, in our repetoire of explanations, a set of standard causes and effects. We know that if a tree has fallen, then some form of extreme weather is a likely cause. We know that if a small child has a bruised knee, then he is likely to have fallen down, and so on. These rules are the basis of the explanation process in that they allow us to not have to try to explain everything. Their role therefore is very much analogous to the role of scripts in language processing.

What is unusual about this example is that the ordinary CAUSE AND EFFECT rule is obviated by the fact that whatever procedure Rather may have used to get rid of his gray hairs was unlikely to be applied only when he was out of New York. We are forced to imagine that he cannot get any Grecian Formula in New York City and whatever supply he does have magically evaporates on his entry into New York.

But, the fact that we can postulate such a thing, well illustrates the nature of explanation process. First we try CAUSE AND EFFECT rules. Next, we try to ACCOMODATE those rules within the confines of what we know about the real world. Thus we are forced to ask ourselves, why, if Rather dyes his hair, he cannot do so in New York. We attempt to find a fact of the world that would make this the case. If we cannot find one, we attempt to invent one. Failing that, we go back and look for other versions of reality.

Thus, the next thing we do is DISTORT reality. By this I mean that we attempt to determine which part of the total picture we have been looking at is in error. In other words, we try to change one of the conditions we had to explain as a way of explaining a situation. This is what I call EXPLANATION BY ERROR CORRECTION. That is, there is an error in the situation to be explained: Rather's hair is not different, it only appears different.

Explanation of 5: The lighting isn't as good in other studios. Studio ceilings outside New York are so high that the overhead lights don't catch the gray hairs.

ADDRESSING THE UNDERLYING ANOMALY

Now let's consider these stories from the perspective of the anomalies that were involved. What is the underlying assertion in the Vermont store closing story? The assertion is that the store owners are crazy. They are in business to make money and they are doing something that will cause them to lose money. Our explanations revolved around the attempt to address this assertion.

What constitutes an explanation here? **An explanation must address an underlying assertion that a given behavior is crazy by showing why it is not crazy.** Therefore, in this case, the store owners must admit to being crazy, or must be discovered to actually be crazy, or else the plan of closing must be seen as a way of making money. The only other alternatives are either to reject the initial claim, or show how the initial data was wrongly perceived. The initial claim here, is that we have, in recognizing this anomaly, been correct in our assumptions about the goals of the store. This could have been in error as well. Thus, we have three basic classes of acceptable explanations. These, plus the category that dismisses the original data, leave us with four **acceptability categories.**

I. CRAZINESS ADMITTED
II. BENEFICIAL RESULT OF APPARENTLY ERRANT PLAN
III. MISASSUMPTION ABOUT GOAL PRIORITIES
IV. DATA MISPERCEIVED

To put this another way, from the point of view of the Monty Python sketch, they can either:

I. *admit their craziness,* (which they do in two of the explanations)
II. *show the benefits of walking around in a tiger suit* (which they don't do—such an explanation might be that walking in a tiger suit in the jungle is an excellent way of losing weight.)
III. *explain why this act is really an important goal in itself.*
IV. *say why what they are doing isn't what it seems* (this is the one they use most often)

For the store in Vermont then, we can say:

I. *That the store is owned by crazy people.*
II. *That closing the store gives some beneficial result.*
III. *That making money is not the highest priority of this store.*
IV. *That the closing isn't really a closing at all.*

The point here is that implicity an understander knows all this. He understands what can be said about this situation in terms of the four acceptability categories above. Recognizing an explanation as an explanation means being able to fit a statement of the explainer into one of the above categories and being able to believe that the substance of the explanation given is likely to be true and is correct.

Recall that the actual explanation of this story was that the store was part of a national chain that was headquartered in Ohio where it was most certainly not the busy season. All the stores in the chain did inventory at the same time. I never found out why but assumed that it had to do with taxes. Thus, for me as an explainer, the basic principle behind the anomaly was unchanged. This business did indeed care about business, but this was how it had to cope.

According to my acceptability categories above then, we have a case of IV (the closing isn't really a closing) and II (that in making money one has to do inventory for a variety of reasons). What is left is why they are doing it at that time. The fact that they are part of a chain makes it clear that *busy season* is a relative term. Thus III is also active, since making money is not the highest priority of *this* store. Their highest priority is doing what their owners dictate.

This is actually a very complicated example, since it combines three different acceptability categories. Example 4 is somewhat simpler:

FROM *The New York Times:*

After dashing down the long flight of stairs to the subway, a woman just missed her train and was exasperated. A guard informed her that she shouldn't worry as he felt a local coming soon.

Here again, the underlying assertion is that the guard is crazy. Any acceptable explanation would therefore have to respond to this assertion. The relevance of the four categories is as follows:

I.   We could find out that the guard really is crazy.
II. There is no plan here.
III. The guard might not care about properly informing people.
IV. His craziness regarding "feeling a local" may not be crazy;—maybe he really can feel one—if so we need to know how.

The viable category is IV. Thus, we formulate the question: *How can the guard feel a local coming?* We know, therefore, before we hear the explanation, what form the explanation will take. We expect a sensible statement about how one can *feel a local.* As long as the facts given make sense, that is, as long as the facts *are or at least appear to plausibly be* facts, and we can be made to see how they would cause the behavior in question to be possible, we will accept them as an explanation. What this means therefore is that we will be accepting a new knowledge structure. In other words, in hearing of someone's knowledge structure that incorporates the event in question, accepting the explanation means a desire to add this structure to our own memories. In this way, accepting an explanation is an important part of the learning process.

Recall that the explanation was simple enough: The guard stated that *You can always tell which train is coming by the strength of the breeze down the platform. The local gives off a weak breeze, the express a strong one.*

This seems reasonable enough and would presumably be accepted by an understanding system because it qualifies as an instance of acceptability class IV. Class IV is a very large catch-all. Essentially what it says is that what seems crazy may not be, because we are not properly informed as to the entire situation.

In fact, we are quite willing to take new information into our understanding system. But, a large problem for an understander is exactly where to put that information. We are willing to hear that the actor whom we are observing isn't crazy after all, but we need to know just what aspect of our understanding of him has to be modified so that we will understand his actions in the future.

Having said all this then, we have our first explanation goal. Recall that the premise here is that in order to recognize an explanation as being valid, that explanation must relate to the goal that was operating when the anomaly that forced the explanation was discovered. Thus, a key part of the acceptance of an explanation is the coordination of that explanation with its explanation goal. Following from what we have said so far, our first explanation goal then, is:

EXPLANATION GOAL 1: To establish if the actor has something coherent in mind when all signs are to the contrary.

In general, the broad categories given above deal with misperception at various levels in the **belief-goal-plan-action** chain. This relates strongly to a second explanation goal, namely:

EXPLANATION GOAL 2: To find the natural context for a given event in the belief-goal-plan-action chain.

To get a better idea of what is going on here then, let's look a little more carefully at what is going on with respect to the types of explanations that one can receive.

Explanation Types

In the following, I consider eleven types of explanations that people give to others and construct for themselves. These are:

1. **Alternative Beliefs**
2. **Laws of Physics**
3. **Institutional Rules**
4. **Rules of Thumb**
5. **New Facts**
6. **Plans and Goals**
7. **Thematic**
8. **Scripts**
9. **Delta Agency**
10. **Lack of Alternative Plan**
11. **Laws of the Universe**

Before we get into a discussion of how these classes are used to produce explanations, it is useful to consider what kinds of explanations these classes produce. Since I have been hearing explanations most of my life as to why a student didn't do what he was supposed to do, consider, as an example, a situation where a professor asks his advisee why he has not been working on his thesis lately. It is possible, using the classes of explanation given above to concoct many different types of explanations.

WHY AREN'T YOU WORKING ON YOUR THESIS?

1. Alternative Beliefs—*I don't think it needs work.*
2. Laws of Physics—*Not enough negative ions in the air here.*
3. Institutional Rules—*Yale doesn't require one any more.*
4. Rules of Thumb—*One of your former students told me that he used the strategy of just hanging around for years until you got annoyed enough that you were willing to sign anything.*
5. New Facts—*It's finished.*
6. Plans and Goals—*If I wrote my thesis, I would have to leave Yale. I like it here and think that it is more important to be where you are happy than to go progress to a place where you are unhappy.*
7. Role Themes—*The money is better in the outside world, and I didn't like being a student, so I've quit school.*
8. Scripts—*I've never done such a thing before and don't know how to begin.*
9. Delta Agency—*My wife is writing it for me.*
10. Lack of Alternative Plan—*The system was down.*
11. Mystical Laws—*My Guru says that that which is not approached directly is first finished.*

Now let's consider these classes in some detail, so as to ascertain which of them is relevant to the problem at hand, and which of them contain explanations that are worth making. One thing to keep in mind while doing this is that, in general, explanations come in two basic flavors: those you think up for yourself, and those that are given to you by others. When we discuss the techniques for explanation therefore, we have two problems: how to come up with an explanation, and how to determine if an explanation (that you or someone else has come up with) is plausible. And, we are interested in the explanation goal that a given explanation type addresses. With this in mind, we can now consider the explanation classes one by one:

1. Alternative Beliefs

When someone does something that we had no reason to expect they would do, we try to find out why by attempting to simulate their reasoning to see what they might have been thinking, as we discussed in Chapter 2. This type of explanation tells us to modify the belief that we thought an individual held. All prediction of behavior stems from what we believe about what another person believes. We are therefore constantly constructing models of why people do what they do, and modifying them. Thus, since we know that we do not know everything that is in another person's belief system, we accept explanations that inform us with respect to our incomplete knowledge.

When someone tells us the reason why he did something, and that reason is stated as a belief that he holds, the issue for an understander is to determine if that belief does, in fact, hold up as a reasonable antecedent for the goal that was supposedly generated from it. Thus, in order to accept the explanation provided to us by another person, we need simply have a model of what beliefs generate what goals. In our present example, believing that a thesis is finished would certainly not generate a goal to work on it, so that would be a valid explanation. Any further discussion would thus be about the ultimate validity of the belief.

Of course, our problem here is not assessing the explanations that other people provide us. Rather the issue is how to generate them ourselves. However, examining the kinds of explanations that other people provide can be helpful here. In generating an alternative belief, we must work backwards. The idea is to attempt to determine what belief could possibly have been the underpinning of a given action, plan, or goal. With respect to the belief-action chain shown in Chapter 2, the issue is simply to fill it in.

We have seen this kind of explanation before in example of the Steak and the Haircut (Schank, 1982):

The Steak and the Haircut

X described how his wife would never make his steak as rare as he liked it. When this was told to Y, it reminded him of a time, 30 years earlier, when he tried to get his hair cut in England and the barber just wouldn't cut it as short as he wanted it.

The argument that I made with respect to this story ran as follows: The understander of the steak story must be using some kind of knowledge structure in order to get reminded of the haircut situation. To do this, he must have been using a structure that was general enough to cover both stories. This structure must have contained expectations about what actors commonly do in situations such as this. For our purposes here we can call this structure **PROVIDE-SERVICE.** The assumption here is that in processing the story about the rare steak, the understander would have used a structure such as PROVIDE-SERVICE as a source of predictions about the actions that are likely to come next in the story.

Since the predictions contained in a structure such as PROVIDE--SERVICE are about the behavior of the participants in the situation governed by that structure, the understander can be assumed to have predicted here that someone assuming the SERVER role in that structure (voluntarily) will do what he has been asked to do if he can and if the request falls within the domain of his normal service.

In the steak story, making steak rare is within the range of abilities of the SERVER, yet she has failed to do so. This is an expectation failure. Our thesis was that such failures must be explained. So, the problem for the understander is to explain why the prediction that was made was in error. The anomaly is: *Why didn't the server do what she was asked?*

There are many possible avenues of explanation here. The SERVER could be feeling hostile, recalcitrant, or whatever. The correct explanation is not important. What does matter is how Y explained things and how that explanation served to remind Y of the experience with the barber. Y must have assumed initially that the SERVER intended to do what the SERVEE wanted, and, having found that assumption to be in error in this case, he had to create an explanation that accounted for the behavior of the wife of X.

There are many possible explanations, but Y seems to have used: *SERVER must not believe that SERVEE wants what he said he wants, he must want something less extreme.* In constructing such an explanation, an index to memory was also created. That is, sometime, thirty years earlier, Y must have explained the haircut story with the same rule. Now that rule has been waiting all this time, to be used as an index to that story if it were ever needed. Or, to put this another way, that rule has been awaiting confirmation all this time. Y wasn't sure that this was the correct interpretation of what happened to him, and he was still wondering about it, in effect. That is, Y decided (subconsciously we assume) to remember that story as an instance of a correction to an expectation he had so that he could confirm the explanation that he had made when more data became available.

The premise then, is that finding the alternative belief constituted an explanation of the anomaly. In this case, the goal of the explanation was to find the alternative belief that would have caused the behavior to be seen as easily explainable had it been known beforehand. This leaves us with explanation goal 3:

EXPLANATION GOAL 3: To find new predictive rules for the behavior of a given individual.

Sometimes it is quite trivial to figure out what someone's belief is. Of course, on occasion it is virtually impossible, especially since many unexplained actions are simply unexplainable when it comes to beliefs. That is, it may not be possible to determine why someone is failing to do his job. He may have a delusional belief system for example. Alternative Belief explanations are really only of great interest to an understanding system when they explain the behavior of groups, and thus can be used predictively in the future.

In general, therefore, there are three kinds of explanations that one can expect to get with respect to beliefs (and this follows for plans, goals, and scripts, as we shall see). The first is **specific to an individual,** namely the beliefs that he has. The second is a set of beliefs that **transcend any given**

individual. The third is a meta-contstruct about **how beliefs are selected.**

To put this more concretely, what we find when we construct an alternative belief can be, first of all, of no more interest than to tell us what one particular individual believes. As such, it is a data item for memory, of value only if we care about that individual and his beliefs.

It is when beliefs transcend a given individual that they become of interest. Thus, in the Steak and the Haircut, both the wife and the barber are in the same PROVIDE SERVICE role. The fact that they both are in the same role is of great significance here because it is that fact that would make the construction of the alternative belief of value. If the alternative belief constructed can be seen as informing us about people who are in serving roles, with whom we interact all the time, as opposed to information about a barber that one will never see again, or a wife at whose home one may never eat, then it might be of value. We are interested in explanations about the beliefs of people performing in various roles or as members of various groups, to the extent that knowing these beliefs helps us to better deal with other people in that role, or with members of that group in the future. Thus, we have rule 4:

EXPLANATION GOAL 4: To find new predictive rules that hold for a group.

The third reason to consider the problem of beliefs is to see how people go about deciding between beliefs. It is quite common for people to have conflicting beliefs in a belief system (see Abelson & Carroll, 1965, or Colby & Smith, 1969) and function happily. The question for an observer is which beliefs get activated at any given time. So for example, one's boss might believe that in order to get you to work hard, he should be especially friendly to you, but that in order to get you to respect him, he should treat his employees at a certain distance. Now, you may want to know that he has these particular beliefs in order to explain his behavior towards you. You would also want to know how he chooses between these beliefs at any given moment, in order to understand how to deal with him. So, one thing to explain within the framework of beliefs is **the decision metric for choosing between operating beliefs** that any individual or group is likely to employ.

2. Laws of Physics

Since we do not know all the physical laws of the universe, we often find ourselves speculating as to why something physical has happened. We change our rules to correspond with experience. Hearing a new law of physics therefore can often satisfy us as an explanation. We expect that the physical rules we know will change over time, not because the world is changing, but because our knowledge of the world is incomplete.

I do not discuss how we make physical explanations in this book. I am much more interested in how people construct models of the social and mental worlds that they inhabit. However, I have collected many explanation examples, quite a few of which I present in this book, and a large portion of the them are physical in nature. People do wonder about the physical world quite a bit, and my avoidance of that topic in any detail is not intended to indicate that it lacks significance.

3. Institutional Rules

When we know that someone is playing according to externally defined rules, we can look for explanations of his behavior in those rules. We assume that we don't know exactly what all those rules are, and therefore we constantly update them. This kind of explanation is analogous to constructing physical explanations except that the rules are defined by people, not by the physical world. Here again, our understanding of these rules is likely to be incomplete.

The main difference between institutional rules and physical rules is that the former are easier for an individual to get a real grasp on. We seek to understand the rules by which institutions operate, and the extent to which individuals whom we know determine what they will do on the basis of their understanding of what a given institution has done or will do. One aspect of understanding institutional rules is identical to understanding individuals. That is, institutions have goals and plans and so on. The aspect which is a problem here, and which thus requires our attention, is the extent to which the explanation of a given person's behavior can be predicted by understanding *his* perception of the institutions that affect his life.

In other words, since the behavior of an individual can often be understood by understanding his perception of the institutions with which he has to deal, one goal of explanation is to determine the institutions that he believes control his life and which do control his decisions. The second problem, with respect to making explanations relevant to institutions, is that, as an understander, it is imperative to explain the actions of institutions so that you can make appropriate decisions when those decisions come under the jurisdiction of that institution.

Essentially there are two goals here. First, explanations must uncover the beliefs, plans, and goals of an institution so as to help predict the actions of that institution. The goal then, is **to add rules about particular institutions to the data base of such rules that one has.** Second, **one must ascertain, again by explanation, the beliefs that particular individuals or groups have about how their actions ought to be affected by a given institution.**

To put this more concretely: *why does Joe support the American presence in Nicaragua?* — because — *Joe is a member of the American Legion and the American Legion supports all actions of the President and the*

Army. Why does Bill always drive at 55? — because — *Bill believes that the police are hiding behind every corner and that he will lose his license if gets a ticket.* It is important to be able to construct explanations such as this. Thus the goal here is to find out the rules by which institutions operate and to determine who believes those rules.

4. Rules of Thumb

There is a set of tricks for living that get people where they want to go. *Ask for advice from superiors,* or *never date the boss's daughter,* are examples. We try to pick them up as we go on in life. We attempt to analyze and generalize the success or failure of various actions or of various individuals. Then, we construct a simple explanation, in the form of a rule of thumb, that will guide us the next time we encounter such a situation. We try to validate our own rules of thumb by fitting the actions of others into our framework.

When we attempt to construct a rule of thumb explanation, we are not attempting to do so because some expectation of ours has failed. Rather, we want to know why a given action has turned out the way it did. We want to know why Joe always does well or why Sam always fails. We look for a rule of thumb explanation when we want a simple heuristic rather than an operating principle. It is not necessary to know why a given rule works in order to use it. What is learned here modifies already extant rules.

As an example of this, I knew a man in a very large and important company who wielded a tremendous amount of power in that company. When he walked into a meeting, people would quake. But yet, he seemed to get along very well with everybody. People seemed to genuinely like him. I asked him how he did it. He responded with a rule of thumb: *never yell at your subordinates, always yell at your superiors.* Whether this explanation really describes his behavior, or really works, is besides the point. The point is that **one of the goals of explanation is to establish rules of thumb that work for others in achieving goals that you yourself would like to achieve.** This man believes that he uses this rule of thumb. It is how he explains his behavior to himself.

I was once asked, as a part of an introduction to a talk to students that I was giving, to give a maxim that they could follow in their careers. I said: *Follow the course of least resistance intellectually, and the course of maximum resistance politically.* Knowing this rule of thumb, it is possible to explain my behavior in terms of it. *Oh he's just using his old rule of thumb in that situation.* But, the rule of thumb itself, was, of course, derived from a different type of explanation entirely.

My maxim means that what is easy to you may not be easy to others so don't demean your own abilities. And, when you find people are angry and nasty about what you have proposed, it often is because you have hit a sore spot where a rational argument doesn't exist. That might just be the right course to follow in that case if you can stand the heat.

Those explanations behind the rules of thumb are explanations of a variety of phenomena. They are explanations about plans, about goals, and about laws of the universe. So, **rule of thumb explanations are derived from other types of explanations.** The goal of a rule of thumb explanation is to get an operative rule without necessarily understanding where that rule came from.

This is as good a time as any to mention explanation goal 5, which, of course, applies to rules of thumb, as well as to decision metrics with respect to beliefs and plans:

EXPLANATION GOAL 5: To get new rules for operating in the world by copying those of others that seem to work.

The point of this rule underlies a great deal of the reason why we bother to explain at all. We explain to learn new rules about the world that may help us to make decisions some day.

5. New Facts

We want to learn about things in the world as well as about people. We need to know about cats, dogs, cars, computers, etc. One of the goals of explanation is simply the acquisition of new facts. People are heavily engaged in building up their own data bases. To do this, we collect explanations of a fairly simple sort. When a dog chases a cat, and we wonder why, the explanation *dogs like to chase cats* will suffice at the level of **new fact explanations.** Anything more profound as an explanation would be anthropomorphizing the dog. There is nothing wrong with this, of course; it is just an explanation of a different type (goals, for example), and with a different goal in mind. Explanations at the new fact level seek to add facts to the data base, and no more.

When we find a new fact, we try to place it in the data base so as to allow it to apply to the largest amount of already extant data to which it could possibly apply. When a machine catches fire, for example, our explanation would be an attempt to add a new fact to the data base that concerned this machine, such as *flammable when exposed to oil*, or *malfunctions in hot weather.* It is possible to look at the physics in such cases, but such explanations are, of course, of the laws of physics type and they have a different goal. Physical explanations satisfy the goals of prediction of a wide range of phenomena. New fact explanations tend to apply to a more limited set of objects, as wide as possible, but limited. In any case, new fact explanations can be fairly superficial. Explanations about new-fangled machinery will sometimes serve many people quite well when attempting to explain why something new has broken down. It is also the case that people are happy with one-shot explanations here. *Just don't use it on hot days* will suffice as an explanation at this level. **The goal of new fact explanations is to add a fact to the data base that will render an incomprehensible event comprehensible. This fact is usually very simple, and rather particular to the specific event being explained.** Thus we have:

EXPLANATION GOAL 6: To add new facts to one's personal data base.

6. Plans and Goals

We can explain the actions of others by understanding where the particular action that we do not understand fits within a broader plan. **Saying that an action is a step on a coherent plan towards a goal, explains that action.** When *John hits Mary* and we want an explanation of why, if he tells us that *that is how he intends to make her fall in love with him,* we can question the wisdom of the plan or its likelihood of success, but we have received an explanation, namely that it was an action in service of a given plan.

Two kinds of learning take place using this type of explanation. We can learn about particular plans and how they are realized with particular actions and how they service particular goals. In other words, we can learn enough about plans to enable us to copy them. Also, we can learn about the kinds of plans that a particular individual is likely to use in a given circumstance. This again helps us in our quest to predict the actions of particular individuals or groups of individuals.

The goal of plan-based explanation then is to render an incomprehensible **belief-goal-plan-action** chain comprehensible. But **it also intended to give us plans to copy and to help us predict plans chosen by others.**

7. Thematic

Knowing what role theme a person is acting under tells us a lot about why he is doing what he is doing, and thus pointing out a role theme can be an explanation. *Why is John asking yet another woman to marry him? John is a bigamist. He wants to have many wives,* is a thematic explanation. Themes come from beliefs, so we can question why a person wants a given theme to generate his goals, but we may not find any satisfactory answer. Why does someone pursue the luxury living theme? They may not know. But, knowing that they are pursuing that theme will certainly help explain their actions.

It can be seen from this brief description that themes compete in some vague way for the same space as beliefs. Themes are, in a sense, inaccessible beliefs. That is, they are ones that are so standardized that we have stopped trying to explain them to ourselves, or justify them in any way. We simply pursue them. The goal of explaining something at the thematic level is that we have also simultaneously explained many future actions that will be driven by the same theme. **The goal of thematic explanation therefore, is to find the pattern that is controlling a person's or a group's actions over a period of time.**

8. Scripts

Since scripts are fossilized plans, script explanations are just simpler versions of explanations for plans. Saying that a person is doing something because he is following a script explains that action in a rather dull way. We accept explanations like this all the time, however. Why do you have to buy a ticket to get on the Paris subway, but a token in New York? Because that's the way it's done. Script-based explanations are uninteresting except to those who need to know how to perform the script. The goal of a script-based explanation is usually to be able to copy the appropriate behavior in order to achieve the goal that the script serves. Although, of course, sometimes we might want to know a script so as to be better able to recognize it and avoid it.

9. Delta Agency

Doing something for someone else does not require a coherent plan of action. It merely requires that one believe that someone who you want to, or have to, please, wants something. It thus explains an action to say that the real explanation is to be found in someone else's plan. **The goal here is to find out who is really in charge.** Delta agency explanations can be quite important in attempting to cope with a bureaucracy, for example. *Why do I have to get this form stamped?* The script-based answer, *because that's the rule,* may not be as revealing as the delta-agency explanation, *because Smith loves stamps and he is in charge.* The second answer at least lets you argue with Smith.

10. Lack of Alternative Plan

Sometimes people do things because they cannot think of a better course of action. Usually there is a goal in mind, but its achievement may not come easily from the action that was implemented. This is a kind of *explain it away* explanation. It doesn't really work in terms of coherency, but sometimes it is the best we can do. In essence, such an explanation is of no value, and we do not seek them. We sometimes receive them anyway, and we sometimes construct them when we are stymied.

11. Laws of the Universe

Not everyone shares the same belief system. Those who are religious or mystical may well believe things that are deemed inappropriate by others. Understanding what others believe is part of the explanation process as we saw in explanation by alternative belief. The difference between that kind of explanation and this one depends upon the difference between the universality of the laws and the individualized beliefs that one may have but not expect others to share. Scientists construct *laws of the universe* explanations all the time. Social scientists do so as well. They are trying to find truths that hold over a variety of phenomena. I do not intend to demean their efforts by lumping them together with religious explanations. However, they do function in the same way.

When we hear that *X happened because the universal law, Y, is true,* what we are hearing is an explanation that is intended to transcend the case that is currently under discussion. The goal of such explanations is to explain as much behavior as possible. An explainer who cites a universal law is saying that *X could not have happened any other way.* The accuracy of his reasoning is not the point here. **The goal of the explainer is to find general truths rather than to understand the particular instance.** This leaves us with our last general explanation goal:

EXPLANATION GOAL 7: To find universal truths that hold across a wide range of phenomena.

Some Examples

Let's look at some actual examples of explanation. I have taken all of these from the newspaper, which is one of the major sources we have of the explanations of others. Sometimes, as in example 6, the newspaper does not attempt to report the explanation, leaving it to the reader. But, especially in columns that express points of view on current affairs, explanations are given quite clearly, as in example 7. In example 8, a type of example which is again quite ubiquitous, the explanations of others are reported.

Example 6

Tokyo, Sept 23, 1985–A Japan Air Lines official who had been negotiating with relatives of the 520 people killed in last month's Boeing 747 crash has killed himself to apologize for the disaster, the police said.

They said Saturday that Hiro Tominaga, 59, a manager at JAL's Haneda Airport maintenance shop near Tokyo, stabbed himself in the neck and chest.

He left a note saying, *I offer my apology with my life,* the police said.

What does one do when attempting to understand an article of this sort? The claim of this book is that any person, or computer program, who would express his understanding of an article such as this by a summary statement such as *A Japanese man who worked for JAL killed himself to apologize for the recent JAL crash,* would be rather inadequate. Or, to put this another way, we have built programs that could create such summaries (FRUMP, DeJong, 1977, and IPP, Lebowitz, 1980, being two). We were, at the time, quite pleased with these programs, since they understood better than any program that existed before them. But, and this is an important *but,* they would have missed what makes this article interesting to most people. And, I claim, it is that pursuit of the interesting aspect of this article that understanding is really about.

The argument is that deep understanding requires understanding the implicit environment, in the **belief-goal-plan-action** chain, in which a new piece of information fits. In attempting to understand an article of this sort, the problem for an American understander is to explain why someone would kill themselves as an apology, especially as an apology for something that they didn't do. The fact of the matter is that this need not be explained (to oneself) by a Japanese understander. A Japanese understander already possesses, in his repetoire of beliefs that can be readily accessed, sufficient information to be able to explain this man's actions.

What does the Japanese understander have that the American does not? Or, to put this another way, what must the American understander do, or think about, to convince himself that he has understood what is going on? The critical point is this: **an understander attempts to convince himself that he understands the context in which a given action has taken place. If he does not understand an action in that sense, he must explain the action.** Explanation in this sense means finding the beliefs that would render such an action comprehensible, and trying to establish a group for which those beliefs are normally held to be true.

The explanation that is done here then is explanation by alternative belief. The reader must assess the beliefs that would render such an action comprehensible. On recognizing that, for an American reader, he does not hold sufficient beliefs to make the suicide comprehensible, he must concoct some belief that some group must hold about life being less important than honor, and he must attempt to ascribe that belief to some group, the Japanese in general being the most likely choice. Even if he already had some belief like this in memory, it would still be necessary for understanding, to reference that belief and think about it a bit, with the aim of adding exemplars to the belief or slightly modifying the belief. Only a person who frequently read stories of this type would be likely to fail to have some conscious reaction to it. And that is the point. **Understanding entails explanation when things are out of the ordinary in some way.** The above example is a real example of **explanation by alternative belief.**

The second article is from a column in The Washington Post by

Michael Barone, written in September, 1985. I only reproduce excerpts here:

Example 7

The evidence is accumulating that America has passed through an Age of Liberation and is now in an Age of Restraint. Statistics on sexual behavior, consumption habits, and social behavior all show this trend.

• By 1982, the steady increase in female teenage premarital intercourse had stopped.

• The number of abortions leveled off starting in 1981, after doubling from 1973–1979.

• The divorce rate declined from 22.8% in 1979 to 21.7% in 1982, ending a long-term upward swing.

• Alcohol use is way down. The liquor industry is in trouble.

• Tobacco use is down.

• Marijuana use among youths aged 12 to 17 declined from 17 to 12% between 1979 and 1982.

• Crime rates have dropped sharply in the U.S.

Not every trend in American society points in the same direction. Cocaine use is probably up in recent years, and there are more single parent families than ever. But these are trends that result mainly from single segments of the population.

The trends I have cited touch the majority of adult Americans. Men and women who were liberating themselves from constraints a decade ago are delaying gratification and imposing restraints on themselves and others.

Why? A better question is, why not? The historian Lawrence Stone argues that people in England became more restrictive in the late 1500s, more permissive after the Restoration of 1660, and more restrictive again beginning around 1770.

Writing in the 1970's Mr. Stone foresaw the cycle of history revolving once more. As the excesses and costs of liberation become plain, people apply restraint.

In the America of 1975–1985, the excesses often appeared as threats to health. Scotch and steaks, cigarettes and marijuana all once seemed the emblems of the affluent, liberated life, but now they are perceived as dangerous.

Thomas tells how the development of penicillin in 1938 meant that physicians for the first time could cure many diseases thought incurable. Americans came to think that there was a pill that could cure any illness and a device that could guarantee risk-free sex.

People may be learning that it is not always best in the long run to maximize pleasure or freedom in the short run.

Americans continue to talk as if they were in an age of Liberation, but the evidence is accumulating, America seems already to be in an age of Restraint.

This article gives us an explanation to work with. We can, of course, simply accept it. But, columns in newspapers present points of view, and, as readers, we do not always accept that point of view. We accept or reject viewpoints by explanation. In this case, the writer of this column presents some data that he claims, implicitly, need to be explained. He offers an explanation and then presents the arguments of others who argued similarly to buttress his claim. A reader, when attempting to understand such an article, considers the data, considers the conclusion drawn from it, and then either accepts that conclusion, rejects that conclusion, or begins to construct his own explanation.

What kinds of explanations are these? They are not explanations by alternative belief, or goals, or appearances. Most of the explanation types given in this chapter relate to the attempt to understand an action in terms of the structures that underlie it. But, here, there is no action to explain. Or, at least, that is the argument that the writer of this article is trying to make. He is saying in effect, don't look for explanations of each action in terms of alternative beliefs or plans, etc. Rather, the correct kind of explanation to make is one having to do with trends. That is, certain forces direct the actions of individuals in ways that we cannot know. We attempt to find out about those forces, and when we uncover one, we can speculate about the truth of it, or just look for examples of it.

This kind of explanation is what I earlier termed explanation by laws of the universe. In this kind of explanation, one attempt to find rules that the mystical force you believe in, from God to science, uses to order things. The assumption is that there is order in the world, and that someone, something, or some principle of science or society, has put it there. The task in this type of explanation is to find the rule. In an argument for the existence of a rule, many exemplars are presented.

The alternative here is, of course, that no such rule exists and that in each of the cases cited as needing an explanation, a different explanation, unrelated to the first, can be found. Such explanations are at the level of alternative beliefs, goals, and so on, for the various groups whose behavior needs to be explained.

The point here is simple enough. Often an opinion has, implicit within it, a single critical argument. In this case, the argument is that explanations of the laws of the universe type, which encompass a wide range of data, are better than explanations of the alternative belief type, which encompass only each piece of data individually. Thus, suppose we argue that premarital sex is less common today because young people are worried about making money, that they believe that making money requires one to not be frivolous, so they consequently exercise restraint with respect to activities they regard as frivolous. Such an argument would take care of some of the data that the author cites, but certainly not all of it. An argument such as this is at the level of alternative beliefs, goals, and scripts, with the group in question being *today's young people.* The argument the author is making is that such a level of explanation is the wrong one to look for.

The third example is taken from the International Herald Tribune, in a column called *From our Sept 24 pages, 50 years ago:*

Example 8

Paris, 1935–*The American people are spiritually ill and there is little hope of change, except for the worse. They have no time for the fine things of life such as wine.* These and other opinions were expressed at the Association of Bordeaux Wine Exporters meeting held in Paris, during which it was decided that the United States is not interested in wine and that the association will make no further effort to sell wine to Americans. Roger Descas, president of the association, declared: *We are sad, not simply because of the loss of a market, but because of the loss of an ideal. Silk stockings, movies, and autos have conquered America. They require too much money to leave scope for the refinement and culture which are necessary to appreciate the fine things of life, such as wine, grand music, and fine literature.*

I put this last article here because I was amused by it. Fifty years later, the Bordeaux wine exporters are exporting tremendous amounts of wine to the United States, but a Frenchman would still say the same things about the U.S. The explanation method, *coordination of anomalies,* is not always very accurate, but it is frequently used. The problem for the exporters was that they had two things they saw as anomalous. One was that Americans, who had the money to do so, weren't buying wine. The second was that they found all the rest of the American life style anomalous. So, they assumed that these two anomalies must have a common ancestor and used one to explain the other.

The explanation that was actually used is a role theme explanation. That is, the argument is that Americans have a luxury living theme that seems to have excluded wine. But, that having been said, the exporters wanted to know why. Explanations of why certain themes have been adopted by various groups are often hard to come by. For example, many people have tried, but it is quite difficult to explain why Americans like big cars and the French don't. So, in the face of no obvious explanation, a coordination of anomalies was tried. As we shall see, even such superficial explanations can be quite useful.

Summary

The goals of explanation are simple enough then. They are:

1. To establish if the actor has something coherent in mind when all signs are to the contrary.
2. To find the natural context for a given event in the belief-action chain.
3. To find new predictive rules for the behavior of a given individual.
4. To find new predictive rules that hold for a group.
5. To get new rules for operating in the world by copying those of others that seem to work.
6. To add new facts to one's personal data base.
7. To find universal truths that hold across wide ranges of phenomena.

And, how do we know if we have found one? That is, how do we know if an explanation is a good one? Remember that no one tells us what explanation type to look for. We look for the explanation that addresses the anomaly we have discovered. If we see behavior as being odd, we attempt to find beliefs, goals, new facts, and so on that would make it not seem odd. We know we have found a good explanation if, in finding the new belief, fact, or whatever, we are now able to relate the anomalous behavior to a pattern of behavior that we were previously aware of. If, after finding out whatever new information was available, we still cannot recognize a coherent pattern of behavior, we do not feel as if the behavior has been sufficiently explained. We can always resort to the assumption that the behavior we have seen is crazy. In a sense it is one or the other. Either we recognize the pattern or we are left to assume that an event or an actor in an event is crazy.

PUTTING IT ALL TOGETHER

The premise of our earlier work on reminding was that learning occurs as we gather up failed expectations and correct them. Explanations, we hypothesized, are used as indices to prior experiences that have failed in similar ways. Comparing two such stories can lead to learning. But, we have seen here that explanation can lead to learning without reminding. It is possible to feel the need for an explanation, find one, and never get reminded at all. What happened to reminding?

It is possible to look at the chain of processes involved in explanation and reminding in two different ways. One can view the significant part of the process of explanation as the correction of an expectation failure. In that case, the problem at hand is to have a memory that contains accurate predictions about the world. When these predictions fail, as they inevitably must if a memory is to grow in any interesting way, the task is to change them. So, in this way a system can change itself by experiencing the world. Learning, in this view, is adaptation to new information, permitting re-organization of that information. The role of reminding is to start the re-organization process. But, as we have seen, finding an anomaly that relates to a particular goal that you have will do as well. When reminding starts the process, then the role of explanation is to label the memories properly so that one will be reminded of them at the appropriate time. In other words, in one view of the learning process, remindings start the process of memory re-organization and explanations are the indices by which remindings occur.

In the second view, it is the object of an understanding system to understand whatever it experiences. Understanding means being able to find a memory structure that will serve as a natural home for a new experience. In other words, understanding means not having to explain, or to put this another way, one feels that one has understood when one's explanations are rather automatic. But, sometimes that is not possible. Events occur that we cannot explain. When this happens, we attempt to create new structures for the events. To do this, we use a number of methods that we have accumulated by which we can construct temporary explanations. In order to make an explanation more permanent, we try to think of other instances that we have experienced that will verify that the temporary explanation we have constructed has some validity beyond the current case. In that case, when the explanation process was started by an anomaly and not by a reminding, the role of reminding, when it occurs at all, is to help provide more data to the understanding system so that more interesting generalizations will become available to it. Remindings in that case, thus have the role of confirming explanations, which allows us to create new memory structures. Learning, in this second view, means finding, or creating, a new structure that will render a phenomenon understandable.

These two views aren't at odds. Rather, they simply have a different focus. Previously we focused on the value of reminding and the correction of expectation failure, whereas now we are focusing on the explanations themselves. The premise is that since understanding is explanation, the issue in explanation is understanding the difficult stuff. So, one question before us is: **Exactly what things do people feel compelled to explain?** Or, the flip side of this question: **What things do people have difficulty understanding?**

We do a great deal of explaining without learning a thing of interest. In other words, explanation is going on all the time, it is a much more pervasive phenomenon that either reminding or learning and we must examine what starts it, how it is accomplished, when the result is pursued to the extent that it is generalized and causes learning to occur, and when a resultant explanation causes us to drop a line of inquiry as a target of further learning. Most important of course, is to establish when and how it is pursued to the extent that the explainer is satisfied that an anomalous situation is no longer anomalous.

One thing about explanation that is important and different from other processes, is that we know the kind of explanation that we seek before we start the process. With reminding and learning we often are surprised with what comes out; we don't really know where we are going. **With explanation, we know one when we see one.** So, what suffices as an explanation is of key importance in discussing the nature of explanation. We must know the nature of satisfactory explanation beforehand in order to be able to be sure that we have one. In other words, a sense of the coherency of what we have processed is critical in the explanation process.

4 The Process of Explanation: Explanation Questions

Our attempts to explain what we don't understand are attempts to make generalizations about various aspects of the world. We don't seek only to know why a given person does what he does, although we may accept an explanation that pertains only to him if that's the best we can do. We also want to know how this new rule that we have just learned can apply to other, similar situations. We seek to generalize the behavior of others in such a way as to create rules that will hold in circumstances other than those we have just encountered. If we are successful at a stock purchase, for example, we wish to know if our success was due to our keen insight, our broker, the day of the week, the industry our stock belongs to, the nature of the market, the weather, or whatever. If we want to replicate successful behavior, then we must know what details of that behavior were criterial to our success and which details were irrelevant. Behavior is so complex that just because the result was successful it doesn't follow that we can easily repeat what we did. We may have done a great many things, most of which were probably irrelevant. (For example, my uncle, who was a successful football coach, always wore the same brown suit to his games. I assume that he knew in some sense that this suit was not the reason that he was successful, but he replicated everything that he could.) We need to know what aspects of an event are significant and which are relevant with respect to what we can learn from the event for the future.

If we wish to account for failures, then when we do fail, we must explain our failures in such a way as to be able to modify the aspect of our behavior that was in error. Finding just which aspect is most significant can be a serious problem, however. We must know how to generalize correctly.

Thus, we must come up with explanations that correctly cover the range of behaviors that interest us. Our explanations must be *inclusive* and *instructive.* They must include more behavior than we just saw and they must instruct us on how to behave in future situations of a like kind. **Establishing what kinds of situations constitute like kinds is one of the main problems of generalization.** It thus is, in some sense, the purpose of explanation.

Not every explanation is instructive or inclusive. Sometimes we explain things to make sure that they are not of interest. This is one reason why the explanation process must be more critically examined than the reminding process. We do not get reminded every time we attempt to explain something. Not all explanations are so significant as to cause a reminding. But any explanation that is intended to be additive, is intended to be additive at a level of generality higher than that of the original phenomenon to be explained. We would like to learn something significant from our efforts at explanation if we can.

Let's now consider the explanation process in some detail:

The Explanation Process

The explanation process involves the following steps:

1. Find an **anomaly**
2. Establish **the explanation goal** that underlies the anomaly
3. Establish **the explanation question** that is active
4. Find **an explanation pattern** that relates to the question
5. Check **the causal coherence** of the pattern as applied to the anomaly:
   if it is coherent—then go to next step
   if it is incoherent—either
                          find new pattern
                     or **tweak current pattern**
6. Take explanation and establish whether it can be generalized beyond the current case by **reminding**
7. If a reminding is found, find breadth of the **generalization** to be formed
8. **Reorganize memory** using new generalized rule.

Clearly, there is a great deal to be explained about the steps in the above chart. First, we must discuss the role of reminding. Then, we shall begin to look at what an explanation question might be and how to determine which explanation questions are active. Then, in the next chapter, we discuss explanation patterns and the tweaking of those patterns in greater detail.

REMINDING AS VERIFICATION

Clear from this chart is the role of reminding in the process of explanation. If reminding occurs, it is one method by which the generalization of an explanation can be justified and through which the new explanation can be used at a high level to reorganize some rules in memory. As an example of this consider the following:

EXAMPLE 1

I was walking along the beach in Puerto Rico and noticed signs saying that it is unsafe to swim yet everyone was swimming and it was clearly safe. I explained this to myself, after seeing a second sign of a different sort, warning about the dangers of walking in a given place, by assuming that the hotel that put up these signs was just trying to cover itself legally in case of an accident.

At this point, that is after the explanation, I was reminded of signs in Connecticut that say *road legally closed* when the road is in full use. I had previously explained these signs to myself in the same way.

Here we have an example of reminding as verification. First an anomaly is discovered. Next an explanation is concocted. When the reminding occurs, it serves to convince the mind that the concocted explanation is reliable. It also gives potential for scoping the generalization that will be formed from the explanation. Here we see that both a state (Connecticut) and an institution (a hotel) can make the same rules for the same reason. Thus our new rule has to be generalized high enough to cover *institutions who could have liability under certain circumstances.* The trick here is to not over-generalize. We learn from these examples that some signs should be ignored. But which signs and under what circumstances? We want to learn to ignore signs some of the time but not all of the time. Should we ignore *stop signs,* or signs asking us to register at a hotel? Clearly not.

Honing the rule so that it correctly applies is an important part of the explanation process. Rules are honed by comparing the intentions of the actors in both cases. Thus, when one is reminded of one sign by another, the issue at hand is exactly what the intent of the sign is. It is not always easy to discern intent from a sign. But, a second sign, presumably put up for a different reason is likely to help one determine the intent of the organization that put up the sign. The claim is that the mind naturally analyzes signs and the like for intent, so that, in some sense, you have already answered this question subconsciously. What reminding does is bring to the conscious processing two examples that have been analyzed similarly but not consciously. Thus, we can make generalizations by looking at two experiences which have already been determined to have some important aspect in common.

The role of explanation-by-example is thus crucial in reminding. People learn better by the use of examples, that much is obvious. Reminding makes it clear that we construct our own examples to help in learning a new rule in memory. What seems obvious is that the rules we know are grounded in sets of examples.

FINDING ANOMALIES

It seems clear that remindings are available as verification in only a small percentage of the explanations that we attempt. In unverified cases (that is, unverified by reminding), we may look for other types of verification, such as seeing if our explanation meets certain standards of coherency for explanation. In other words, without a reminding to help us, we are on our own, so to speak. We discuss this more in Chapters 5 and 6 where we see yet another role of reminding in the explanation process.

People have powerful models of the world. Through these models, which are based on the accumulated set of experiences that a person has had, new experiences are interpreted. When the new experiences that a person perceives fit nicely into the framework of expectations that have been derived from experience, an understander has little problem understanding. However, it is often the case that a new experience is anomolous in some way. It doesn't correspond to what we expect. In that case, we must reevaluate what is going on. We must attempt to explain why we were wrong in our expectations. We must do this or we will fail to grow as a result of our experiences. Learning requires expectation failure and the explanation of expectation failure.

But, expectation failure is not a simple process. When we have only a few expectations and they turn out to be incorrect, finding which one failed is not that complex a process. In the real world, however, at any given moment we have a tremendously large number of expectations. In fact, people are constantly questioning themselves and each other, in a quest to find out why someone has done what he has done and what the consequences of that action are likely to be. Thus, in order to find out how we learn, we must find out how we know that we need to learn. In other words, we need to know how we discover anomalies. How do we know that something did not fit?

The premise here is that whenever an action takes place, in order to discover what might be anomolous about it, we have to have been asking ourselves a set of questions about the nature of that action. In other words, during the course of processing, we are constantly asking certain questions about that event in order to fully understand it. Anomalies occur when the answers to one or more of those questions is unknown. It is then that we seek to explain what was going on. It is then that we learn.

To get a handle on this process, we must attempt to sort out the kinds of anomalies that there are. Knowing the kinds of anomalies that there are gives us two advantages. In order for us to find something to be anomalous we must have been unable to answer a question about some circumstance. So, first we must discover the questions that are routinely asked as a part of the understanding process. Second, in finding out what anomalies there are, we also have the basis for the kinds of explanations that are created to take care of those anomalies. Thus we understand what can be learned.

Since we learn from everything, by the reasoning presented in the preceding it follows that everything can be anomalous. But what is *everything?* The *things* we seek are the types of events that there are in the world. For example, we observe the actions of others in the world around us. To find anomalies (or more directly, to understand what they are doing), we ask questions of ourselves about their actions. For actions by individuals, I propose the following set of questions, which are asked in some sense, every time that an action is observed:

1. **PATTERNS:** Is this an action that this person ordinarily does? Have I seen him do it? If not then. . . .

2. **REFERENCE TO SELF:** Is this an action that I would do? If not then. . . .

3. **RESULTS:** Is this an action that will yield a result that is clearly and directly beneficial to the actor? If not then. . . .

4. **PLANS:** Is this action part of a plan that I know to be a plan of the actor's? If not then is this an action that is part of an overall plan that I was previously unaware of that will, in the long run, be beneficial to the actor? If not then. . . .

5. **GOALS:** Is this an action that might be determined to be effective in achieving a goal that I know this actor has? If not, then is this action helpful in achieving a goal that I did not know he had but might plausibly assume that he might have? If not then. . . .

6. **BELIEFS:** Is there a belief that I know that the actor holds that explains this action? If not, is there a belief that I can assume he might hold that would explain this action?

The result of this process is either a new fact, (a plan, goal, or belief that one did not know that a given actor had), or else that the action is unexplainable.

Every time that someone does something, an observer, in his attempt to interpret the action that he is observing, checks to see if that action *makes sense*. But, actions do not make sense absolutely. That is, we cannot determine if actions make sense except by comparing them to other actions. In a world where everyone walks around with his thumb in his mouth it is not necessary to attempt to explain why a given individual has his thumb in his mouth. In a world where no one does this, we must explain why a given individual has his thumb in his mouth. Clearly, making sense, and thus the idea of an anomaly in general, is a relative thing.

Relative to what? Naturally the answer is, relative to events in memory that we have seen before. The additive explanations that we discussed before pertain to the kinds of norms that there are, namely, norms for intent behind actions, norms for patterns of actions, and the normal causal chains of events that allow us to make predictions about the world in general. These were, as we saw earlier:

PREDICTIVE EXPLANATION

INTENT EXPLANATION

PATTERN EXPLANATION

We are satisfied, as observers of actions, when the action that we observe fits into a known pattern; has known consequences that we can determine to be beneficial to the actor; or is part of an overall plan or view of the world that we could have predicted that the actor would be part of. When we are trying to understand our thumb-sucking adult therefore, we can explain his action by pointing at the advantages of thumb-sucking (intent); we can explain it by reference to the group to which he belongs that normally does this behavior, perhaps neurotics or Martians (predictive); or, we recognize the pattern that is functioning here, for example, maybe he has just gone through a Rolfing session, and one always thumb-sucks afterwards (patterns).

The claim in the chart outlined earlier is that there is an order to this process. The one I just used for thumb-sucking is not optimal, for example, since known patterns either come to mind immediately or not at all. When we see that someone has done something, we first try to find the pattern to which it belongs. Failing that, the consequences that will result become an issue. If those consequences are beneficial to the actor then nothing needs to be explained since there is no anomaly. If those consequences are not obviously beneficial, then we need to find out why the action has been attempted in the first place. This requires ascertaining what goals an actor has, what plans he believes will effect those goals, or what beliefs he has from which a goal may have been generated.

People are not processing information with the intent of finding out whether something is anomalous and needs explaining. In fact, quite the opposite is the case. An understander is trying to determine the place for an action that he observes. To do this, he must find a place in memory that was expecting this new action. Of course he may not find one since not everything in life can be anticipated.

So, an understander asks himself the question, **what structure in my memory would have been expecting this action had I reason to believe that that structure was active?** It is at this point that the above issues arise. We are always asking ourselves why things have happened the way they have, but we usually know most of the rudiments of the answer since what we are observing is usually fairly ordinary. When things are unusual and must be explained, it is because some of our routine questions have gotten some strange answers.

EXPLANATION QUESTIONS

To understand how to create an explanation for an event, one must know the kind of explanation that one is seeking, and that entails knowing what kinds of questions people ask that need explaining. In order to talk about how to establish what explanation questions are of interest, we must, of course, examine what an explanation question is.

Once it has been determined that something needs to be explained, we formulate a particular question, the answer to which, presumably, will constitute the explanation we were seeking and make us feel that we have understood what was previously impossible to understand. We call the question that starts the explanation process, an Explanation Question or **EQ**. The claim here is that there exists a set of standard EQs from which particular EQs are determined to be active at any given point. We do not really formulate wholly original questions each time we demand an explanation. In fact, we tend to know what we are looking for before we start to look. EQs are, in a sense, indices to memory. It is the role of the EQ, therefore, to provide its own answer.

To the extent that there exists a standard set of questions, there must also exist a standard set of answers to those questions. This notion is at the core of what we are saying in this book. The claim is that explanation, creativity, learning, and such seemingly complex notions have at their core a rather simple base. That base is a reference to what has gone before. That is, we are constantly using what we have previously done as a way of extending what we can do. One phenomenon that we have seen that exemplifies this process is reminding. Another is the adaptation of old, seemingly erroneous patterns to new situations where they seem not to apply. We discuss this latter method in some detail in the next two chapters. First, however, we must discuss how EQs are selected.

Finding an Active EQ

There exist a large set of standard EQs, as we shall see. These can be quite useful for determining an answer to a specific question by transforming that question into a more general standard one for which there already exist some standard answers. Faced with an anomaly, the entire range of possible EQs is available to us. The task of the explainer is to determine which EQs are active at any given point. One way to delimit the EQs such that they become active or inactive is by features that uniquely characterize them. Features of the anomaly help determine the indices for the EQs. Any anomaly has many possible features. Hence, **part of the variability in the explanation process comes from the great deal of choice we have in picking features to focus on or to assume in the anomaly that will determine the EQs that are posed and which, in turn, will determine the explanation patterns that can be considered as the basis of possible answers.**

In the following are a set of examples of real explanations. The examples were collected over the course of a year by asking graduate students at Yale to send me an electronic mail message any time that they had an experience where they found themselves explaining something to themselves. For each of these examples, one important issue is, **what question was the explainer seeking to answer when he came up with his explanation?** Another issue is, **how might that question be more easily answered by seeing it as an instance of a more standard general question** (an EQ)?

These examples are categorized by the features that are involved in selecting EQs. EQs correspond to the combination of all these features. Thus, in principle, there are $3 \times 3 \times 7$, or 63 possible EQs. We only discuss some of these, of course.

A: TYPE OF FAILURE: As we discussed in Chapter 2, an event can be anomalous in three ways. Either a prediction explanation is needed, an intent explanation is needed, or a pattern-based explanation is needed:

A1: WRONG PREDICTION: We predicted some event and something else (or nothing at all) happened. Or, some event violates what we would have predicted. Here the question was formulated: *Why do the primaries drag on so long, when one would imagine that that is very costly for the parties involved?* This specific question is then more easily answered by transforming it into the general EQ: *How is this apparently ineffective plan in reality a good plan for some unseen goal?* for which their exist standard answers and strategies for applying those answers to specific situations.

EXAMPLE 2 (Simultaneous Primaries)

Jim questioned why the primaries dragged on so long, complaining about how they dominated the news, making it harder to find out what ELSE was happening in the world. He advocated a much shorter primary season, suggesting that best of all would be if they were all the same day. My explanation: The primaries are under the control of each political party. It's in the interest of the political parties to drag this on as long as possible, because it is a way of getting free press coverage. The candidates don't have to PAY for advertisement, just hold yet another debate, and the media will compete over who can cover it most.

A2: UNPREDICTED (events): Something happens where we hadn't expected anything to occur. The question in this story is *"What's causing that strange noise?"* That question is answered with the help of the EQ: *What are the underlying causes of this bad event?*

EXAMPLE 3 (The Ice Storm)

During the ice storm last night, Suzie and I were in my apartment. Neither of us had realized that the snow had turned to freezing rain. We heard a long series of crackles and whooshing sounds. I said that it sounded like trees falling. During the ice storm of '79 (my first real winter) I was nearly killed by a falling limb, and I suppose I am now sensitized to that noise. Suzie was sure it wasn't trees because there were so many similar noises. When we awoke, it turned out to be dozens of fallen trees.

A3: LACK OF CONTEXT (reasons): Someone did some-thing and we cannot figure out why, here, *Why would a Jew choose to be a reporter in Lebanon?* This corresponds to the more general EQ: *What caused the actor to behave this way?*

EXAMPLE 4 (Reporter in Lebanon)

This morning, watching the Reuters newswire on TV, one of the headlines at the beginning read *American TV network reporter feared kidnapped in Beirut.* Immediately, Jerry Levin, CNN's reporter in Beirut, came to mind, not as a conscious prediction, but just sort of idly. When I first noticed that he had been posted as Beirut bureau chief for CNN, I remember thinking that it was a bit risky for a Jew to take that assignment. Sure enough, it turns out that it's Jerry Levin who is missing and believed kidnapped.

B: TYPE OF EVENT: An event can occur in one of several broad *worlds* or classes of events. In general, people have questions about the physical world they inhabit, the social world that is made up of various institutions with their rules, and the personal world that concerns the individuals that one knows.

B1: PHYSICAL WORLD: Inanimate objects and causations cause us to wonder about why things happen the way they do. We have a simple model of the physical world that consists of a set of predictions about what will happen and a set of standard explanations for why things fail to work on occasion. One EQ that occurs in the physical world is: *What factors caused this event and can they happen again?* The specific question here is: *"Why did the gate keep moving?"* in the following story:

EXAMPLE 5 (The Parking Lot Gate)

Yesterday, walking to my car, I approached the automatic parking lot gate to my parking lot. The gate is the type where you insert a plastic card to get in, and that automatically opens when you approach the gate in your car to get out.

At a distance of about 50 feet I noticed that the gate rose about half way up and went back again. I also noticed that there were no cars moving in the vicinity. The spontaneous spasm of the gate was highly unusual. I have approached this same gate on foot countless times and this never happened before.

I tried to explain why the gate behaved in this way. The first thing I did was to check again that I did not miss a car that was approaching the gate. I saw no car, but I did see a government police car parked in the distance in a place where cars do not usually park. I then wondered if the police car had something to do with the gate's behavior. Did they have some device that triggered the gate? Were they watching the gate? I decided that this was unlikely and paranoid.

I then wondered if I had not in some way triggered the gate in my approaching it. I was reminded of the times that I passed through airport metal detector gates and triggered the alarm due to something I was carrying. This seemed to make more sense so I pursued it further. Was the parking gate triggered by some sort of metal detector? This seemed plausible, but cars have a great deal of metal in them and I do not. Was I carrying something with metal in it? Yes, but no more than I usually carry and the gate had never mysteriously moved before when I passed it. Furthermore, if a car were the distance I was from the gate it would not have triggered the gate. I rejected the metal detection explanation as well.

I decided that for the purposes of the moment the gate was acting unusually because it might be broken. I hoped that the gate would work when I tried to get my car out of the lot. Fortunately, the gate did work.

I told my wife the story of the gate and she came up with two explanations that I hadn't thought of. One was that someone left their card in the device that reads the cards and this was causing the aberrant behavior. The second was that it had been raining heavily that day and perhaps the rain caused some electrical problem in the gate.

B2: PERSONAL WORLD: The various people who we know on occasion do things that we would not have anticipated and cannot quite comprehend. These require us to formulate specific questions, such as *"Why were people walking without shoes?"* in the example below. The general EQ is: *What previous behavioral change led to this event?*

EXAMPLE 6 (Shoeless Student)

Yesterday I walked into a graduate student office and saw David sitting down reading the paper with no shoes on. I chalked it up to idiosyncratic behavior. Ten minutes later, I was walking down the hall and saw Jonathan walking toward me barefoot. At that point I decided that there must be an explanation. I realized that it had been raining very hard that day and that David and Jonathan must have gotten their shoes and socks soaked. They had then taken them off to let them dry. Jonathan confirmed my hypothesis.

B3: SOCIAL WORLD: We also concern ourselves with the institutions that are part of our lives and seek to formulate accurate models of them. When they do something that violates our model we ask what we have misunderstood. The specific question here is: *Why did Yale give up on its principles in a tenure case?* The general question is: *What are the policies of this institution?*

EXAMPLE 7 (Yale and Tenure)

At dinner last night, we were talking about the woman who was denied tenure at Yale (History Dept.) and sued the university. Yale settled out of court.

• The woman claimed that she was denied tenure because she is female, and that they gave her position to someone less qualified.
• For academic reasons, the woman did not deserve tenure (opinion of the history faculty). Her position was given to another woman. Courts cannot decide academic qualifications. One would have thought that Yale would have fought it out in court, defending principles. Why didn't they?

Some explanations I thought of:

1. It's cheaper to settle out of court than to let the case drag through the courts.

2. Yale settled out of court precisely BECAUSE courts can't decide academic qualifications, so Yale gets to say (implicitly) that the woman was a poor scholar, although they chose to pay her off.

C: GOAL OF EXPERIENCE: Anomalies are explained for a reason, and these reasons conform to the goals that we examined in Chapter 3, namely: coherency; context; prediction of individual behavior; prediction of group behavior; copying strategies; adding facts; and the seeking of universal truths. Each of these goals spawns questions related to them.

C1: COHERENCY: To establish if the actor has something coherent in mind when all signs are to the contrary, we ask appropriate questions. We saw some of these questions in the discussion of the Monty Python sketch. One EQ here is: *What are the plans of this institution?* Here is an example:

EXAMPLE 8 (Hairdressers and Credit Cards)
Diane was trying to figure out why hairdressers won't take credit cards. She thought that maybe they had a poor clientele but realized it was also true in Westport. She never found an answer.

C2: CONTEXT: To find the natural context for a given event in the belief-action chain, we often must formulate appropriate questions, e.g., *Why don't TV commentators attempt to be more analytical in their presentations?* This is answered with respect to the EQ: *What are the goals of this institution?*

EXAMPLE 9 (Campaign Predictions)

I noticed with Hart all the news people yesterday were saying that *that's what he's been predicting for two years* **as though he had such a sage understanding in advance of how the campaign was going to work. That's how they explain the situation, or at least provide background.**
I got very annoyed as different news shows repeated this and I wondered why NONE of them were swift enough to look at other predictions made by other candidates of how THEY would do and blow the whole notion away. I explain this anomaly by positing that

they just want something to say to fill up air time and are too dumb to think about what is really going on.

C3: PREDICTION OF INDIVIDUAL BEHAVIOR: To find new predictive rules for the behavior of a given individual we must inquire as to why they do what they do. This can apply to why particular animals do what they do, as well as to why we ourselves do what we do. For example, the question below is: *Why did I talk to the dog like that?* which relates to the EQ: *How is this action typical of this actor?*

EXAMPLE 10 (Barking Dog)

Walking home, I was deep in thought when I heard the sound of a dog barking fiercely and saw it coming at me. Without stopping to think, I slipped my hands into the pockets of my coat and, without breaking my stride, made eye contact with the dog and asked: *Just what do you think you're doing? Hunh? HUNH? Just WHAT do you think you're doing?!* **Startled by the sound of my own voice, I suddenly felt quite foolish. What was I doing speaking out loud (asking silly questions, no less!) to strange, hostile dogs in public places? Discretely glancing around, I was relieved not to detect any witnesses. Then I realized that it had worked—the dog had shut up, backed out of my way, and was looking totally cowed and confused.**

C4: GENERALIZATION FOR GROUP PREDICTION: To find new predictive rules that hold for a group, so as to eliminate the sense that certain events are anomalous, we ask about anomalies that we find, e.g., *"Why do underdogs win in New Hampshire primaries?"* and find answers by relating to the EQ: *How does this behavior fit in with a group of behaviors?* in this instance.

EXAMPLE 11 (New Hampshire Primaries)

Political postmorteming over the Gary Hart win in New Hampshire reminded me of McCarthy in 1968. In February in New Hampshire, not much is happening other than waiting for the sap to rise in the maples, so voters are receptive to the energy and youth of young campaign workers. Similarly for the weather. It was snowing, so the candidate with the most 4-wheel drive vehicle owning supporters was likely to win.

C5: ADDITIVE FACTS: To add new facts to one's personal data base that will better enable one to function in the future, we ask about whatever circumstances we cannot control or understand. For example, the question below is: *Why won't the door close?* This is related to *What were the underlying causes of this bad event?*

EXAMPLE 12 (Car Doors)

I've been spending more time in Alex's little Honda these days, and I never seem to be able to close the door completely. Whenever I get in or out of the thing, the dome light stays on to tell me that I haven't managed to close the door tight. Alex, on the other hand, never seems to have this problem. Last week, for the first time, I slammed the door hard enough to close it, but Alex didn't close his all the way. It struck me then that the problem wasn't me, but the second person to close a door can't do it. After pondering a moment, I decided that it must be air pressure—when the car is sealed save one door, the pressure in the car keeps that last door from closing all the way. When another door is opened, the air has another place to go.

C6: COPYING STRATEGIES: One way to get new rules for operating in the world is by copying those of others that seem to work. To do this, we ask about the strategies of others. *How does IBM manage to make money on computers by doing what seems to be odd?* relates to an EQ we have seen before, *How is this apparently ineffective plan in reality a good plan for some unseen goal?*

EXAMPLE 13 (IBM Policies)

The conflict:
• IBM sells foreign-language versions of their word-processing software in foreign countries, but refuses to sell them in the U.S.
• There are people in the U.S. who would buy the foreign-language programs.

My explanation: Since IBM has a vast and sophisticated marketing department, they must have determined that it's not cost-effective to distribute the foreign-language software in the U.S.

C7: TRUTH SEEKING: The goal is to find universal truths that hold across wide ranges of phenomena. Thus, we seek to understand, for its own sake, the anomaly, e.g., *Why is my friend doing this odd behavior?* This question brings up the EQ: *Is this actor a member of any group that is known to do this anomalous behavior?*

EXAMPLE 14 (Holding the Pillow):

I was spending a quiet evening with Suzie, who is in the midst of an internship in midwifery. She had had a difficult day (delivered her first dead baby) and was finally relaxing a little. We were sitting on the bed and she was hugging a pillow to her breast. It was not a focus of her attention, she was just holding it there as we talked. This reminded me of the fact that I had seen someone holding a pillow

like that before; I didn't remember the particular scene, but I did remember that the other person had also been a woman. I asked her why women do that—she was surprised, and said she hadn't even noticed she was holding it, but that it somehow made her more comfortable. The feeling was quite palpable, and changed when the pillow was held differently. My explanation, which she agreed with, was that it affected the level of some hormone associated with nursing; that would make holding things in that position feel good. The pillow is roughly baby sized, and the phenomenon only worked in a narrow range of positions. There should be some sort of biological mechanism for making nursing attractive. Suzie's might have been activated by her work (or always present in women of that age) and she could have been sensitized to the feeling by her stressed-out, emotional condition. We had no other explanation of why that sensation should be so strong, or why neither of us could think of a man in a similar position.

One point to be made from looking at the above examples is the difference between the question that was asked directly and the EQ from which it was derived. Questions can be fairly difficult to answer if they are posed in the wrong way. EQs serve to focus questions by pointing the way to answers. Thus, in example 14, for example, just asking why Suzie is doing what she is doing may not be very helpful. But, considering what group that she is a part of that shares the behavior to be explained may help a great deal in coming up with an answer. The assumption here then is that the specific question is generated first, but that in answering it, one must make reference to some EQ. The general EQ then helps provide the answer by pointing to known answers stored with it. In general, the process of question transformation, that is the deriving of more answerable questions from less answerable ones, is critical to explanation. We discuss this further in Chapter 8.

SOME QUESTIONS

Perhaps one of the most important observations one can make from looking at the foregoing examples of explanation is how ubiquitous a phenomenon explanation is. People seem to be explaining all kinds of things to themselves all the time. These examples were gathered from a rather intelligent group of people over a fairly short period of time. And, of course, the examples shown here are only a small sample of what was sent to me. Do unintelligent people do as much explanation? It seems likely that they do, but it is my belief that intelligence and the need to make explanations are linked phenomena.

But, what to make of the fact that at least one group of people seems to be explaining things to themselves quite frequently? The answer, I think, is this: People have a large set of questions to which they do not know the answer. They do not concern themselves with the facts of their ignorance at every moment of the day, but, when an opportunity comes to find the answer to an extant question, they take it. Perhaps more interestingly, they seek to generate new questions as new phenomena appear. What is the significance of this? First, with respect to understanding anything — written text, other people's actions, whatever — **one must be able to generate and answer large sets of questions.** Second, it seems clear that **learning is dependent upon the successful generation and answering of these questions.** Explanation therefore, can be seen as a phenomenon whose role it is to answer questions that have been generated by an understanding system in response to a lack of information about a given subject.

The next step, after posing questions is to attempt to answer them, of course. But, our problem now, in terms of the problem of defining the process of explanation, is how exactly such questions were posed. Further, after posing a question, since many possible questions could be posed, one must determine which questions are sensible enough to pursue, and which should be abandoned. Consequently, we now discuss the issue of where questions such as these come from.

GENERATING AN EXPLANATION QUESTION

Consider the following:

In the summer of 1984, Swale, the best thoroughbred racehorse of that year, the one who had been winning the most important races for three year old horses, was found dead in his stall. Newspapers around the country concerned themselves with the issue of why Swale had died.

The problem here is not figuring out how Swale died. Most people, when confronted with a story or situation such as this, can figure out, or invent, a theory of what happened. That is, it is possible to explain Swale's death in many different ways. The issue for us here is how we come up with potential explanations. There is no right answer. It might seem that there is only one cause of death and therefore there is only one explanation. But, for our purposes, there are as many right answers as there are coherent hypotheses. And, in fact, different explanations satisfy different questioners. Thus, the first issue is what different questions there might be from which different hypotheses could be derived. To examine the problem of answers, one must first look at the questions.

To see how the explanation process begins then, let's consider what standard Explanation Questions might exist from which specific questions could be generated. The list presented here is by no means exhaustive. As I noted earlier, theoretically there are 63 different types of EQs. Moreover, these types can be further and further specified. An EQ is, in principle, an old favorite type of question that has been useful in the past for helping one to find answers. Thus, we could expect that different individuals would have different idiosyncratic questions that they prefer to ask. There is no right set. Rather, EQs are useful to the extent that they can help transform specific questions for which no answer exists into general questions for which a standard answer exists. Thus, the EQs presented here simply relate to this example in some way. The intent here is to give the flavor of how EQs function, the real test of that coming in how they are used to find Explanation Patterns.

PHYSICAL EXPLANATION QUESTIONS

The first set of Explanation Questions that we discuss are all about physical causal sequences, involving both simple physical events and human behavior. The basic concept is that one event causes or enables another event. In contrast, the explanations in the two sections that follow are based on concepts such as *typical behavior for an individual (group, institution)*.

EQ1: "WHAT CAUSED AN UNEXPECTED EVENT?"

The goal is to UNDERSTAND an UNPREDICTED event. EQ1 includes the question applied in Example 3 (The Ice Storm), which is *What caused the loud noises during the storm?* In that case, the unpredicted event of loud noises has potentially harmful CONSEQUENCES, because whenever we hear loud noises we think that something dangerous might be happening.

EQ2: "WHAT FACTORS CAUSED THIS EVENT and CAN THEY HAPPEN AGAIN?"

The goal is to AVOID an UNPREDICTED event. EQ2 is relevant in Example 15 (Lightbulbs).

EXAMPLE 15 (Lightbulbs)

The lightbulb in the hall blew for the second time in a month. Diane said that we must have put in an old bulb. I decided that it was a 100 watt bulb in a closed container and that heat blew it. I put in a 60-watter and decided to give more strength to my belief that light bulbs in a closed space cause too much heat to accumulate which causes them to blow out.

This EQ is simple enough to explain. When something doesn't work the way we expected it would, we want to know why. One reason that we want to know why, is that we want to correct the aberrant situation so that it doesn't happen again. Thus, the issue is how to avoid this continuing in the future.

EQ3: "WHAT THEORY OF PHYSICAL CAUSES EXPLAINS THIS EVENT?"

The goal is to UNDERSTAND an UNPREDICTED event. The issue here is to differentiate EQ3 from EQ2. For example, when an object fails to function properly, we can ask either *How do I fix it so it works right the next time?* or *What principle is governing the continuing failure here?* The first is EQ2 in simple English. The second is EQ3.

EQ3 is common enough among technically-oriented people. Example 12 (Car Doors) is an instance of it. The person posing the problem was worrying about why things tend to work the way they do. He found himself posing theories of the physical phenomena involved. In fact, in Example 12, both EQ2 and EQ3 are active. The problem was to get the car door to close properly as well as to understand why. It was possible to learn a rule about why doors of Honda's don't close easily, or simply to learn that opening the window will fix the problem without learning why. This difference reflects the difference between EQ2 and EQ3.

EQ3.1: "WHAT WERE THE UNDERLYING CAUSES OF THIS BAD EVENT?"

This is a special case of EQ3, where the event was a bad, or dangerous event, and hence our goal in understanding is to be able to avoid it. It differs from EQ3 in that EQ3 is understanding for curiosity's sake, while EQ3.1 has a serious purpose. We might give up on EQ3 before we give up on EQ3.1. EQ3.1 differs from EQ4–EQ6 in that EQ3.1 does not begin with any assumption that the victim in the bad event was at fault. For example, if someone were mugged several times, it would be possible to explain why that individual tended to get mugged by creating a theory about the victims of a mugging. If the theory were constructed that only short people get mugged, maybe elevator shoes might be a good solution.

This having been said, let me now introduce the remaining physical EQs with minimal additional comment.

EQ4: "HOW DID THE VICTIM ENABLE THIS BAD EVENT?"

The goal is to AVOID by MODIFYING OWN BEHAVIOR. This is the behavioral analog of EQ2. The observer wants to learn how to recognize the conditions of danger before they occur so that the danger can be avoided. Thus, for example, if he got hurt in icy conditions (Example

16—Slipping on Snow), then deciding not to go out on a snowy day would work here.

EXAMPLE 16 (Slipping on Snow)

This morning, as I stepped out the door into the snow, I expected it to be slippery but found instead that the snow was nice and crunchy— better than average traction. Walking to my bus stop, I became aware that it was a bit late and I had better hustle if I wanted to make the bus. I started to speed up to a jog and went into a skid, almost falling. I wondered what had happened to my nice crunchy traction. I thought that it might be that the weather was changing. This didn't seem likely since it had only been three minutes. I then thought that maybe the snow on this block was different. I have noticed in the past surprising differences in this few-block-area of how early flowers bloom, how soon snow melts, etc. This reminded me of ice I had noticed in that part of my route the previous day. While most of the way was clear, I had detoured around a bad-looking patch. Then I decided that the snow itself was still high-traction. What was slippery was the ice underneath. I was slipping on old ice, which I had easily avoided when I could see it, but which now looked the same as where there was concrete under the snow.

EQ5: "WHAT DID THE VICTIM DO WRONG IN THIS BAD EVENT?"

The goal is to DECREASE EFFECTS by MODIFYING OWN BEHAVIOR. In this case the observer worries about how to cope with the same situation if it occurs again. In the slipping on snow example, the observer would want to generate some rules about how to walk in snow.

EQ6: "WHAT CIRCUMSTANCES LED TO THIS EVENT?"

Here the goal is to AVOID by REARRANGING CIRCUMSTANCES. If something you value is threatened, you might take steps to preserve it. Thus when trying to explain a robbery, there are many explanations one could construct. One of these exemplifies EQ6, namely the creation of set of impediments for the robber. In this case, *there weren't enough good locks* might be all the explanation that was required with respect to a robbery.

The point of EQs in general is to establish what kind of explanation is necessary so that an explanation can begin to be constructed. One cannot come up with elevator shoes as a hypothesis unless one has asked the question: *What can I do to change my behavior that fits in with my theory of why I am in danger in this circumstance?*

This is, actually, a rather important point. Asking the right question is critical in science, as any scientist knows. It is also critical in daily life. We return to this point again, especially in Chapter 7, but it worth noting here that one simply cannot come up with creative answers without creative questions. The premise here is that creativity is, in fact, guided by the EQs presented here. In other words, **there exist standard methods of finding creative solutions to problems. These methods are embodied in the selection and use of EQs.**

SOCIAL EXPLANATION QUESTIONS

EQ7: "WHY DID THIS INSTITUTION ACT THIS WAY?"

As we have said, we try to understand why the institutions that we interact with do what they do. Thus, we seek to understand corporate or institutional policies when they affect us. In EQ7 we are trying to understand what the social factors are that cause a given institution to act the way it does. In other words, we need to know about the environment that an institution operates within in order to appreciate why it has evolved into its present shape.

This is specified more particularly in the following set of EQs:

EQ8: "WHAT ARE THE POLICIES OF THIS INSTITUTION?"

The goal is to UNDERSTAND institutional behavior, focusing on its PROTOTYPIC policies. We are seeking to know how an institution makes its decisions. Examples 7, 8, and 13 include speculation about the policies at Yale, small businesses, and IBM. The need to explain institutional behavior can revolve around an attempt to understand the policies of that institution. Policies are prototypic in that the explanations have the form *Institutions of this type always do such and so.*

EQ9: "WHAT ARE THE GOALS OF THIS INSTITUTION?"

The goal here is to UNDERSTAND institutional behavior, focusing on PREDICTIVE goal-based behavior. In general, we seek to understand the institutions we deal with. In this case, understanding means being able to explain past actions as well as being able to predict future actions. As we shall see, the EQs above, plus the others given at the end of this chapter, give one the opportunity to do that.

EQ10: "WHAT PLANS WAS THIS INSTITUTION CARRYING OUT?"

EQ11: "WHAT DID THIS INSTITUTION DECIDE WAS MOST IMPORTANT?"

EQ12: "WHAT WILL THIS INSTITUTION DO NEXT?"

These three EQs all relate to the treatment of an institution as if it were a human actor.

PERSONAL EXPLANATION QUESTIONS

We seek personal explanations as well. These include particular observations about particular individuals as well as an attempt to understand stereotypical groupings of individuals. A great deal of this type of explanation involves seeing the action that needs to be explained as prototypical of actors who are members of a particular group, and attempting to place the actor of this action into that group. An explanation that is already extant can then be used as the basis for constructing a new explanation. We see how this works shortly.

EQ13: "WHAT CAUSED THE ACTOR TO BEHAVE THIS WAY?"

This is the basic question of behavior, focusing on the actor as an individual. The goal is to UNDERSTAND the event as a REACTION to some prior event.

EQ14: "IS THE ACTOR A MEMBER OF ANY GROUP THAT IS KNOWN TO DO THIS ANOMALOUS BEHAVIOR?"

This is the basic question of behavior, focusing on the actor as a member of some group. The goal is to UNDERSTAND the event as typical of certain GROUP behavior by finding the applicable group. If we can find a group, then the behavior is no longer anomalous. We can predict future actions of that individual by resorting to a standard pattern of actions associated with the group to which we have determined that our actor belongs.

EQ15: "WHY WOULD THE GROUP THAT THIS THE ACTOR IS A MEMBER OF DO THIS ANOMALOUS BEHAVIOR?"

Of course, we may not have a set of predicted actions associated with every group. Thus, we can attempt to understand a particular group better by creating a hypothesis about the theory of that group. That is the role of EQ15. In essence, it begins the process of theory formation. The result of answering EQ15 leads to knowledge that can, in the future, answer EQ14.

EQ16: "WHAT MAKES THIS PARTICULAR GROUP BEHAVE DIFFERENTLY FROM OTHER GROUPS?"

In order to create a theory about a group, it is sometimes necessary to speculate about that group in comparison to other groups. Concluding that group A is like group B can be a way of explaining the actions of group A if those of group B are known.

EQ17: "HOW DOES THIS BEHAVIOR FIT IN WITH A GROUP OF BEHAVIORS?"

Sometimes we need to find out if various actions are related by virtue of having the same cause. Viewing an anomalous action together with other actions can render the general phenomenon more understandable. Knowing which actions to compare a given action to is the hard part here.

EQ18: "WHAT PLANS DOES THIS GROUP HAVE?"

Knowing that an actor is a member of a group can help us to predict the plans that he will use if it is the case the plans of the group are known. Understanding that someone is a pacifist, for example, will help to explain why he backed away from a particular fight.

EQ19: "WHY DOES THIS GROUP HAVE THE GOALS THAT IT DOES?"

We may want to know how a particular group came to have given goal. In the terms we used in Schank and Abelson (1977), we need to know the *themes* that drive the goals. In general, any goal or plan-related EQ for an individual actor has a group equivalent, where the actor has that goal or plan by virtue of belonging to some group known to have that goal or plan. Thus an individual actor can have many diverse and possibly conflicting sets of goals, coming not only from the actor's personal needs and experiences, but also from the needs and experiences of the groups to which the actor belongs.

Other EQs for personal behavior can be derived from the nature of goals and plans (Schank & Abelson, 1977, Carbonell, 1979):

EQ20: "WHAT COUNTERPLAN WAS THE ACTOR PERFORMING?"

Counterplans are actions done to block the plans of other actors that this actor is known to be in conflict with. Seeing that an action fits a standard set of counterplans may help to explain it. For example, two politicians in a debate will always claim to disagree on every answer, even though what they actually say may mean the same thing. This is because each politician has to block his opponent's plan of appearing to be right.

EQ21: "WHAT PREVIOUS BEHAVIORAL CHANGE LED TO THIS EVENT?"

Since we are relying here on standard patterns of behavior, we must also know about changes in patterns. When a pattern changes, we expect it to affect future events and behaviors.

EQ21.1 "WHAT LED TO THE CHANGE IN BEHAVIOR?"

If we interpret an event as a change in behavior, then we have different explanations from those we use to explain a single action.

EQ22: "HOW IS THIS ACTION TYPICAL FOR THIS ACTOR?"

Just as we must know the actions of an individual to the extent that they are explained by his membership in a group, we must also know when they are explained by his simply being who he is. *That's just the way John is* is not a very deep explanation, but recognizing a pattern in a set of actions does give some comfort.

EQ23 "HOW IS THIS EVENT A TYPICAL COUNTERPLAN APPLIED TO THIS ACTOR?"

Sometimes, a salient feature of an actor is not what that actor does, but what happens to that actor. In EQ23, it is assumed that some other actor has done a typical counterplan against this actor. For example, in the movies, at least, detectives are always being led into traps.

EQ24: "HOW IS THIS APPARENTLY INEFFECTIVE PLAN IN REALITY A GOOD PLAN FOR SOME UNSEEN GOAL?"

Reclassification can be an effective method of explanation. Things seem odd on occasion because they were misclassified in the first place. EQ24 allows for looking at an action as effecting a positive outcome by reconsidering the goals that were assumed to be operating.

ESTABLISHING POTENTIAL EXPLANATION QUESTIONS

Now, having listed a general classification of types of EQs that can be active, we can consider how to determine which of them might be active at any given time. For example, in trying to ascertain why Swale died, the problem is determining which of the general types of EQs could possibly be active here. An EQ is active if it in any way relates to the problem at hand. To establish if an EQ is active in the Swale case, let's examine them one by one:

1-POSSIBLE QUESTIONS

Each of the EQs have goals associated with them. Explanations are goal-driven. The task at hand in the process of explanation is to determine whether the goal within an EQ is relevant to the goals of the understander. In other words, there is no correct explanation. Rather, we must decide the kind of explanation that we want and pursue it. Seen that way, the EQs given above yield questions that we can ask about the situation that we have failed to understand.

For example, EQ2 (*How can I keep an unexpected physical event from happening again?*) translates, in the particular context of the Swale situation, into the question:

> *How can I keep Swale from dying again?*

This is a rather odd question. Thus, EQ2 is not an active EQ for this example.

EQ3.1 (*What theory of physical causes explains this event?*) becomes, in this example, the actual question:

What were the underlying medical causes of Swale's death?

Clearly, such a question could be active, in the sense that it makes sense to ask it. Of course, it might not make sense for any given individual to ask it. That issue however, is taken care of in later steps of the explanation algorithm. Initially, we only want to know which EQs are active. Later, we seek to determine which EQs are of interest to us personally.

EQs—GOOD AND BAD

Below are the EQs that make sense to think about with respect to Swale's death, in terms of the question that EQ translates into in this case:

EQ1: WHAT CAUSED SWALE'S DEATH?

is derived from "WHAT CAUSED AN UNEXPECTED EVENT?"

This is the basic question. It does not need to be active because the more specific versions, such as EQ1.1, are active.

EQ1.1: HOW WILL SWALE'S DEATH BENEFIT OTHERS?

is derived from "HOW WILL AN UNEXPECTED EVENT BENEFIT OTHERS?"

This is a reasonable question. We can at this point create some convoluted plan that might have resulted in Swale's death. The trick here is the correct characterization of the event. Is it a *"death,"* a *"horse death,"* a *"racehorse death,"* or a *"valuable object theft?"* The point is each of these might be the index to a pattern. For example, there is a movie called *The Killing* about the killing of a racehorse as a subterfuge for a robbery at the racetrack. People have been reminded of that movie when discussing Swale when the idea of *"horse death for profit"* comes up

EQ2: HOW MIGHT SWALE'S DEATH HAPPEN AGAIN?

is derived from "WHAT FACTORS CAUSED THIS EVENT and CAN THEY HAPPEN AGAIN?"

This is not a reasonable question, although it could be transformed into a different question, *"How might the same thing happen to another racehorse?"* that *is* reasonable. That happens below, with the institutional EQs.

EQ3.1: WHAT WERE THE MEDICAL CAUSES OF SWALE'S DEATH?

is derived from "WHAT WERE THE UNDERLYING CAUSES OF THIS BAD EVENT?"

This is a reasonable question.

EQ4: HOW DID SWALE CAUSE HIS OWN DEATH?
is derived from "HOW DID THE VICTIM ENABLE THIS BAD EVENT?"

Since horses do not control what happens to them, this is not a reasonable question.

EQ5: HOW DID SWALE INCREASE THE EFFECTS OF HIS DEATH?
is derived from "WHAT DID THE VICTIM DO WRONG IN THIS BAD EVENT?"

Since we don't know how Swale died, it is not reasonable to ask how Swale made things worse.

EQ6: WHAT CIRCUMSTANCES THAT SWALE HAD CONTROL OF LED TO HIS DEATH?
is derived from "WHAT CIRCUMSTANCES LED TO THIS EVENT?"

As with EQ4, this is not a reasonable question.

Institutional EQs

The institutional EQs focus on Swale as part of the "racehorse" institution.

EQ7: IS EARLY DEATH A TYPICAL EVENT IN THE LIFE OF A RACEHORSE?
is derived from "WHY DID THIS INSTITUTION ACT THIS WAY?"

This is a reasonable question.

EQ8: IS EARLY DEATH A POLICY FOR RACEHORSES?
is derived from "WHAT ARE THE POLICIES OF THIS INSTITUTION?"

EQ9: IS EARLY DEATH A GOAL FOR RACEHORSES?
is derived from "WHAT ARE THE GOALS OF THIS INSTITUTION?"

EQ10: IS EARLY DEATH A PLAN FOR RACEHORSES?
is derived from "WHAT PLANS WAS THIS INSTITUTIONS CARRYING OUT?"

EQ11: IS EARLY DEATH MORE IMPORTANT THAN OTHER THINGS FOR RACEHORSES?
is derived from "WHAT DID THIS INSTITUTION DECIDE WAS MOST IMPORTANT?"

EQ12: WHAT DO RACEHORSES DO AFTER DEATH?
is derived from "WHAT WILL THIS INSTITUTION DO NEXT?"

All of these questions are not reasonable, if for no other reason than that racehorses are not planners.

EQ13: WHAT MADE SWALE DECIDE TO DIE?
is derived from "WHAT CAUSED THE ACTOR TO BEHAVE THIS WAY?"

Not a reasonable question.

The personal explanation questions based on groups would consider Swale as a racehorse, but treat "racehorse" as a kind of animal, rather than an institutional actor. Hence, these questions are more likely to be reasonable.

EQ14: IS SWALE A MEMBER OF SOME GROUP FOR WHOM EARLY DEATH IS NORMAL?
is derived from "IS THE ACTOR A MEMBER OF ANY GROUP THAT IS KNOWN TO DO THIS ANOMALOUS BEHAVIOR?"

EQ15: WHY MIGHT RACEHORSES DIE YOUNG?
is derived from "WHY WOULD THE GROUP THAT THIS THE ACTOR IS A MEMBER OF DO THIS ANOMALOUS BEHAVIOR?"

EQ16: WHY MIGHT RACEHORSES, AS OPPOSED TO ANY OTHER KIND OF ANIMAL, DIE YOUNG?
is derived from "WHAT MAKES THIS PARTICULAR GROUP BEHAVE DIFFERENTLY FROM OTHER GROUPS?"

EQ17: IS SWALE'S DEATH RELATED TO SWALE'S OTHER ACTIVI-TIES, e.g., HIS WINNING ALL THOSE RACES?
is derived from "HOW DOES THIS BEHAVIOR FIT IN WITH A GROUP OF BEHAVIORS?"

These are all reasonable questions.

EQ18: IS SWALE'S DEATH A COMMON PLAN FOR RACE-HORSES?
is derived from "WHAT PLANS DOES THIS GROUP HAVE?"

EQ19: WHY DO RACEHORSES HAVE THE GOAL OF DYING YOUNG?
is derived from "WHY DOES THIS GROUP HAVE THE GOALS THAT IT DOES?"

EQ20: IS SWALE'S DEATH A COUNTERPLAN OF SWALE'S?
is derived from "WHAT COUNTERPLAN WAS THE ACTOR PER-FORMING?

EQ21: IS SWALE'S DEATH PART OF A CHANGING PATTERN OF BEHAVIOR FOR SWALE?
is derived from "WHAT PREVIOUS BEHAVIORAL CHANGE LED TO THIS EVENT?"

EQ22: IS SWALE'S DEATH SOMETHING SWALE DOES ALL THE TIME?

is derived from "HOW IS THIS ACTION TYPICAL FOR THIS ACTOR?"

These are not reasonable questions, since they all assume a planner is involved.

EQ23: IS SWALE'S DEATH THE RESULT OF SWALE BEING THE VICTIM OF SOME COUNTERPLAN?

is derived from "HOW IS THIS EVENT A TYPICAL COUNTERPLAN APPLIED TO THIS ACTOR?"

This is not only a reasonable question, but one that many people come up with after thinking about the problem a little.

EQ24: IS SWALE'S DEATH, WHICH WE NATURALLY ASSUME TO BE A BAD THING FOR SWALE, REALLY A GOOD THING FOR HIM IN THE END?

is derived from "HOW IS THIS APPARENTLY INEFFECTIVE PLAN IN REALITY A GOOD PLAN FOR SOME UNSEEN GOAL?"

Notice that in some cases, the bad EQs translate into questions that are absurd, in other cases, they may be impossible even to state, and in still others there are sensible questions, if you relax your definition of "sensible" a bit. In other words, crazy ideas can come from pursuing a bad EQ seriously. Sometimes, of course, crazy ideas aren't so crazy after all.

RESTRICTING EXPLANATION QUESTIONS TO THOSE OF INTEREST

The next step in the explanation process is to restrict the theoretically possible explanation questions to those that actually might produce a reasonable answer. Once the active EQs are determined, the question that that EQ generates has to be put into terms that reflect the goals of the explainer. Not all active EQs are equally interesting, especially not to every explainer.

Now let's consider the active EQs for this example. Consider, for example, the question that would be derived from EQ1.1, namely: *How will Swale's death benefit others?* In this phase of the explanation process we take the active EQ and determine where the interests of the explainer match the goals inherent in the EQ. Thus, for example, if you are a detective or an insurance investigator, the question generated by EQ1.1 is very relevant. EQ1.1, under this view, is quite common, and we call it **the FOUL PLAY hypothesis.**

This is a critical point. Each of the active EQs generate a hypothesis that can be eventually translated into an explanation. The FOUL PLAY hypothesis is a fairly standard hypothesis that should be called up in some standard situations. It is what I call an **EXPLANATION PATTERN (XP),** about which I shall have more to say shortly. EXPLANATIONS PATTERNS are indexed under EQs. In fact, one of the primary purposes of having standardized questions such as EQs, is to enable the finding of standardized answers, derived from XPs. Thus, FOUL PLAY is indexed under EQ1.1. It is not the only pattern under EQ1.1, but it is the only one we shall consider right now.

In order to correctly match active EQs with the goal of the explainer, therefore, what is really needed is a goal-biased version of the EQ. In other words, if goals are part of the EQ, then they can be matched to goals that are part of the interests of the explainer.

Now, the task of determining the relevant EQs is really one of establishing how the goal-biases inherent in the active EQ relate to one's interests. So, the FOUL PLAY pattern would be activated by EQ1.1 because detectives and other investigators are, by definition, people interested in who benefits from some crime or event. A random explainer, who just had a curiosity about Swale could, of course, adopt the perspective of such an investigator, which means, in this case, no more than a decision to keep EQ1.1 active.

The EQ3.1 perspective (*"What were the medical causes of Swale's death?"*) is goal-biased towards a theoretical explanation. Here again, there are people whose perspectives are inherently oriented towards a EQ3 point of view. Often these people are scientists, for example. Or, in this case, a veterinarian might look for this kind of explanation. The point is that in an automatic explanation system, the bias of the explainer would be pre-set. That is, if we had the task of saying what kind of explanation a veterinarian might look for, we would have classified a veterinarian as someone whose goals included theoretical explanations, and would follow the line of EQ3.1 in that case.

Is It Really Exhaustive Search?

One might get the impression from what has preceded that I am suggesting that the way we determine which EQs are possible is by testing each one in turn to see if it makes sense. To some degree, this is a viable algorithm. It may well be that there are occasions in which one is well off to consider each possibility in turn. This is especially likely to be worthwhile when the payoff is large. That is, sometimes an issue is significant enough to warrant an exhaustive search of that type, testing every possibility in its turn. And, one would expect that computers might well employ such a technique when looking for especially important explanations and when time is of no consequence. However, there is little reason to suppose that humans employ such algorithms.

But, as in the old joke about the woman who agrees to sex for a million dollars and then is offended with a suggestion that she do it for five dollars, we are just arguing about price. The cost of search is the issue. One can devise numerous methods by which only some EQs will be considered. These methods would presumably employ various indexing schemes that would call some EQs to mind if various conditions were met. Such conditions would include, one would assume, some of the features that I mentioned earlier. But, it is important to understand that we are just arguing about price. The cost of search is high, but one is willing to pay that cost at various times. On other occasions, one is willing to consider one or two alternatives and then further search is not worth the effort. Determining how much to search and what to consider when is an interesting topic, but probably not one of great theoretical interest.

The Next Step in The Process

And so, we find ourselves ready to make explanations by accessing explanation patterns. Explanation Patterns are stored under Explanation Questions. When a good EQ has been generated, it is highly likely that it will point the way to a relevant XP. What exactly XPs are, and how they are used, are discussed in the next chapter.

5 The Process of Explanation: Explanation Patterns

FINDING THE XP INDEXED UNDER THE EQ

The major value of Explanation Questions is to use them to find Explanation Patterns that are stored under them. Once a standard question has been found, a standard answer will not be too far away. There is no correct path to follow in deciding which Explanation Questions to pursue. One follows the interests that one has. In any automatic explanation system, goal-biases would be useful for deciding how to create an explanation within a certain perspective. So, for example, to get a veterinarian's perspective one would follow the EQ that matched according to the goal-bias that would be part of such a system's definition of a veterinarian.

In what follows we assume that we are interested in creating many possible explanations so that we can illustrate the apparatus of explanation. The key point in explanation is that there really is nothing new under the sun in most cases of explanation. Certainly, there are occasions in which a brand new explanation is created, but understanding relies upon pre-established reference points that are learned over a period of time and applied in novel ways as needed, and thus, so does explanation.

Scripts and other knowledge structures (Schank & Abelson, 1977) are useful for placing events that are not obviously casually-related into pre-established causal chains. The point is that one does not have to compute everything as if it had been seen for the first time. Understanding relies upon our ability to take shortcuts by assuming that what we have just seen is not that different from something with which we were already familiar. All we need do, in many cases, is say "A is just like B, so I will proceed as if it were B." Not all understanding is script-based of course, but planning mechanisms also exhibit this reliance on past experiences that have been codified and fossilized.

The same is true of explanation. A great many of our explanations rely upon other explanations that we have previously used. People are inherently lazy in this way, and this laziness is of great advantage, as we shall see. Much of the point behind the work on memory reported in Schank (1982) was to show how people use past experiences to help them interpret new experiences. Reminding is one of the key methods by which this is accomplished. Seeing A as an instance of B is helpful in making generalizations and thus in learning about both A and B. The fact that generalizations are often inaccurate does not stop us from making them and does not lessen their value. In explanation, a similar phenomenon occurs. We rely upon **EXPLANATION PATTERNS (XPs)** to create new explanations from old explanations. This at once makes the process of explanation easier and makes its precision considerably less than ideal. Nevertheless, it makes creativity possible, and that is the point.

EXPLANATION PATTERNS

An Explanation Pattern is a fossilized explanation. It functions in much the same way as a script does. When it is activated, it connects a to-be-explained event with an explanation that has been used at some time in the past to explain an event similar to the current event.

Explanation Patterns are stored under EQs. Once an EQ has been determined to be of interest, various indices associated with the event to be explained can be used to activate one or more Explanation Patterns that may apply.

The value of an EQ is best understood by analogy to the primitive actions in Conceptual Dependency Theory (Schank, 1972, 1975). The real value or meaning of the primitive actions was the set of inferences that they fired off. ATRANS has no inherent meaning. It means the sum of all its inferences. ATRANS is interesting in that it is a convenient shorthand for grouping together a set of inferences that have a great deal in common. What they have in common mostly is that they fire off whenever ATRANS is present. Thus, ATRANS is a kind of index that relates words that refer to it to events that are true when the right sense of those words is present. Thus, the real value of a primitive action is in reference to a set of other actions also likely to be present when ATRANS is present.

The same situation exists with EQs. An EQ's real value, or its meaning in some sense, is in the Explanation Patterns that are indexed under it and which are caused to fire as likely hypotheses under the right conditions. To put this another way, in the case of EQ1.1 ("How will Swale's death benefit or hurt others?"), various Explanation Patterns may *"come to mind"* to be used in the current case, if they are indexed correctly. For example. EQ1.1 has within it the concept of a BENEFICIARY of the action. Thus the index BENEFICIARY OF DEATH is useful if there is an Explanation Pattern with that title. An Explanation Pattern is a standard stereotyped answer, with an explanation, to a question. In this case, the question is: *Who would benefit from a particular death?*

Most people have an Explanation Pattern for such a question. It is what we called FOUL PLAY earlier. FOUL PLAY essentially provides an answer, together with an explanation, to the above question. It says, for example, that one beneficiary is someone who stands to inherit money from the death. It also says that another beneficiary of a death is someone who has an insurance policy made out to him on the life of the dead individual.

We can see that there are really two Explanation Patterns here (actually there are probably many more). One is **FOUL PLAY; INHERITANCE,** and the other is **FOUL PLAY; INSURANCE.** Each of these is proposed as a hypothesis as the result of finding the XP indexed under a plausible EQ. The next step in the explanation process, therefore, is the evaluation of the reasonableness of the hypothesis indexed under the EQ. Thus, an EQ is valuable for suggesting to us that FOUL PLAY;INHERITANCE should be considered. Whether or not this is a reasonable hypothesis, we want to have it suggested to us, as there is no way of knowing a priori if it is reasonable until we have considered it for a while. Thus EQs force us to consider their inherent hypotheses. We can always choose to abandon those hypotheses, of course.

THE STRUCTURE OF AN EXPLANATION PATTERN

An Explanation Pattern consists of a number of parts. First, we have an **index to the pattern.** This index is made up of a combination of states and events. Second, we have **a set of states of the world under which those indices can be expected to be active.** When those states of the world are achieved, the indices fire. The next part is **the scenario.** The scenario is essentially a little story that is a carefully constructed causal chain of states and events that starts with the premise of achieving the combination of states and events in the index and presents a plan of action for achieving that combination. The fourth part is **the resultant state that follows from the scenario.** This state may also be used as an index initially (*early death* in the Swale case, for example.) Also, **attached to an XP are explanations that have been previously compiled from that XP.** In this way, one can be reminded of similar cases. Thus, XPs are themselves a means of traversing memory. Last, **every XP has a reason attached to it that can both serve as an index and as the ultimate explanation behind the use of the explanation embodied in an XP.** (In other words, every explanation can cause us to demand an explanation at a higher level.)

To make this simpler to understand, the EQ poses a question, and the Explanation Pattern answers that question. But, this is all in the most general of terms. The question is not about Swale's death, but about beneficiaries of death in general. The answer is not about Swale, but about prior experiences with the general phenomenon. It could not be any other way, of course. Memory cannot concern itself with storing patterns about Swale. Such patterns, once encountered, are not likely to be of use ever again. Rather, memory stores patterns in the most general terms, and thus we must access them in the most general terms. This is the value of the EQ. Then, after having received our answer in general terms (the XP), we can begin to try and alter that answer so as to make it relate to the particulars at hand. Thus, **the algorithm is, take a particular question, generalize from it in order to find a general question under which is indexed a general answer. Then, take the general answer and particularize it to find the specific answer that you were after originally.**

The next step then, is to match the particulars. Thus, we would reason in the Swale case, under FOUL PLAY;INHERITENCE that horses don't usually inherit money so that that hypothesis is a bit silly. But, this false XP might bring to mind that horse owners do have insurance policies on their horses so that this hypothesis might yet be viable. From bad hypotheses often come good ones. This is the ultimate value of the XP with respect to creativity.

FINDING ADDITIONAL PATTERNS

The key to inventing creative explanations lies in intelligently indexing the Explanation Patterns. It would be nice if everything we would ever want to explain about Swale were listed under *horse death,* but this is unlikely to be the case. One way to explain something unusual is by reference to something different for which there exists an explanation. So, one way to find a candidate set of Explanation Patterns is by changing the event that is to be explained into one that is like the original event but is different enough to possibly bring up a new idea that is relevant. In this way we have the possibility of finding additional Explanation Patterns that are not connected to the indices at hand but might be relevant. Thus, for example, we might know of an XP that relates to cars or elephants. We might want to test it to see if it might relate to a horse as well. Therefore we attempt to change the event that needs to be explained into another event that we can explain.

To do this, we use a set of rules that I call **tweaking rules.** Tweaking rules are very important for the process of the transformation and adaptation of XPs into answers that are relevant to specific questions. To get a feel for what these rules look like, let's consider three of them here:

Rule 1: **Transpose objects that are alike in function.**

The idea behind a tweaking rule is to change what we were looking at into something else that might give us new ideas. So, since we are interested in horses, let's consider a different aspect of a horse from the obvious aspects that are relevant in Swale's case. For example, a horse is transportation and so is a car. Thus, one thing to consider would be rules relating to the "death" of cars. We can try this in any of the EQs. For example, "death of cars" plus EQ2 (*What factors caused this event that might happen again?*) would index Explanation Patterns that we might try to apply to horses.

Here's a possible answer to the specific question about cars that came to mind as I considered that above EQ: It happens that in my car there is a hose that pops out fairly frequently. I don't know what this hose's function is, but I know what to do when the car fails to go—I put the hose back in place. This is my own personal Explanation Pattern for "car death." Notice that this particular XP doesn't explain too much. This is true of many XPs, as we shall see. This one does its job in helping me fix my car however, and that is what matters. I was reminded of it while thinking about Swale and considered for a moment the idea that **Swale's hose had disconnected and no one put it back in time.** Such a hypothesis can then be checked for credibility, of course. And, naturally, it is quite silly. But many times this kind of application of an XP and subsequent tweaking is not so absurd.

Rule 2: **Transpose objects in similar environments.**

For example, if we consider Swale to be a person who chose to live the way he lives, i.e., in a stall, then EQ6 (*What circumstances led to this event?*) becomes relevant, and we can consider what would happen if a person had had the experiences that Swale had. If he were a person and he lived in a stall, we would assume that these cruel conditions killed him. Thus, the hypothesis **Living in a stall would kill anyone** can be generated by this rule.

Rule 3: **Transpose objects that are alike in behavior.**

Suppose that we consider racehorses to be like star performers, in that they both constantly exert great effort for short periods of time and can become extraordinarily rich and famous. This makes EQ14 (*Is the actor a member of any group that is known to do this anomalous behavior?*) relevant, and we might be reminded of star performers who have died young, such as Janis Joplin and Jimi Hendrix. This reminding enables the proposal that **Swale died from overdosing on drugs taken to relieve the pressures and boredom of stardom and available because of wealth.**

There are many more rules than those of course. The real problem here is finding suitable Explanation Patterns. Heuristics for bringing up likely candidates are thus an important part of the task of explanation.

INDEXING EXPLANATION PATTERNS

The major value of EQs, as we have said, is in their connection to XPs. XPs often have a trite and boring form, like that of clichés or proverbs. Normally such frozen patterns might bear little relation to any creative process. But, taken out of context they can often shed light on new domains of inquiry. That is the philosophy behind the *misapplication of Explanation Patterns.* When one applies patterns where they do not obviously belong, interesting things can result.

For example, let's consider EQ7 (*Is early death a typical action for racehorses?*). To be useful, EQ7 would have to be a pointer to relevant XPs that might help answer this question. In other words, what we require of EQ7 is that it somehow point us to explanation patterns that will tell us about early death, this time from the perspective of the societal factors involved. To put this another way, the question we really want to consider is *what kinds of things normally bring early death?* That is, we can ignore racehorses entirely. (This is another tweaking rule, listed as T1 in Chapter 6, which says that one can eliminate set membership constraints from consideration.) What we want to know is, *what societal conditions cause early death?* Then, after getting some XPs from that question, we can begin to consider if they might be relevant to Swale at all.

Since Explanation Patterns have a way of looking like clichés or proverbs, let's consider some clichéd XPs that might relate here. So, for example, here are some Explanation Patterns that are fairly standard that can be found under EQ7:

"Early death comes from being malnourished as a youth."

"High living brings early death."

"An inactive mind can cause the body to suffer."

"High pressure jobs cause heart attacks."

What we are arguing here is that once these Explanation Patterns are found, they can be adapted to serve as explanations of the event under consideration. Now, clearly, some of these Explanation Patterns sound pretty silly when applied to Swale. On the other hand, they are possibilities. Some of them are represent humorous possibilities and some of them are bizarre hypotheses that might just have something to them. It is not unusual that weird ideas start the creative juices flowing, and that is just what I am suggesting here. People, and computers, can get their weird ideas from playing with standard XPs in unorthodox ways, and this is how fossilized explanations, derived from explanation patterns, can serve as the beginning of the creative process.

Could Swale have felt the pressure of being "Horse of the Year" and have had this pressure contribute to a heart attack? Sounds silly but who knows? The point of course, is that we have just generated a hypothesis. We took an XP unrelated to Swale, found under the index *early death* which EQ7 uses, and related it back to Swale's life. We can now consider the legitimacy of this hypothesis.

Was Swale taking one too many "uppers"? Was he living high? He was a "star" after all. And stars do live high. So the XP fits the case, at least superficially. Where would this hypothesis come from? The argument here is that one would want to be reminded of a rock star or a star athlete. Should Swale remind you of Janis Joplin? Maybe not immediately, but Explanation Patterns can cause that reminding to occur. The task is first to cause those remindings to occur, thus bringing to mind various hypotheses, which later may be discarded. First, they must be invented. This kind of reminding can be the source of real creativity.

We can see this kind of "creativity by reminding" with respect to EQ14. In a seminar that I was running on explanation, one of the students was reminded, while discussing Swale's death, of Jim Fixx, the author of a book on the health benefits of jogging that was widely read and respected. The irony is that Jim Fixx died while jogging at a comparatively young age. This kind of reminding can be very valuable for its ability to bring to mind questions, in this instance, of the possible health hazards imposed by excessive running. And, it is from the formulation of such questions that creative thoughts can occur, Formulating new questions is as important as formulating new answers.

In EQ14 (*Is Swale a member of some group for whom early death is normal?*), we are trying to learn something new that will both explain the event under consideration as well as tie together one or more unrelated facts into some kind of explanatory whole. Thus, for example, if it were the case that many three year old racehorses die, we would want to realize that and use that fact as an explanation of Swale's death. That would, of course, not be an interesting explanation, but it is one kind of explanation that XPs provide, namely, routine ones that match the conditions of the XP perfectly.

Thus, not only clichés or proverbs are indexed as Explanation Patterns. We would also expect, as a rather standard form of Explanation Patterns, general truths. That is, one thing that we do when we explain something is to create a new rule that we can use in the future to help us understand. Such new rules are also indexed under Explanation Patterns to be used in the understanding process. Thus, Swale's death is in no way anomalous if we have the rule that many three year old race horses die young regardless of whether we know a fact that explains that rule.

Similarly, if Swale is a member of a class of actors known to die young or to be subject to heart conditions, then Swale's death is explained in the sense of explanation that we are discussing. So, we might have a rule that says that *finely-tuned running atheletes suffer more physical problems than others*. This rule would render Swale's death non-anomalous.

Alternatively, we would like to be able to construct such a rule as a way of explaining the anomaly. To do this requires us to find a class of actors for whom we have information that is connected to *early death*. The reminding about Jim Fixx is an instance of this kind of rule-search. In order to be reminded in this way, the student would have had to have created a class of actors into which he could place Swale and into which he had already previously placed Jim Fixx. Then, having indexed Jim Fixx in the same way that he indexed Swale (presumably with something like *early death*), he would be reminded. The value of the reminding is to start the process of creating a new rule incorporating both events.

EQ16 (*Why might racehorses, as opposed to any other kind of animal, die young?*) is enough like EQ14 that we can avoid getting too detailed in our discussion. We might like to understand why athletes who run have heart problems. Or, we might want to investigate the issue of whether these problems could have been predicted better. Thus, we might want to consider other athletes with heart problems to see if taken all together they might all have something in common that enabled a deeper understanding of the general phenomenon. Is early death a factor in athletes in general, or just runners, or just dark-haired athletes?

In EQ23 (*Is Swale's death the result of Swale being the victim of some counterplan?*) the question is whether Swale was in some way preventing the goals of someone else. Since Swale was entered in races, obviously he was preventing the losers from winning. Known counterplanning techniques, that is, the Explanation Patterns indexed under EQ23, include *killing one's opponent in a contest*. Thus, we have another possible explanation.

MODIFYING ASPECTS OF THE HYPOTHESES

The next step in the explanation process, after a hypothesis has been derived from an XP, is to begin to **Modify Aspects of the Hypotheses.** Thus, we must take the hypotheses created in the last step, and see if they make sense. The hypotheses, recall, were created by simply copying what seemed to be relevant Explanation Patterns. Now the task is to see if they really are relevant. We must alter the parts of the Explanation Pattern that have nothing to do with the actual case.

The **INHERITANCE** idea doesn't seem viable since horses don't have relatives who fight for inheritances. The **INSURANCE** idea makes sense if and only if the beneficiary of the policy that insured Swale stood to make more money from his death than from his being alive. The evidence with respect to that issue is just the opposite, so this hypothesis can be disregarded.

The **MALNOURISHED** hypothesis seems wrong given what we know about how valuable racehorses are treated. However, before totally discounting this, or any other hypothesis, we should recall that explainers can have different goals, rendering various explanations more or less viable relative to those goals. So, someone who wanted to make up an interesting story might consider a racehorse who died early to have died from an earlier maltreatment for use as a possible story line. Creative hypotheses are useful for things other than detective work, of course.

LIVED TOO HIGH might be viable, again it depends upon our goals. We cannot discount it as a real explanation without investigating exactly how Swale did live. But, it is a good candidate for a joke explanation. Humorists find good material from such exaggeration, and this kind of humor often originates from the construction of explanations in this manner. The same is true of **MIND INACTIVE; BODY SUFFERED.**

HIGH PRESSURE JOB CAUSED HEART ATTACK seems viable if we change "job" to "situation" and assume that Swale "knew" about the pressure on him. Since this last assumption seems a little tenuous, we again have a candidate for a joke, although this explanation seems more plausible since one cannot really know what a horse knows.

RUNNING ATHLETES SUFFER PHYSICAL PROBLEMS allows us to speculate on whether there really are any similarities between Jim Fixx and Swale that ought to be looked into. Swale didn't die while running of course, nor did he write a book. Plenty of racehorses live to a ripe old age, as do plenty of runners. Nevertheless, it is possible to hold on to this hypothesis as viable.

DARK-HAIRED ACTORS ARE PRONE TO HEART ATTACKS is lighthearted and probably irrelvant. If it were true, we could speculate on the cause, but presumably it would be because of something other than hair color.

The **PLOT TO LET OPPONENT WIN** is entirely viable, however. Here we can assume that the owner of the second best horse in Swale's next race was a serious possibility as the murderer if it was found that he was murdered (which it wasn't).

The end of this step in the explanation process, therefore, is the retaining of the few hypotheses that remain viable as possible explanations. The next task is to consider if any of these new, viable hypotheses ought to be retained as *"beliefs."*

TESTING THE NEW BELIEF

There isn't anything particularly unique about the process of testing the new belief. We are left with viable hypotheses for which we can attempt to find counterexamples. Or, we can try to find other facts that correlate with each new hypothesis that serve to strengthen it. We can try to test the causalities involved. That is, if we have asserted that A caused B, we can try to find other things like A that have caused other things like B.

The most important part of this process is *living with the new fact.* Recall that what we are trying to do here is create an additive explanation. That is, we are trying to learn something. And, what we are trying to learn is a set of expectations that, had we had them in the first place, would have caused us to have never noticed the anomaly. An event is anomalous, after all, only by reference to what we already know about the world. An event that is anomalous to one person, will not be to another, if the second person had the appropriate expectations for that event. So, we are looking to learn new facts that will resolve current anomalies. But, we are looking for the new fact that we learn to do more than simply resolve the current anomaly. We want to be able to explain events that we may encounter in the future. After all, once an anomaly is resolved, it ought not seem anomalous to us the next time we encounter it or anything like it. In other words, we want to be able to understand more than we were able to understand before confronting the current anomaly.

Thus, for example, we want to be able to use the explanation **PLOT TO LET OWNERS WIN** at some future time. Or, to put this another way, we want the Swale episode itself to become an Explanation Pattern such that when a baseball player who was likely to have been selected as Most Valuable Player for the year suddenly gets injured in an unusual way, we might suspect his nearest rival for the award.

In order to do that, we would need to first have verified that this was the case with Swale (which there is no reason to believe really, but just suppose it for a while). Then, we would have to correctly index the Swale case such that it was something to be reminded of when a debilitating circumstance took a prized competitor out of action. We would also want to find this episode only when the circumstances were in some way unusual. We certainly wouldn't want to think about Swale every time a star football player got injured.

A new explanation need never be verified in actuality. We can keep whatever Swale hypothesis we like, for as long as we like. The real issue is how often the explanation we have concocted is used to help us explain something else.

CREATING NEW FROM OLD

We can see then that the major role of Explanation Patterns, ironically, is not in their intended use. XPs are fossilized reasoning. They represent our intention not to think very profoundly about a subject. When we use an XP in its intended role, we are deciding to forego complex reasoning of our own in favor of using a well established reasoning chain that is in favor amongst a particular group of reasoners.
Essentially, the normal use of an XP is of the following form:

1. **Identify event sequence needing explanation**
2. **Establish index that is likely to lead to an XP**
3. **Find relevant XP attached to that index**
4. **Substitute XP into event sequence**

This is the normal situation, as we have seen. But, what is interesting about XPs is their abnormal use. That is, it is in the misapplication of an XP that possibilities for creativity arise. *Misapplication* is a bit of a misnomer here, since that misapplication is often quite intentional.

A LOOK AT SOME XPS

Before we can get into the details of how to *misapply a pattern correctly,* we must specify exactly what an XP looks like. In general, one would expect that any explanation pattern will have been used quite frequently by an understanding system in the normal course of processing various commonplace events. Additive explanation by use of explanation patterns, (as opposed to everyday understanding or explaining away by explanation pattern) is done when an uncommon event is being processed, and no applicable knowledge structure is found. To remedy this lack of understanding, an explanation pattern is considered for direct application or adaptation.
Let's consider what information must be represented in an XP by examining the normal functioning of one. First, there must be **indices** to be used in calling up an XP. Second, there must be **relevance-conditions for verification** of the applicability of an XP. Since creative explanation involves tweaking an XP we don't quite believe to be relevant, we also need to have some information about the **potential usefulness of tweaking** a given XP

that doesn't apply directly. For this, we need to know some key features whose presence suggests that it's worthwhile to tweak the XP. For the tweaking process, we need to know what the **belief-support relationship** of the parts of the packaged explanation is. That is, when we're dealing with a situation which isn't quite what the XP explains, we must know which parts of the XP's explanation are inviolate and which can be patched up.

The next part of an XP is the **set of episodes** for which it has previously been used. As we have seen when considering reminding, explanations revolve around the expectation failures they explain, so, an XP can relate one episode to another. That is, once one thinks of a given XP it is not too difficult to come up with examples of the use of that XP in prior situations. Thus, XPs must point to the episodes that they have been previously used to explain.

Finally, we should be able to apply the knowledge from an XP when we are planning as well as when we are correcting failures. This is done by storing a **stereotyped summary** of the explained situation in the XP. This summary tends not to be stated in the language of expectation failures or explanations; instead, it's often a proverb or rule of thumb.

Thus the parts of XPs must include:

Indices

verification information

information on when it's worth tweaking the XP

the explanation chain, for use in tweaking

prior episodes explained by the XP

a stereotyped description of the XP

Thus, every explanation pattern has the following parts:

1. **An anomaly that the pattern explains (which is the main index into the XP)**
2. **A set of relevant indices under which it can be retrieved**
3. **A set of states of the world under which the pattern is likely to be a valid explanation**
4. **A set of states of the world under which the pattern is likely to be relevant, even if it isn't immediately applicable**
5. **A pattern of actions, with the relationships between them, that shows how the event being explained could arise**
6. **A set of prior explanations that has been made possible by use of this pattern**
7. **A reason that stereotypes the behavior being explained**

As an example, a classic explanation pattern is: **KILLED FOR THE INSURANCE MONEY.** This pattern is useful when it is necessary to explain why someone was killed. If the person who is dead is worth more money dead than alive, it is reasonable to assume that he was killed for the insurance money. The pattern is as follows:

1. **An anomaly that the pattern explains:** *untimely death*
2. **A set of relevant indices under which it can be retrieved:** *untimely death; death heavily insured*
3. **A set of states of the world under which the pattern is likely to be a valid explanation:** *one of the conditions of 2 and one of the conditions from 3*
4. **A set of states of the world under which the pattern is likely to be relevant, even if it isn't immediately applicable:** *deceased was rich; relatives didn't love him; beneficiary is suspicious character*
5. **A pattern of actions, with the relationships between them, that shows how the event being explained could arise:**
   beneficiary dislikes policy-holder
   dislike makes beneficiary want to harm policy-holder
   beneficiary has goal to get a lot of money
   inheriting is a plan for getting inheritance
   insurance means that inheritance will include a lot of money
   inheriting requires that the policy-holder dies
   beneficiary kills the insured to get rid of him and to get money
6. **A set of prior explanations that has been made possible by use of this pattern:** *deaths seen in movies, mafia killings*
7. **A reason that stereotypes the behavior being explained:** *a good way to get rich and get rid of someone you don't like at the same time.*

The explanation pattern shown above is what we can call a **CULTURALLY SHARED pattern.** That is, we would expect that many people might have such a pattern and that talking about that pattern would not require a great deal of explanation in itself. In other words, it is like a restaurant in the sense that one needn't think much about it in order to operate with it.

The second major type of explanation pattern is called an **IDIOSYNCRATIC pattern.** These patterns are quite prevalent in human reasoning processes and thus it is rather important to study them and to employ them in any explanation system. **IDIOSYNCRATIC patterns** are often ill-formed in that they may constitute no actual explanation of anything. Examples of such patterns must come from real live individuals, so here are two, one gathered while I was politicking against the Viet Nam War, and one gathered from a friend:

> The first: When I was recruiting voters for an anti-war candidate, one of the people I contacted began to argue with me about the war. He said that the reason that I was against the war was that I was a coward and was just trying to avoid fighting in it. I argued my point of view but he just ended up saying: *I fought in World War II when I was your age and now it is your turn to fight in your war.*

> The second: A friend of mine told me his views on how to pick up women. He claimed that it was absurd to even try to pick up a woman who was under the age of 28. He had a complex series of reasons for this, most having to do with the shaky reasoning abilities of young people, but in the end it became clear to me that he had just not had any success with women under the age of 28.

There are two explanation patterns here. The first is: *this generation should fight a war because past ones did.* The second is: *older men can't pick up women under 28 because the women are too immature to appreciate them.* Now clearly both of these patterns are absurd. Nevertheless they are in use by at least two real people. Let's take a look at how the second one looks in the format given above for explanation patterns:

1. **An anomaly that the pattern explains:** *failures with young women*
2. **A set of relevant indices under which it can be retrieved:** *chance meetings; failures with women; singles bars; loneliness*
3. **A set of states of the world under which the pattern is likely to be a valid explanation:** *the man is successful with older women; he fails with young women*
4. **A set of states of the world under which the pattern is likely to be relevant, even if it isn't immediately applicable:** *problems with relationships; questions of maturity*
5. **A pattern of actions, with the relationships between them, that shows how the event being explained could arise:**
   woman has chance meeting with man
   quick meeting means she has to evaluate him immediately
   she's not old enough to see his good qualities that fast
   bad impression means she's doesn't want to continue with him
6. **A set of prior explanations that has been made possible by use of this pattern:** *all past failures with young women*
7. **A reason that stereotypes the behavior being explained:** *young women expect too much from a new relationship*

A key point is that the summary need not be a rational conclusion from the conditions, nor is there any reason that the XP has to have the correct explanation of the situation. It's also important to note that in the pattern of actions, the relationship between steps which we're representing is belief-support, not deduction. In most people's picture of the world, there's seldom an absolute causal link between a supporting fact and what it supports; it may be necessary to accumulate a lot of independent evidence for a condition before we believe it. For example, in the **KILLED FOR THE INSURANCE MONEY** XP, either the beneficiary wanting to get rid of the policy-holder or his wanting to inherit money is support for his killing the policy-holder, and for some people, either would be enough motivation for murder. We wouldn't normally believe that either one alone resulted in a murder, while the two together are fairly convincing evidence.

Even when a pattern is idiosyncratic and ill-formed, it is useful for reasoning. That much is obvious, since people do use such rules to explain the behavior for which they were concocted. The question with respect to explanation patterns however, is whether and how those patterns can be applied to situations other then those for which they were originally intended. **The real issue in the use of explanation patterns is how to misapply them.**

The issue in misapplication must be embodied in the notion of a partial match. It is all well and good to establish that someone has been killed and that he had a large estate that was to go to his evil son-in-law and to thus suspect his son-in-law. Such a suspicion comes from matching the pattern, KILLED FOR THE INSURANCE MONEY, and there is really no more to say about such a match other than such patterns must exist in memory in order for such matches to occur.

But the really interesting case is when KILLED FOR THE INSURANCE MONEY is used to explain a set of circumstances that are superficially quite different than those of son-in-law, rich man killed, and so on. Thus, we can see that there are three overriding issues with respect to explanation patterns:

1. What culturally shared explanation patterns exist in memory?
2. How are these patterns accessed for normal application?
3. How are these patterns accessed such that they can be misapplied to foster novel or creative explanations for events that are unusual to the extent that they have no obviously applicable pattern?

We begin our discussion, therefore, with a look at some culturally shared patterns and their application. Since there are a great many possible explanation patterns, and their normal application can be somewhat dull to consider, we discuss here one kind of explanation pattern only, namely the application of proverbial advice to planning. (We discuss the misapplication of a pattern for the creation of novel explanations in Chapter 6).

PROVERBIAL ADVICE

Consider the following situation:

A friend was telling me about a job opportunity that she was trying to arrange for herself. She had asked the people where she worked to arrange something for her in a new place in which she was going to live temporarily. They seemed amenable to this idea, even considering it a good opportunity for them. But, the senior people who make such decisions were all away until the end of the summer and my friend was leaving before that. One day my friend heard that the only remaining senior person had been joking with another employee about her job opportunity in a way that made it seem that he thought it was a very good idea to arrange some work for her with the company. My friend asked my advice. I told her to go see him right away. *Make hay while the sun shines,* I said.

I began to think about the advice I had given. I thought about why I had said what I said. Specifically, I wondered about the literal meaning of what I had said. Having grown up in a city, I had no idea about why one should make hay in the sunshine, although I could make some guesses about it. I also wondered about how this phrase came to be in my, or anybody else's, vocabulary. Somehow, some good old farm wisdom had worked its way down into the everyday vocabulary of an urban professor. Moreover, I knew that this phrase was going to be readily understandable by my friend.

But the key point here is not where this proverb came from, or why I happen to know it, or how it was understood. The real issue is: how did I know to say it at that moment? Or to put this in a way that reveals its true significance: **How can memory be organized so as to enable situations to be analyzed such that proverbs that characterize them can be found?** Clearly, a proverb is one type of explanation pattern. Thus, giving proverbial advice is a rather stereotypical way of applying an explanation pattern in everyday life.

Whatever indices characterize a proverb such that it can be retrieved when needed, it is likely that those same indices are used to characterize and retrieve explanation patterns when they are needed. Since finding relevant explanation patterns is such an important part of creativity, it seems clear that determining the set of indices that can be used for the storage and retrieval of XPs is of critical importance. Examining one class of XPs that are readily available in written form, with an eye towards how one might represent them, is a fairly important thing to do.

What exactly does one do in order to retrieve and apply an explanation pattern, such as *Make hay while the sun shines?* Or, to put this question back into the realm of this example, what was I doing in this situation? What I was doing while listening to my friend's story was analyzing what she said in terms of her goals, and plans to achieve those goals, and integrating that analysis with my knowledge of how people in various situations are likely to behave and my beliefs about what plans work best in various situations. As a result of listening to all this, I decided that my friend had to take her opportunity when it arrived, and that as long as the man in charge was thinking about her favorably, it would be a good time to ask. This much is fairly obvious. The issue is: what happened next?

The next thing I had to do was express my advice, and, suddenly, this proverb occurred to me and I said it. Yes, yes, but so what?

In order to use an explanation pattern, one must first be reminded of it. Proverbs that embody culturally-shared explanation patterns are applied by reminding, but somehow this form of reminding does not feel exactly like the remindings that I discuss in Schank (1982). One doesn't *feel* reminded of the proverb exactly. It is more like the proverb *comes to mind.* Also, one is aware, when this proverb comes to mind, that the reminding is not unique to oneself. It is reasonable to assume that the person you are talking to knows the proverb and will readily appreciate the wisdom in it. We can call this kind of reminding **CULTURALLY SHARED REMIND-ING (CSR).** It is a type of *pre-compiled* reminding in that one expects to be reminded of it in situations where it might be useful. Thus, one would expect that there exists method by which the mind pre-indexes explanation patterns, knowing quite well that these indices will determine the future applicability of the pattern. This is in contrast to expectation-failure based remindings where one is, in some sense, surprised to discover an old memory still lurking about.

In expectation failure-based reminding (Schank, 1982), a failure of an expectation about what was going to happen next causes the memory of another event involving a similar expectation failure to be called to mind, if the explanation of the expectation failure in both cases is identical. In other words, the problem is to figure out why a wrong expectation was generated by memory and the solution is to keep around potential explanations of why the expectation failed, so that if, in the future, the same thing occurs, memory can be updated. Reminding, in this case, entails holding past mistakes at the ready so that learning can occur. The key problem, as always, is indexing. How can these memories be found later? The answer, we found, was to index them with the explanation that was concocted as the potential resolution of the failure.

In CSR reminding, the problem is not learning but planning. We are not trying to recover from a wrong expectation. Rather, we are trying to effectively plan. But, in planning as in any other mental activity, the object is to find old experiences and use them to guide in the planning of new ones. That is, the best plan is one that one has been used effectively before. The trick in planning therefore is to get reminded well: **if you are reminded of an effective plan, you can use it.** But, as always, getting reminded means having a well-organized memory, one that is indexed by means that enable retrieval.

In planning then, one wants to find a specific relevant experience. And, this is often the point of human conversation. One person tells another a problem, and the other, having gotten reminded, will relate his most germane experience to the first. And what if you don't have a germane experience? The next best thing is a pre-compiled, culturally shared experience. That is, we can give advice in terms of tried and true wisdom that may not be from our own personal experience but is generally agreed upon to be wise. Often such advice is quite clichéd and subject to funny looks. Nevertheless, such things do come to mind. The question for us is: how?

It would seem obvious that the indexing scheme that the mind employs must be strongly connected with the parameters that define a proverb of this type in the first place. That is, once I determined that I thought that my friend should ask for what she wanted right away, I was able to find the proverb to express it. So, first I analyzed her situation in terms of the characteristics that happen to be expressed by the proverb. The analysis would have had to have been in the form of unique identifiers that would be associated with each proverb. These identifiers, I claim, would be exactly the same as the ones the mind would have to use in order to be able to use those proverbs at a given point. And, more importantly, since correctly using proverbs isn't my point, these would be the very same abstract characterizations in terms of which the mind is storing explanation patterns and in terms of which new inputs were being analyzed. If an XP comes to mind after the formulation of an EQ, then these indices would have to be used by the EQ as well. The indices expressed by proverbs ought to be quite natural in the sense that they ought to be expressive of the indices naturally used by the mind.

Culturally shared remindings are thus exactly the same thing as explanation patterns. Either we can attempt to explain something in brand new terms, or we can use an explanation pattern and tweak it, in order to make life simpler. The same is true with reminding. Either we can get reminded of a particular individual event that was stored in terms of an expectation failure, or we can get reminded of a culturally shared experience with its associated proverb. In the former case, the work we do is much harder and the possibility for a creative solution is therefore much greater. In the latter case, the answer about what to do is much simpler (just follow the advice of the proverb), but the possibility of producing anything creative is much less.

Thus, for the general question: *what should I do?* the answer is either: *consider this other case that is quite like it as an example to guide you* (expectation failure-based reminding), or *follow the generally accepted wisdom on the subject* (culturally shared reminding).

Proverbs can be seen as the labels of various baskets of memories, in this case culturally shared memories. In other words, proverbs are found during the processing of various situations, which would indicate that the analysis of those situations was related to the analysis of the proverb. Therefore, proverbs are themselves indicators in use in organizing memory at its simplest level.

A LOOK AT SOME PROVERBS

There are, of course, a great many kinds of proverbs, many of which are irrelevant for the problem at hand. For example, there are **explanatory proverbs** (the proverbs I am using here are taken from a book of Yiddish proverbs, Kogos, 1970):

The apple doesn't fall far from the tree.
When the stomach is empty, so is the brain.
If the student is successful, the teacher gets the praise.
A second wife is like a wooden leg.

There are also **observational/philosophical proverbs:**

By day they're ready for divorce, by night they're ready for bed.
Bones without meat is possible; meat without bones is not possible.
When a poor man makes a wedding, the dog gets the shivers.
If everybody looks for pretty brides, what's to become of the ugly girls?

And, of course, there are other kinds as well. Here we are interested in proverbs that are intended to give **planning advice,** because such proverbs relate situations to prescriptions for action in such situations. Thus, they are quite like XPs that relate states of the world to events that follow from those states. Some examples of these are:

It's a good idea to send a lazy man for the Angel of Death.
If one has nothing to answer, it is best to shut up.
If you can't go over, go under.
If you come for the legacy, you often have to pay for the funeral.
If you invest in a fever, you will realize a disease.

If you dance at every wedding, you will weep at every funeral.
When you beat a dog, be sure to find a stick.
If you stay at home, you won't wear out your shoes.
The just path is always the right one.
With honey you can catch more flies than with vinegar.
With nets you catch birds, and with presents—girls.
You can't make cheesecake out of snow.
It's not the stick that helps but the kind word.
Neither with curses nor with laughter can you change the world.
It's good to learn to barber on someone else's beard.
If all men pulled in one direction, the world would topple over.
If you are going to eat pork, let it be good and fat.

I have selected these proverbs precisely because they may not be familiar to everybody. The issue is, when would you want to say one? The answer that I intend to give to this question must be in terms of the analysis of a situation wherein the proverb is a plan, or a commentary on a plan, that might apply to that situation. The intent therefore, is to use the same features in the analysis of the proverb that we might expect to find in the analysis of the situation.

To analyze these proverbs, a framework that uses the vocabulary of plans and goals is necessary. Each of these proverbs refers to an implicit goal. Some refer to possible problems with the normative plan to achieve that goal, others with what to pay special attention to in the plan, and still others with how to choose between plans. Thus, any analysis we do must start with goals and include information about the normative plans, choices of plans, and impediments to plans that one might expect. For example, the indices relevant for:

When you beat a dog, be sure to find a stick

are as follows:

GOAL TYPE: violent action against dangerous actor

CAUTIONARY ADVICE: proper instrument for action would provide some degree of protection from possible retaliation

The just path is always the right one

GOAL PROBLEM: choice between two goals

CHOICE PROCEDURE: choose morally justified goal

The problem with these analyses is that they do not seem any more like indices than the original proverbs, so let's rewrite each proverb in terms of a culturally neutral, problem-independant proverb:

When you beat a dog, be sure to find a stick

becomes:

When you tackle a dangerous situation and decide to take action, be sure to steer clear of side-effects.
and

The just path is always the right one
becomes:
When choosing, bad side-effects will be avoided if decisions are based on doing the morally right thing.

Looking at these proverbs in this way makes what was once unrelated seem quite similar. Both are talking about side-effects of the choice of bad plans. Each defines *bad* differently however. For the first *bad* means potentially dangerous, and in the second, *bad* is left undiscussed.

Here are some other proverbs in the list that talk about side-effects, directly or indirectly:

It's a good idea to send a lazy man for the Angel of Death.
If one has nothing to answer, it is best to shut up.
If you come for the legacy, you often have to pay for the funeral.
If you invest in a fever, you will realize a disease.
If you dance at every wedding, you will weep at every funeral.
If you stay at home, you won't wear out your shoes.
It's good to learn to barber on someone else's beard.
If all men pulled in one direction, the world would topple over.

All of these are about side effects, as follows:

It's a good idea to send a lazy man for the Angel of Death.

This proverb refers to the side-effects of deliberately choosing a bad plan for something you really don't want to accomplish. It says in effect: *The side-effects of a bad plan are good if you didn't want the plan to work.* Or, to put this another way, if you do want a plan to work watch out for side-effects that will cause it not to work. Therefore, I paraphrase this as: **If you want a plan to work, avoid choosing one with bad side effects.**

The next proverb discusses the side-effects of doing something when one doesn't know what one is doing. Thus, *If one has nothing to answer, it is best to shut up,* means, in effect that **the side-effects of acting are often worse than those of not acting.**

The next proverb, *If you come for the legacy, you often have to pay for the funeral* is more directly about side-effects. It says in effect that **there are side-effects to seemingly positive events that can be quite negative.** The next one says almost the same thing. *If you invest in a fever, you will realize a* *disease* means in effect that **if you think that an event might be negative, stay away because it could have even worse side-effects than you might have anticipated.**

The next also plays upon this theme. *If you dance at every wedding, you will weep at every funeral* means that there is a side-effect to emotional commitment in that sharing people's pleasures also means sharing their sorrows. A more callous way of putting this is that **the side-effect of feeling pleasure to is to feel pain.**

The next one, *If you stay at home, you won't wear out your shoes* means, in terms of side-effects, that the side-effect of action is the general possibility of misfortune. Of course, there is a sense in which this proverb, as it is stated, is making fun of people who don't take chances. But, it is important when analyzing proverbs such as this, to not be swayed too much by their surface expression. So this means, in effect, that **the side-effect of taking a chance is that you might lose.** *It's good to learn to barber on someone else's beard* means that **the side-effect of learning is the possibility of mistakes, so avoid the more costly ones while learning.**

The next one is a little peculiar. In essence *If all men pulled in one direction, the world would topple over* means two different things. First it means that **there are bad side-effects to even seemingly wonderful actions.** Secondly, it means that **things that seem bad often have good side-effects.** These are basically different sides of the same coin of course.

So, in sum, these proverbs have said the following things about side effects:

1. **When you tackle a difficult problem, be sure to steer clear of side-effects.**
2. **When choosing, bad side-effects will be avoided if decisions are based on doing the morally right thing.**
3. **If you want a plan to work, avoid choosing one with bad side effects.**
4. **The side-effects of acting are often worse than those of not acting.**
5. **There are side-effects to seemingly positive events that can be quite negative.**
6. **If you think that an event might be negative, stay away because it could have even worse side-effects than you might have anticipated.**
7. **The side-effect of feeling pleasure to is to feel pain.**
8. **The side-effect of taking a chance is that you might lose.**
9. **The side-effect of learning is the possibility of mistakes, so avoid the more costly ones while learning.**
10. **There are bad side-effects to even seemingly wonderful actions.**

11. Things that seem bad often have good side-effects.

One thing that seems quite clear in reviewing the above generalizations is that, as with most generalizations, they can be true some of the time and false some of the time. Or, to put this another way, planning by proverb is not necessarily the best planning method available. But I am not trying to find a good planning method here. The intention is to discover how explanation patterns can be applied by examining the features that might be used for indexing them. The generalizations embodied within these proverbs contain within them something very special—the features that are used in composing indices to the patterns. Such generalizations occur cross-culturally because this analysis of events and experiences in terms of plans and goals is at the core of being human.

INDEXING PROVERBS

The trick here then, is to establish the set of primitives that embody the generalizations inherent in the proverbs. The premise is that if a language of representation of the elements in these proverbs can be found, it would likely have some relationship with the representation scheme employed by the mind for the comprehension and storage of events. Or, to put this another way, if proverbs come to mind when events are being processed, the representational elements in terms of which those events are processed must bear a strong relationship to the representational elements of the proverbs. So, we work backwards and see how we can represent proverbs. At the end we should have a vocabulary that can be used by an indexing scheme for this type of explanation pattern.

The first thing to do in finding a representation for proverbs is to start with what we have. Consequently, let us assume that the eleven *language-neutral* proverbs given earlier (by *language-neutral* I mean that there are many ways to express these proverbs in many different languages and cultures) are the only ones that we have to represent. So, what elements are in them?

First, they all make reference to an **action in the service of a goal.** *Second,* they all refer to, at least implicitly, **the choices available for possible actions.** *Third,* they all refer to **possible side-effects of the actions chosen.** *Fourth,* they all refer to, at least implicitly, the **side-effects of the actions that were not chosen** as a comparison to the action that was chosen. *Fifth,* they all refer to **benefits and hazards** associated with the overall event. And, of course, this specific set of proverbs are all about side-effects, and that must be represented as well.

The next step therefore is to put all of these aspects of the representation together. To represent these proverbs, we must have:

MAJOR HEADING:
GOAL:
INTENDED ACTION:
INTENDED RESULT:
PREMISE:
ALTERNATIVE ACTION:
NEGATIVE SIDE EFFECTS OF INT–ACT:
POSITIVE SIDE EFFECTS OF INT–ACT:
NEGATIVE SIDE EFFECTS OF ALT–ACT:
POSITIVE SIDE EFFECTS OF ALT–ACT:
RECOMMENDED CHOICE:

So, let's try this representation out on one of the proverbs. Consider the proverb *If you stay at home, you won't wear out your shoes:*

MAJOR HEADING: side effects

GOAL: any

INTENDED ACTION: any

INTENDED RESULT:

PREMISE: fear of acting

ALTERNATIVE ACTION: doing nothing

NEGATIVE SIDE EFFECTS OF INT–ACT: many

POSITIVE SIDE EFFECTS OF INT–ACT: many

NEGATIVE SIDE EFFECTS OF ALT–ACT: none

POSITIVE SIDE EFFECTS OF ALT–ACT: none

RECOMMENDED CHOICE: INT–ACT

For the proverb *If you come for the legacy, you often have to pay for the funeral* we have:

MAJOR HEADING: side effects

GOAL: A–POSS

INTENDED ACTION: show up

INTENDED RESULT: get money

PREMISE: receipt without work

ALTERNATIVE ACTION:

NEGATIVE SIDE EFFECTS OF INT–ACT: might cost more than you get

POSITIVE SIDE EFFECTS OF INT–ACT:

NEGATIVE SIDE EFFECTS OF ALT–ACT:

POSITIVE SIDE EFFECTS OF ALT–ACT:

RECOMMENDED CHOICE:

And for *If you invest in a fever, you will realize a disease:*

MAJOR HEADING: side effects

GOAL: A–POSS

INTENDED ACTION: effort expended in activity A

INTENDED RESULT: reap rewards

PREMISE: A is a bad thing

ALTERNATIVE ACTION:

NEGATIVE SIDE EFFECTS OF INT–ACT: very bad

POSITIVE SIDE EFFECTS OF INT–ACT: none

NEGATIVE SIDE EFFECTS OF ALT–ACT:

POSITIVE SIDE EFFECTS OF ALT–ACT:

RECOMMENDED CHOICE: don't do A

Assuming that this representation suffices for side-effects, the next problem in our examination of an indexing scheme for proverbs is to look at some proverbs that do not relate to side-effects to see how they compare and to see if the representation used for side-effects has to be modified in some way. So, let's consider some proverbs about planning that are not about side effects:

> If you can't go over, go under.
> With honey you can catch more flies than with vinegar.
> With nets you catch birds, and with presents—girls.
> You can't make cheesecake out of snow.
> It's not the stick that helps but the kind word.
> Neither with curses nor with laughter can you change the world.
> If you are going to eat pork, let it be good and fat.

These proverbs are about planning, but not directly about side effects.

Let's try to represent some of them using the format generated earlier. Let's first look at representing *With honey you catch more flies than with vinegar:*

MAJOR HEADING: plan selection

GOAL: PERSUADE(X)

INTENDED ACTION: A

INTENDED RESULT: X does what you want

PREMISE:

ALTERNATIVE ACTION: B

NEGATIVE SIDE EFFECTS OF INT–ACT: makes X unhappy

POSITIVE SIDE EFFECTS OF INT–ACT: none

NEGATIVE SIDE EFFECTS OF ALT–ACT: none

POSITIVE SIDE EFFECTS OF ALT–ACT: makes X happy

RECOMMENDED CHOICE: ALT–ACT (B)

This format seems to work well enough in this instance, and indicates that proverbs about planning can be seen as advice about how to choose between alternatives. This can be seen again in the next proverb, which, as before, isn't directly about side effects but indirectly deals with them by a discussion of choices. This time we discuss *If you are going to eat pork, let it be good and fat.* Obviously, this refers to the idea that once one has chosen to do wrong, one may as well enjoy oneself:

MAJOR HEADING: plan selection

GOAL: A–ENJOYMENT

INTENDED ACTION: A

INTENDED RESULT: pleasure

PREMISE:

ALTERNATIVE ACTION: B

NEGATIVE SIDE EFFECTS OF INT–ACT: many

POSITIVE SIDE EFFECTS OF INT–ACT: none

NEGATIVE SIDE EFFECTS OF ALT–ACT: equally many

POSITIVE SIDE EFFECTS OF ALT–ACT: many

RECOMMENDED CHOICE: ALT–ACT (B)

In this format then, the proverb has been reduced to something like: *If you are going to choose between two plans for pleasure, both of which have bad side effects, you may as well choose the plan that has maximum positive side effects.*

THE ROLE OF PROVERBS

The proverb with which we started this discussion was *Make hay while the sun shines.* In this representation it would look as follows:

MAJOR HEADING: plan selection

GOAL: any

INTENDED ACTION: appropriate to goal

INTENDED RESULT:

PREMISE: preconditions are in place now

ALTERNATIVE ACTION: do nothing

NEGATIVE SIDE EFFECTS OF INT–ACT:

POSITIVE SIDE EFFECTS OF INT–ACT:

NEGATIVE SIDE EFFECTS OF ALT–ACT:

POSITIVE SIDE EFFECTS OF ALT–ACT:

RECOMMENDED CHOICE: choose to act now

This proverb has nothing to do with side effects, of course. It just talks about the right timing of an action. Nevertheless, it can be seen as a choice between two plans, *do nothing now,* and *act now.*

As I have previously argued (Schank, 1982), memory is organized in terms of the very same features with which we process new information. If this were not so then we would have difficulty finding old memories or experiences to guide us during processing. The fact that we are often guided by past experiences, our own when we are thinking, and those of others when we are asking advice or engaging in conversation, would indicate that those experiences are readily available.

The proverbs that we have been looking at indicate that we are capable of processing events that are told to us in terms of plans, side-effects of plans, intended consequences of plans, and so on. The point then is that we represent experiences in terms of indices of that type. Or, to put this another way, the correct representation of events concerned with planning must be in terms of the plans, consequences, side-effects, and such that those events entail, in a way that has been abstracted from the content of the problem itself. Specifically, this means that I had represented my friend's problem as a choice between the plans *act now* and *act later,* with the idea that (in my view) the preconditions necessary to what she wanted were present now. In other words, my analysis of her situation was in terms of the kinds of indices we have been discussing here.

If one were to attempt to establish all the possible configurations of the indices that we have been using, with appropriate choices as to which of two plans is the better under which circumstances, it would seem reasonable to assume that there could exist, in many cultures, proverbs for all of them. Or, if they did not exist, we could predict that they would get invented (with a language and style that reflected the culture.) That is, in a farming culture we might expect that the language about planning would be couched in terms and ideas that relate to farming.

The point of course, is that all the possible configurations can exist in the head, in principle, in service as the basis for memory organization.

RETURNING TO EXPLANATION

The proverbs we have been discussing have all concerned advice for planning. Clearly it is proverbs of explanation that relate most strongly to the notion of an explanation pattern. Let's see then, how two of the explanatory proverbs cited above fit into the format for explanation proverbs that we used earlier:

When The Stomach Is Empty, So Is The Brain

1. **An anomaly that the pattern explains:** *stupid actions*
2. **A set of relevant indices under which it can be retrieved:** *someone does something stupid; they might not ordinarily be expected to act that way; they are also hungry*
3. **A set of states of the world under which the pattern is likely to be a valid explanation:** *short term goals valued over long term goals by actor*
4. **A set of states of the world under which the pattern is likely to be relevant, even if it isn't immediately applicable:** *poverty; ignorance*
5. **A pattern of actions, with the relationships between them, that shows how the event being explained could arise:**

actor is poor
actor is hungry
actor does stupid action
action has short term value of getting him fed
action has long term bad consequences

6. **A set of prior explanations that has been made possible by use of this pattern:** *theft; irrational violence*
7. **A reason that stereotypes the behavior being explained:** *hunger is an overwhelming feeling*

If the student is successful, the teacher gets the praise

1. **An anomaly that the pattern explains (which is the main index into the XP):** *lack of praise for a success*
2. **A set of relevant indices under which it can be retrieved:** *masterful performance at some task*
3. **A set of states of the world under which the pattern is likely to be a valid explanation:** *music performances; acting performances; scholarly performances; athletic feats*
4. **A set of states of the world under which the pattern is likely to be relevant, even if it isn't immediately applicable:** *whenever a task requires great amounts of training*
5. **A pattern of actions, with the relationships between them, that shows how the event being explained could arise:**

teacher trains student
students works hard
student performs
student succeeds
people praise teacher

6. **A set of prior explanations that has been made possible by use of this pattern:** *continued success of some teams under same coach; great musicians, artists, scientists who have had same teacher*
7. **A reason that stereotypes the behavior being explained:** *in many instances, teaching is harder than performing; consistent success of students can best be understood by looking at teacher*

Now, looking at the above, we can see that there is no difference between an explanatory proverb and an explanation pattern. The next question to ask, therefore, is what the relationship is between the indices that were developed for the planning advice proverbs and the explanatory proverbs.

Any lesson to be learned from examining either of these kinds of proverbs must have relevance to the general problem of the application of an explanation pattern. Thousands of explanation patterns exist in memory, and each is indexed according to the kind of explanation that it represents. In Chapter 3 we discussed a variety of types of explanations. But, there exist explanation patterns for each and every type of explanation. Within each of these patterns there are a standard set of indices associated with a particular type of explanation that connects it to the pattern. There are, of course, sub-types within the types. And, connected with those are a standard set of indices. The indices we listed earlier were:

MAJOR HEADING:
GOAL:
INTENDED ACTION:
INTENDED RESULT:
PREMISE:
ALTERNATIVE ACTION:
NEGATIVE SIDE EFFECTS OF INT–ACT:
POSITIVE SIDE EFFECTS OF INT–ACT:
NEGATIVE SIDE EFFECTS OF ALT–ACT:
POSITIVE SIDE EFFECTS OF ALT–ACT:
RECOMMENDED CHOICE:

The question is then, do proverbs such as the two listed above fit into that framework? Obviously, not exactly. The above framework is one that relates to plan side effects and choice between plans. It has very little to do with explanation. Then why have we gone into the detail that we have with respect to representing proverbs that relate to planning.

Basically there were two reasons. First, I wanted to show, in a domain away from the concept of planning, how linguistically encoded sayings had to refer to indices that were language-neutral and related to mental representations that must be used in memory. Second, I wanted to press the basic claim that there is nothing new in the general framework of creativity. The point for planning is that there is no new planning as such. Rather, we plan by adapting old plans. In the case of planning, as well as in the case of explanation, there exists old standards, often stated as proverbs, that encode various points of view about how to go about planning or explaining. One of the most common methods of creating new plans and explanations is the adaptation of these old standards to a new situation. But, one cannot apply them if one cannot find them. So, a big problem is indexing the old standards.

Indexing, at least in the case of planning proverbs, can be seen as a problem of the juxtaposition of goals, intended actions, intended results, alternatives, side effects, and choices, considering the conditions. The indices for explanation patterns are also in terms of the format that was presented for them; that is, in terms of anomalies, conditions when those anomalies are likely to occur, conditions when the explanation is likely to be valid, and prior explanations that remind one of the pattern.

Creativity Through
The Misapplication of
Explanation Patterns

Now we come to the third question posed in Chapter 5. For our purposes in this book, it is really the most important question:

How are explanation patterns accessed such that they can be misapplied to foster novel or creative explanations for events that are unusual (where unusual means that they have no obviously applicable pattern)?

Just how do we know that we have a *proper misapplication* of an XP, and exactly how do we misapply the XP? Or to put this another way, what exactly is it that we have when we have an explanation pattern that mis-matches? The answer is that we have a candidate for **TWEAKING.** The real usefulness of culturally shared patterns and idiosyncratic patterns is in their adaptation to new situations. The question is how this adaptation takes place.

There are two separable processes in the creative misapplication of an XP. The first is **finding a candidate XP for consideration.** The second is **altering the constraints of that XP so that it applies to the current problem.** Both of these processes require what we shall call *creativity.*

CREATIVITY

What is creativity? Needless to say this is a non-trivial question. In fact, it is at least three separate questions, depending upon the field of inquiry that generates the question. In general, laymen tend to think of creativity as something mystical, beyond the reaches of the explainable. But, what this really means is that there seems no obvious algorithm to describe creative processes. Our premise here is that such an algorithm must exist, in principle. In fact, this is really the operating philosophy behind all of AI. Even though very few people in AI work on creativity per se, AI is based upon the premise that there is nothing mystical in the processes that underlie intelligence. Arguments against the tenets of AI, such as that of Searle (1980) or Dreyfuss (1972) always seem to be based on the idea that some things are unknowable in principle about the nature of mind. Philosophers and others often seem to believe, without ever quite saying so, that one cannot just write down the rules that underlie intelligent processes. Often these arguments get transformed into a discussion of whether, once a machine was capable of operating on the basis of rules that describe an intelligent process, it was reasonable to claim that that machine was *intelligent,* or *understood,* or was *creative,* or whatever.

What I shall term the **philosopher's question** concerns the issue of whether just following rules qualifies as embodying the process that those rules describe. In other words, the issue for them is, if a machine had all the rules for creativity, and it could follow them so as to enable it to create new ideas, things, or whatever, would it actually be reasonable to claim that that machine was creative? Clearly, AI believes that if a machine creates then it is creative. So, let us leave the philosophical arguments to the philosophers and address the **AI question** here, namely: can we write a set of rules, that, if a machine followed them, it would be able to create something new? Later, we can address the **psychological question,** which is: assuming that AI has given us a set of rules that enable machines to create, is it reasonable to assume that those rules are also used by people, and, if so, how do they acquire them?

Is it possible that there exist a set of rules that embody the method by which ideas are created? This seems like a tall order, but looking at the kind of creativity we are talking about, namely, the creation of novel explanations, and dividing that task into two sub-processes, can make the problem seem tractable. Let us look at the sub-processes. The first, which is inherently *a search process,* is finding a candidate XP. The second, which is inherently *an alteration process,* is modifying and adapting the XP.

What would it mean for search, or alteration, to be considered to be a creative process? In a sense, any creativity that would exist in those processes would be a function of the novel application of techniques used in them. And, of course, novelty being relative, the issue becomes one of the degree to which a particular use of a given technique is regarded as novel. This seems like an odd measure of creativity. Or is it? Perhaps creativity means no more than the application of a technique or rule where one would not expect to apply it. Perhaps creativity is, in some sense, purely a relative term. Let us consider this idea for a moment, with respect to the problem of search.

In the Swale example the problem, for the search phase of the explanation process, was to find an XP that might apply to the index *early death*. To do this, explanation questions were generated that focused the search on different aspects of Swale's situation so as to bring to mind appropriate XPs indexed under a given explanation question. The creativity inherent in the explanations proposed in the Swale example depends critically on the questions generated in the first place. **The novelty of the search process depends upon the novelty of the question asked.**

In discussing the Swale example, we took the standard set of EQs and generated from them a set of questions that might apply in Swale's case. The issue here is *where is the creativity in this process?* Let's look at what we did. We took a standard set of questions, which can be seen as a standard set of search techniques, and we attempted to establish which of these questions made sense with respect to Swale. Some questions were found to be silly or irrelevant, and others were discovered to be quite useful. So far, the issue of where the creativity lies is quite simple. It is not creative to take a standard list of questions and apply them. It is also not creative to decide that certain questions are silly or irrelevant, except to the extent that one can perceive that a given question that on the surface seems irrelevant ought to be considered. It is further not creative to take the standard XP indexed under an EQ and assume that the explanation provided by the XP is correct. Let's look at the process again. The first question found to be relevant was:

EQ1.1: HOW WILL SWALE'S DEATH BENEFIT OTHERS?
(derived from "HOW WILL AN UNEXPECTED EVENT BENEFIT OTHERS?")

This question is a fine starting point. The intent of the question is to focus search on actors who might have had a motive to do away with Swale. As for the issue of *creativity in search,* we have yet to begin. The first step is to generate a candidate set of actors who might fit the bill. There are, of course, the old standards, such as *rival owner, beneficiary of insurance policy,* and so on. And where would the creativity lie here? Clearly, **creativity in search is dependent upon indexing.** And, it is also relative. It might seem creative to come up with the idea of wondering if someone was holding a large insurance policy on Swale's life if it weren't such a common line of inquiry in murder cases. Why then, is such an idea not creative? The answer is simply one of reference to standard XPs. **Killed for the insurance** is a standard XP indexed under EQ1.1. Or, to put this another way, the reason that EQ1.1 is useful is because it points to XPs such as *Killed for the insurance.*

However, and here is the critical point, EQ1.1 also points to a great many other XPs. They are less obviously relevant than *Killed for the insurance.* Thus, two important points emerge. First, we need some measure of obvious relevance. Second, one key point in creativity is to not be turned off by obviously irrelevant XPs, or to put this more positively, **being creative entails allowing oneself to generate seemingly irrelevant indices in response to an EQ.**

There are then, two obvious ways in which creativity happens within the context of the search for an explanation. They are:

1. **Creativity depends upon finding an unusual index from which XPs can be found under an EQ.**
2. **Creativity depends upon keeping in consideration an XP that seems obviously irrelevant.**

With respect to EQ1.1 then, the issue is *who benefits from the misfortune of others, in general? Someone who will get money as a direct result of the death* is the index that is attached to EQ1.1 as a common answer and it is linked to the XP *killed for the insurance.* In order to creatively misapply an XP, we must first generate that XP as a candidate. So, the question to ask is: *what kinds of benefits are there, in general, and how can I relate those benefits to a death?* To put this another way, the task is to relate sad events to happy ones, in particular, we wish to find an XP that relates sad events to happy ones. So, let's think of some happy benefits, in general:

Things that might make you happy:

1. getting a lot of money
2. becoming successful in your work
3. falling in love
4. having someone you care for become happy
5. curing adversity (such as an illness)
6. making a new friend
7. having a pleasant sensual experience
8. achieving a goal

The next step is to find a way that a negative event might cause one of these positive events to occur. For example, it is possible to achieve a goal because someone else has failed to achieve it. This is the XP, **backed into victory,** and it is a common XP in sports (in winning the championship of a division in a sport) and in work situations where someone is promoted because someone else was fired or quit. And, it is *backed into victory* that generates the *rival owner plot* hypothesis. Similarly, *backed into victory,* can call to mind another XP when the positive benefit is *fall in love,* namely the XP **fall in love on the rebound.**

The nice thing about *fall in love on the rebound* with respect to our purposes here is the obvious irrelevance of it. What could it have to do with Swale's death? That, of course, is the second part of creativity. Once a seemingly irrelevant XP has been found, it may be possible **to tweak it into relevance.** To do this, one must begin to relax the constraints on the XP such that Swale fits. There are a number of heuristics for tweaking, some of which, such as *transpose objects that are alike in function* were presented in Chapter 4.

There are no rules for tweaking in the sense that there are no proscriptions about what you cannot do. For example, even though *love on the rebound* was generated with respect to a plot against Swale, it need not be used that way. Once the pattern is in memory, it would be perfectly reasonable to think that Swale died of being lovesick after being the victim in the *love on the rebound* XP. The problem here is only one of evidence. It is fine to suggest this, but there is no evidence to support it, and it would seem silly (but unfortunately not funny) to say it. Thus, there must exist in all this, **an editing function,** whose job it is to decide if an XP that has been tweaked into a new, creative explanation, has been tweaked into a reasonable explanation as well.

Now let's consider another EQ from the Swale example:

EQ14: IS SWALE A MEMBER OF SOME GROUP FOR WHOM EARLY DEATH IS NORMAL? derived from "IS THE ACTOR A MEMBER OF ANY GROUP THAT IS KNOWN TO DO THIS ANOMALOUS BEHAVIOR?"

Under this EQ, there are, of course, a number of XPs. The issue for a creative explainer is how to find them. The question for an explainer is *what XPs exist in memory that link the members of a group with early death.* The problem, in essence, becomes one of trying to think of various groups that often die early and then attempting to see Swale as a member of that group. Or, to put this back into the terminology that we were using, one must search for candidate XPs, and then tweak those XPs. According to this view then, creativity is defined in a six step process:

1. **Consider EQ**
2. **Generate candidate set of indices relating to the EQ**
3. **Find XPs that answer EQ for each index**
4. **Consider XPs**
5. **Tweak XP**
6. **Consider new explanation**

By *consider* here, I mean the process by which one examines a question, pattern, or explanation and determines whether or not to pursue that particular line of thought. If it is decided not to pursue that line of thought, the process stops and returns for a new candidate.

In view of the above algorithm, it should be clear where creativity lies. There is a measure of creativity in each step, but the *consider* steps, being basically acceptance or rejection are not all that creative. As I said earlier, of course, rejecting everything is a certain way to avoid creativity. For humans then, one might say that creativity means *keeping an open mind about possible candidates that do not obviously apply.* For machines, an algorithm that rejected a reasonable percentage of candidates while keeping alive enough would be sufficient for these purposes.

Creativity is a function of one's ability to generate candidates in the first place and to attempt to tweak them into an acceptable state. There are two forms of acceptable states, which we call the **realistic** and the **artistic.** In the realistic state, we have found a candidate that sounds plausible as an explanation. In the artistic state, we have found a candidate that is plausible as a fun candidate, perhaps as a joke, perhaps as a metaphor, perhaps as the basis of work of art. The process of creativity is the same in both cases. It is the acceptability criteria that set them apart.

Now let's return to EQ14. This EQ must be transformed into a question whose intent it is to discover XPs that might be relevant. The transformed question is *what groups die young?* The hard part is answering this question. Here are a few answers: *people who were malnourished as youths, alcoholics, drug addicts, professional criminals, poor people, people in countries with poor sanitary facilities, people who put too much pressure on themselves, people who are overweight.* For each of these candidates, there exists an XP that explains it. In other words, in essence we have already generated a set of XPs simply by considering indices under the EQ under consideration. It is trivial to find the XP for each of these candidates. The hard part is finding the candidates.

I shall, however, have nothing more to say here about how these candidates are found. For one thing, finding them requires a complex, complete, and highly interconnected memory. We have not yet learned how to build such a memory. Psychologists who tell us that such memories are associative are not of much help here. It is clear that discovering the principles upon which such memories are built, and expand over time, is one of the main critical areas in both Artificial Intelligence and Psychology. But, it is fairly difficult to just decide to discover the right memory organization. First, one has to know of what things, precisely, that memory must be capable.

Although there is complexity associated with the generation of candidates, it is clear that one could build a creative computer by simply listing sufficient XPs under each EQ. I am not suggesting that people have long lists of XPs under each EQ. Rather, I assume it is the case that they generate possible candidates by interesting search techniques. Nevertheless, a computer system that simply had access to lists of XPs would have to be considered solely by its output. If it were, in fact, capable of creative explanations, then it would be reasonable to consider it to be creative. It would not, I assume, be reasonable to consider such a machine to be capable of understanding, by the arguments of Chapter 1, however. That would require it to understand the content of what it had created, a far more complex task.

Returning to our example then, in the tweaking phase, one must examine candidate XPs to see which could possibly apply to Swale. First, of course, Swale is not a person. This bothers us not at all in these instances because the XPs involved do not depend upon aspects of personhood exactly. Thus, we have our first tweaking rule:

T1: Set membership constraints can be relaxed.

The next step, after assuming that *Swale was an alcoholic, Swale was a professional criminal, Swale pushed himself too hard, Swale was raised in poverty,* and so on, are active possibilities, is to test each one to see what its difficulties might be. To do this, one must find a set of conditions under which the XP might be reasonable. Let's look at a couple of these XPs and see how this might work.

We said in Chapter 6 that an XP had the following form:

1. **An anomaly that the pattern explains (which is the main index into the XP)**
2. **A set of relevant indices under which it can be retrieved**
3. **A set of states of the world under which the pattern is likely to be a valid explanation**
4. **A set of states of the world under which the pattern is likely to be relevant, even if it isn't immediately applicable**
5. **A pattern of actions, with the relationships between them, that shows how the event being explained could arise**
6. **A set of prior explanations that has been made possible by use of this pattern.**
7. **A reason that stereotypes the behavior being explained.**

Specifically then, let's consider two patterns, **Poverty brings early death,** and **Mob Killing:**

Poverty brings early death

1. **An anomaly that the pattern explains:** *early death*
2. **A set of relevant indices under which it can be retrieved:** *early death; poverty; lack of food*
3. **A set of states of the world under which the pattern is likely to**

be a valid explanation: early death; prior lack of health; poor childhood

4. **A set of states of the world under which the pattern is likely to be relevant, even if it isn't immediately applicable:** *shortage of necessities; harsh conditions*
5. **A pattern of actions, with the relationships between them, that shows how the event being explained could arise:**

lack of money prevents buying enough food
lack of money prevents adequate health care
lack of food causes bad health, as does lack of health care
bad health causes early death

6. **A set of prior explanations that has been made possible by use of this pattern:** *lives of immigrants; people in Africa*
7. **A reason that stereotypes the behavior being explained:** *the body can't be treated poorly early on without eventual repercussions.*

Mob killing

1. **An anomaly that the pattern explains (which is the main index into the XP):** *untimely death*
2. **A set of relevant indices under which it can be retrieved:** *untimely death; injury of gang member*
3. **A set of states of the world under which the pattern is likely to be a valid explanation:** *killing of gang member and one of the conditions: gang warfare rampant; turf being taken over by enemy; previous killing by rival gang*
4. **A set of states of the world under which the pattern is likely to be relevant, even if it isn't immediately applicable:** *rivalry; revenge*
5. **A pattern of actions, with the relationships between them, that shows how the event being explained could arise:**

gang member commits crimes for gang
during crimes, he steps on toes of rival
rival seeks revenge
rival kills gang member

6. **A set of prior explanations that has been made possible by use of this pattern:** *The Untouchables TV show; gangland slayings in New York; horse's head scene in The Godfather*
7. **A reason that stereotypes the behavior being explained:** *he who lives by the sword dies by the sword.*

The key part of the XP, for the purposes of misapplication, is *step five which lists the sequence of events that the XP describes. When trying to apply* **Poverty brings early death** to the case of Swale, it is clear immediately that the step *no money to buy food* which starts the process is very unlikely to be true. Racehorses are rather well treated from birth. So, if we are looking for a realistic explanation, we can either look elsewhere, or else we can *suspend the condition* that we don't like. This is tweaking rule number 2:

T2: If a condition is clearly false, ignore it temporarily, make it true later if the rest works out.

Using T2 allows us to assume in any case that Swale's problem was that he ate poorly as a youth and that his body suffered for it later. There is no reason to believe this, of course, but let's not let that deter us. Assuming that we like this line of reasoning, the problem becomes one of creating a scenario whereby the offending condition might have been true. There are many ways to do this: we can assume an eating disorder that Swale had as a youth, we can give him a female horse who he knew who was poorly fed and to whom he gave all his oats, and so on. The point is that, especially if we want to create an artistic explanation, it is possible to keep alive a clearly wrong line of inquiry by using T2. T2 has a companion rule therefore, which is:

T3: To make an unworkable condition viable, substitute another EQ and XP.

This means, in effect, that one must ask the question, *why would Swale not have had the right food when he had access to good food?* Thus, we must find candidate indices and relevant XPs, such as **disease prevents action,** or **donate to a good cause** to explain why one would think he had eaten well when actually he hadn't.

The first point here is that it is possible to make any XP viable if you want to, but one may have to resort to numerous suspensions of conditions. This may cause an explanation to be created that is so fanciful that it is absurd. Nevertheless, the second point that follows from the first is quite powerful. There is a procedure for the suspension of belief from which creative explanations can be constructed, and that procedure is fairly straightforward in its application.

Now let's look at the next XP. In **Mob Killing,** the conditions in step three are even more absurd, on the face of it. Surely, Swale wasn't a member of a rival gang. Further, one can of course, construct a story in which there are horse gangs, but this is soley an artistic explanation, and probably not a very good one. So, we can safely abandon this line of inquiry. Or can we? One important point about XPs is that they contain pointers to others episodes in which they have applied. This leads to rule T4:

T4: Use relevant remindings in XP to find other XPs

Recall that the difficult part of the explanation process is finding the XPs to consider. We said earlier that this problem was part of the more general problem of memory organization and that therefore we could not solve it here. Nevertheless, it is possible to find some techniques that allow us to find indices more easily. Here the trick is to not abandon the original XP without allowing oneself to think about that XP in the context of the original index, in this case *horse death*. I have listed as an exemplar of the *Mob Killing* XP, the *horse head scene from the movie The Godfather*. From this point, we can reconstruct an explanation wherein Swale is now seen as an object of revenge between rival gangs. Now, this explanation should not have come from this EQ, officially. That is, there is an appropriate EQ here, namely:

EQ23: IS SWALE'S DEATH THE RESULT OF SWALE BEING THE VICTIM OF SOME COUNTERPLAN? derived from "HOW IS THIS EVENT A TYPICAL COUNTERPLAN APPLIED TO THIS ACTOR?"

Using EQ23, we should have, more naturally come upon the idea of a revenge killing. But there is nothing proscribed about the process of wandering around in memory. We take remindings when we can get them. For example, it is possible to get what has come to be called at our laboratory, *The Janis Joplin Memorial Reminding*, from two entirely different places. In Chapter 5, when we discussed how to find additional XPs, we introduced Rule 3: *transpose objects that are alike in behavior.* This rule was used to find candidates under EQ 14 as well. Thus, one could find the above reminding by seeing Swale as a *successful performer who died young* or by seeing Swale as a *drug addict.* In the first case we have the **Early Success Brings Early Death** pattern. In the second case, we have the **Addiction Brings Early Death** pattern. These look like this: **Early success brings early death**

1. **An anomaly that the pattern explains (which is the main index into the XP):** *early death*
2. **A set of relevant indices under which it can be retrieved:** *dangers of success; early success; life in the fast lane; stardom*
3. **A set of states of the world under which the pattern is likely to be a valid explanation:** *early death and either great success or life in the fast lane*
4. **A set of states of the world under which the pattern is likely to be relevant, even if it isn't immediately applicable:** *high-stress environment; extreme change in social status; wild living*

5. **A pattern of actions, with the relationships between them, that shows how the event being explained could arise:**

achieve success fast
ease of accomplishment causes boredom
success gives lots of money
boredom causes you to look for kicks
money makes drugs available
drug overdose causes death

6. **A set of prior explanations that has been made possible by use of this pattern:** *Janis Joplin, Jimi Hendrix, John Belushi.*
7. **A reason that stereotypes the behavior being explained:** *it's difficult to cope with success when you're young.*

Addiction brings early death

1. **An anomaly that the pattern explains:** *early death.*
2. **A set of relevant indices under which it can be retrieved:** *addiction to something; junkies; alcoholics*
3. **A set of states of the world under which the pattern is likely to be a valid explanation:** *early death and drug addiction.*
4. **A set of states of the world under which the pattern is likely to be relevant, even if it isn't immediately applicable:** *difficulty coping; dependence on something; trying to escape reality*
5. **A pattern of actions, with the relationships between them, that shows how the event being explained could arise:**

be unhappy
look for escape from unhappiness
find escape in addiction
require escalating dosages
overdose

6. **A set of prior explanations that has been made possible by use of this pattern:** *junkies in alleys; alcoholics.*
7. **A reason that stereotypes the behavior being explained:** *people who try to escape their lives eventually do away with themselves.*

Either of these patterns may be used in the Swale case to come up with something relevant. The trick in the first is to be able to suspend belief on the issue of how Swale could have decided to obtain, and have been able to ingest, drugs. Using rules T2, and T3, we can decide to believe the rest of the XP. Thus we are faced with resolving the problem of the suspended belief. The trick is, again, to find an XP that will resolve the new EQ. So for the EQ, *who could have helped Swale with drugs and why would he do it?*

we get a few obvious patterns: **dope peddler hooks youth, friend can't prevent self-destruction,** and **evil person uses another in schemes of his own.** The third one of these allows us to toy with the idea that Swale actually was a drug addict, because someone else, perhaps his trainer or his owner found some reason to do this to him. Of course, at this point, one should get reminded that in fact *horses do take drugs* and one can consider the realistic explanation that Swale was a great racehorse because he was on drugs and that the drugs finally took their toll. This brings to mind tweaking rules T5 and T6:

T5: If one is reminded, while tweaking, of a related fact, suspend tweaking and apply fact to original XP.

T6: In choosing XPs to tweak, choose the one with the most ordinary characters first.

Had we used the other XP, we would have arrived at the same place, of course. One does not need to think of Janis Joplin to get this idea about Swale being an addict. One need only think about how Swale might have had access to drugs. Again, the key point is in asking the right question. One must transform the question about whether Swale took drugs into one that asks how or why someone else would have given him drugs. This is rule T7:

T7: If an actor could not have done an action, hypothesize an agent who could have.

The *tweaking rules* have the form of heuristics, the purpose of which it is to bring to mind a new event from which one can derive a working XP that can adapt the originally proposed XP into one suitable for the situation. Thus, it is unlikely that one could give an exhaustive list of them since there is no reason to suppose any limit to the possible methods of reminding. The issue here, it should be clear, is a kind of intentional reminding. When we are faced with the problem of explaining something, and no easily fitting XP exists, the adaptation of another, superficially unsuitable XP to the current situation is attempted. However, during the process of adaptation, it may come to pass that alternative XPs suggest themselves that are more suited to adaptation. Thus, the process of creative explanation is very much one of search, as we said earlier. That is, we are searching for XPs to adapt. Thus, creative explanation is dependent upon intentional reminding. And, adaptation of XPs found by intentional reminding, is controlled by a set of heuristics. This suggests that **creativity depends upon two primary factors,** namely, **a set of methods for getting reminded,** and **a set of methods for adapting remindings in such a way as to fit the new situation.** Plus, one must also have a creative attitude. This attitude manifests itself in the ability to keep alive *obviously errant remindings* or *obviously irrelevant XPs* long enough to see if they really are useless.

If this is true, what does it tell us about computers and their possible creativity? The creative attitude is easy. All we need do is be willing to compute a great deal. Of course, we might do nothing else, so some heuristics for knowing when to abandon a hypothesis might be nice. Thus, we are left with the notion that creativity in a computer means supplying the computer with three types of heuristics, namely:

CREATIVITY HEURISTICS

1. **Heuristics for the intentional reminding of explanation patterns**
2. **Heuristics for the adaptation of old patterns to the current situation**
3. **Heuristics for keeping alive seemingly useless hypotheses**

SOLVING TERRORISM

One way to see how the whole process works is to try to solve an inherently difficult or unsolved problem, by computer. Of course, we have not yet fitted a machine with all the heuristics necessary for creativity, so we shall first do this as a *thought experiment.* Consider the problem of international terrorism. If a person came up with a novel solution to this problem, we would consider him creative indeed. Could we get a machine to suggest solutions? Of course I am going to suggest that we can, by supplying that machine with a great many explanation patterns; the heuristics to find reasonable candidates to adapt to the current situation; the heuristics to do the adaptation; the ability to recognize a viable solution; and the patience to try. Of these, the ability to recognize viability is probably the most difficult because it depends upon a more or less complete world model. Nevertheless, the recognition of viability is not something one ordinarily considers to be all that creative.

The first step in creative explanation is to find the thing that needs to be explained, of course. Here we will attempt to explain *why the terrorists are fighting and how it can be stopped.* This initial question must be transformed into a set of EQs by taking the standard EQs, and adapting them. The EQs we used in the Swale example were:

EQ1: "WHAT CAUSED AN UNEXPECTED EVENT?"

EQ1.1: "HOW WILL AN UNEXPECTED EVENT BENEFIT OTHERS?"

EQ2: "WHAT FACTORS CAUSED THIS EVENT and CAN THEY HAPPEN AGAIN?"

EQ3.1: "WHAT WERE THE UNDERLYING CAUSES OF THIS BAD EVENT?"

EQ4: "HOW DID THE VICTIM ENABLE THIS BAD EVENT?"

EQ5: "WHAT DID THE VICTIM DO WRONG IN THIS BAD EVENT?"

EQ6: "WHAT CIRCUMSTANCES LED TO THIS EVENT?"

EQ7: "WHY DID THIS INSTITUTION ACT THIS WAY?"

EQ8: "WHAT ARE THE POLICIES OF THIS INSTITUTION?"

EQ9: "WHAT ARE THE GOALS OF THIS INSTITUTION?"

EQ10: "WHAT PLANS WAS THIS INSTITUTIONS CARRYING OUT?"

EQ11: "WHAT DID THIS INSTITUTION DECIDE WAS MOST IMPORTANT?"

EQ12: "WHAT WILL THIS INSTITUTION DO NEXT?"

EQ13: "WHAT CAUSED THE ACTOR TO BEHAVE THIS WAY?"

EQ14: "IS THE ACTOR A MEMBER OF ANY GROUP THAT IS KNOWN TO DO THIS ANOMALOUS BEHAVIOR?"

EQ15: "WHY WOULD THE GROUP THAT THIS THE ACTOR IS A MEMBER OF DO THIS ANOMALOUS BEHAVIOR?"

EQ16: "WHAT MAKES THIS PARTICULAR GROUP BEHAVE DIFFERENTLY FROM OTHER GROUPS?"

EQ17: "HOW DOES THIS BEHAVIOR FIT IN WITH A GROUP OF BEHAVIORS?"

EQ18: "WHAT PLANS DOES THIS GROUP HAVE?"

EQ19: "WHY DOES THIS GROUP HAVE THE GOALS THAT IT DOES?"

EQ20: "WHAT COUNTERPLAN WAS THE ACTOR PERFORMING?"

EQ21: "WHAT PREVIOUS BEHAVIORAL CHANGE LED TO THIS EVENT?"

EQ22: "HOW IS THIS ACTION TYPICAL FOR THIS ACTOR?"

EQ23: "HOW IS THIS EVENT A TYPICAL COUNTERPLAN APPLIED TO THIS ACTOR?"

EQ24: "HOW IS THIS APPARENTLY INEFFECTIVE PLAN IN

REALITY A GOOD PLAN FOR SOME UNSEEN GOAL?"

We now attempt to adapt these questions to the current situation, eliminating those that are irrelevant:

EQ1: too general

EQ1.1: HOW DOES TERRORISM BENEFIT PEOPLE?"

EQ2: "WHAT MOTIVATES THE TERRORISTS?"

EQ3.1: "WHAT IS THE REASONING OF THE TERRORISTS?"

EQ4: "HOW DO THE VICTIMS GET INTO THE SITUATION IN THE FIRST PLACE?"

EQ5: "DO THE VICTIMS MAKE AN ERROR OF SOME KIND?"

EQ6: "WHAT EVENTS TEND TO PRECEDE TERRORIST ACTS?"

EQ7: "WHAT ARE THE MOTIVES OF THE INSTITUTIONS WHO BACK TERRORISM?"

EQ8: "WHAT ARE THE POLICIES OF THOSE INSTITUTIONS?"

EQ9: "WHAT ARE THE GOALS OF THOSE INSTITUTIONS?"

EQ10: "WHAT PLANS ARE THOSE INSTITUTIONS CARRYING OUT?"

EQ11: "WHAT DID THIS INSTITUTION DECIDE WAS MOST IMPORTANT?"

EQ12: "WHAT WILL THIS INSTITUTION DO NEXT?"

EQ13: redundant

EQ14: "WHAT OTHER GROUPS BEHAVE IN A SIMILAR MANNER?"

EQ15: "WHY DO SUCH GROUPS BEHAVE THAT WAY?"

EQ16: "WHAT MAKES THIS PARTICULAR GROUP BEHAVE DIFFERENTLY FROM OTHER GROUPS?"

EQ17: since we are considering a group of behaviors, this is irrelevant

EQ18: "WHAT GENERAL PLANS DO GROUPS THAT THE ACTORS BELONG TO HAVE?"

EQ19: "WHY DOES THIS GROUP HAVE THE GOALS THAT IT DOES?"

EQ20: "WHAT EVENT IS TERRORISM TRYING TO PREVENT?"

EQ21: "WHY IS THERE SO MUCH TERRORISM NOW?"

EQ22: irrelevant

EQ23: irrelevant

EQ24: "DOES TERRORISM SUPPORT SOME GOAL THAT ISN'T OBVIOUS?"

The next step is to find the XPs indexed under the above EQs. Of course, some of these yield fairly standard explanations that we have all learned for explaining terrorism. Since what we are interested in here is creative explanation, we must focus on the EQs that have no XP indexed directly under them, or which ask a question that is unusual enough that one would have to give some thought to it. Looking at the list in this way, yields:

EQ1.1: HOW DOES TERRORISM BENEFIT PEOPLE?"

EQ4: "HOW DO THE VICTIMS GET INTO THE SITUATION IN THE FIRST PLACE?"

EQ5: "DO THE VICTIMS MAKE AN ERROR OF SOME KIND?"

EQ6: "WHAT EVENTS TEND TO PRECEDE TERRORIST ACTS?"

EQ14: "WHAT OTHER GROUPS BEHAVE IN A SIMILAR MANNER?"

EQ15: "WHY DO SUCH GROUPS BEHAVE THAT WAY?"

EQ16: "WHAT MAKES THIS PARTICULAR GROUP BEHAVE DIFFERENTLY FROM OTHER GROUPS?"

EQ18: "WHAT GENERAL PLANS DO GROUPS THAT THE ACTORS BELONG TO HAVE?"

EQ20: "WHAT EVENT IS TERRORISM TRYING TO PREVENT?"

EQ21: "WHY IS THERE SO MUCH TERRORISM NOW?"

EQ24: "DOES TERRORISM SUPPORT SOME GOAL THAT ISN'T OBVIOUS?"

Now let's consider what XPs are under these EQs or, what XPs might be brought to mind by transforming these EQs slightly. We will look at each question in turn, indicating some XPs that might be relevant:

EQ1.1: HOW DOES TERRORISM BENEFIT PEOPLE?"
  war brings plunder; revenge brings happiness; recognition brings importance;

EQ4: "HOW DO THE VICTIMS GET INTO THE SITUATION IN THE FIRST PLACE?"

vacations bring risk; travel brings risk; homesickness causes disturbed behavior; change upsets routine

EQ5: "DO THE VICTIMS MAKE AN ERROR OF SOME KIND?"

bullies pick on cowards; people who are into symbols pick victims who are symbolic

EQ6: "WHAT EVENTS TEND TO PRECEDE TERRORIST ACTS?"

full moon arouses werewolves; revenge

EQ14: "WHAT OTHER GROUPS BEHAVE IN A SIMILAR MANNER?"

nations at war; marital disputes; professional infighting; office politics; children's disputes; revolutionaries

EQ15: "WHY DO SUCH GROUPS BEHAVE THAT WAY?"

jealousy; inability to share; dominance problems; arrested development; general unhappiness

EQ16: "WHAT MAKES THIS PARTICULAR GROUP BEHAVE DIFFERENTLY FROM OTHER GROUPS?"

poverty; lack of control of own lives; political oppression; pawns in the games of others; religious differences; true-believer mentality

EQ18: "WHAT GENERAL PLANS DO GROUPS THAT THE ACTORS BELONG TO HAVE?"

Moslems-kill infidels; Lebanese-fix country; young people-let off steam; young people-be idealistic

EQ20: "WHAT EVENT IS TERRORISM TRYING TO PREVENT?"

violence disturbs status quo; violence brings repression which brings revolution; fanaticism disrupts boredom

EQ21: "WHY IS THERE SO MUCH TERRORISM NOW?"

new breeding grounds; frustration over lost wars; loss of power of Arab block because of oil price drops; new fanatics gain power; religious resurgance in moslem world

EQ24: "DOES TERRORISM SUPPORT SOME GOAL THAT ISN'T OBVIOUS?"

somebody gets rich through terrorism; someone gets power through terrorism;

The above XPs all came from my own head as I thought about the situation. Obviously, a great deal of the creative process is hidden in the ability to think up XPs at the right time. One method for doing this is to try to see the original issue as if it were something else. For example, by considering irrelevant features that precede events that are dastardly, the idea of full moons and werewolves occurred to me. Such silly ideas are the stuff of which creative explanations are made, of course.

However, my intention here is twofold. I am interested in the creative process in people and in how that process might be applied to machines. Thus, to make machines creative we must do careful work on the heuristics by which one comes up with candidate XPs, as I have said. Until that complete set of heuristics is developed, there are other alternatives. For example, just seeing *terrorism* as a member of a class of actions, one can begin to come up with XPs in a fairly standard way. Therefore let's consider this list again, but this time in a different way. This time, I have chosen a book of proverbs, which have been classified under various major and minor headings. Below are the original EQs again, this time followed by the major and minor headings and proverbs that correspond to the EQs, listed under them, that I found to be relevant from *The Penguin Dictionary of Proverbs*. Not all the EQs had proverbs that were relevant, of course. Here again, one can see that the trick is in the indexing. In this case, the proverbs in this book were classified under headings that forced me to decide whether or not they were relevant to the case at hand. In other words, here again, I had to decide what ideas best related to the issue of terrorism seen from any possible perspective.

EQ1.1: HOW DOES TERRORISM BENEFIT PEOPLE?"

ADVERSITY-value:	**He that is down need fear no fall.**
	Adversity is the touchstone of virtue.
ADVERSITY-effects:	**Adversity makes a man wise, not rich.**

EQ2: "WHAT MOTIVATES THE TERRORISTS?"

BADNESS-sources:	**Covetousness is the root of all evil.**
	No mischief but that a woman or a priest is at the bottom of it.
	When the weasel and the cat make a marriage, it is a very bad presage.
CRIME-sources:	**Poverty is the mother of crime.**
	He that is suffered more than is fitting, will do more than is lawful.

EQ7: "WHAT ARE THE MOTIVES OF THE INSTITUTIONS WHO BACK TERRORISM?"

TROUBLE–MAKING:	**Pouring oil on the fire is not the way to prevent it.**
PEACE:	**The stick is the surest peacemaker.**

HYPOCRISY: **If you want to see black-hearted people, look among those who never miss their prayers.**

EQ8: "WHAT ARE THE POLICIES OF THOSE INSTITUTIONS?"
ASKING-effects: **Ask and it shall be given to you. He that demands, misses not, unless his demands be foolish.**
AUTHORITY-advantages: **Better to rule, than be ruled by the rout. It is better to be the hammer than the anvil.**
WAR-tactics: **Cities are taken by the ears.**

EQ9: "WHAT ARE THE GOALS OF THOSE INSTITUTIONS?"
CORRUPTION-religious: **No penny, no paternoster.**
-causes: **He who squeezes in between the onion and its peel picks up the stink. Keep not ill men company unless you increase their number. Fish begin to stink at the head.**

EQ10: "WHAT PLANS ARE THOSE INSTITUTIONS CARRYING OUT?"
FEAR-power: **Fear is stronger than love. There is no remedy for fear but cut off the head.**
ENEMIES: **For a flying enemy make a golden bridge.**

EQ11: "WHAT DID THIS INSTITUTION DECIDE WAS MOST IMPORTANT?"
BELIEVING-value: **Faith will move mountains**
-doubt: **The more one knows the less one believes.**
DEEDS-value: **Tis action makes the hero.**
intention: **The good intention excuses the bad action.**

EQ12: "WHAT, WILL THIS INSTITUTION DO NEXT?"
DANGER-effects: **You may play with the bull until you get his horn in your eye. Danger makes men devout.**

EQ14: "WHAT OTHER GROUPS BEHAVE IN A SIMILAR MANNER?"

CRIME: **Show me a liar and I will show thee a thief.**

COWARDICE: **Some have been thought brave because they were afraid to run away.**

Having been reminded of these proverbs, by whatever method, the issue is whether they can be adapted to be of use in understanding terrorism and perhaps finding a solution for it. In other words, can one make use of these proverbs in such a way as to create a new idea from them? The claim is, of course, that one can, in the following way. Consider the following proverbs taken from the above chart:

EQ1.1   **Adversity makes a man wise, not rich.**

EQ2:   **Covetousness is the root of all evil.**
            No mischief but that a woman or a priest is at the bottom of it.
            He that is suffered more than is fitting, will do more than is lawful.

EQ7:   **Pouring oil on the fire is not the way to prevent it.**

EQ8:   **It is better to be the hammer than the anvil.**
            Cities are taken by the ears.

EQ9:   **No penny, no paternoster.**
            He who squeezes in between the onion and its peel picks up the stink.
            Fish begin to stink at the head.

EQ11:   **The more one knows the less one believes.**
            Tis action makes the hero.

EQ12:   **You may play with the bull until you get his horn in your eye.**
            Danger makes men devout.

EQ14:   **Some have been thought brave because they were afraid to run away.**

The above proverbs constitute an explanation for a number of things, and within them a suggestion of what to do to fix the situations to which they refer. Here then, is where the second part of the creative process comes in. After finding an XP (and proverbs are very standard and usual XPs), one begins to adapt it. This may require using it solely as a vehicle for finding other, more relevant XPs. In other words, an XP is, in one of its most important roles within the process of *creative* explanation, a source of indices to remindings or to other XPs. That having been said, let's look at each of the above proverbs to see what they suggest:

From EQ1.1 we found **Adversity makes a man wise, not rich.** This was a reference to the effects on the victims of terrorist acts. Thus, one can come up with the idea that people who suffer from terrorism become wiser because of it, but while this may well be true, it is rather useless as is. However, suppose that we reversed the problem here. As we said in Chapter 3, one of the goals of explanation is to find rules of the world that seem to work so as to be able to adapt them to one's own circumstances. Using the following tweaking rule:

T8: If a rule applies in given situation, try reversing its actors and objects and see what happens.

we come up with the idea that perhaps if the terrorists would suffer some more adversity, they would get wiser. This brings to mind the idea, using the XP **divine retribution,** of *hijacking or kidnapping some of them for a change.*

Using the first XP derived from EQ2, **Covetousness is the root of all evil,** we get the simple idea that the reason the terrorists do what they do is that because they want something, money and power being two prime things that people tend to want. As we said, one of the prime purposes of the search for XPs is to find appropriate indices to other XPs. In this case, since we are looking for plans of action, those too can come to mind. Thus, two plans come to mind here, connected to *covetousness,* namely, **give them what they want,** and, **convince them they can't have what they want.** Thus, we now have the idea of *giving a large grant to the PLO, in exchange for an agreement to stop terrorism,* or *giving Israel nuclear weapons to use in their retaliation for terrorist attacks.*

The next proverb, **No mischief but that a woman or a priest is at the bottom of it,** is of interest because it brings up two rather unusual new indices. Using tweaking rule T9:

T9: Whenever you have a character in an XP, try changing the character to a different one within the same set, in order to find a reminding or relevant rule.

we can begin to think of mothers, teachers, and so on, and for priests, we can think about any clergyman. The latter notion leads easily to Moslem clergyman, and might bring up Ayattolah Khomeini, suggesting that *killing Khomeini would end the terrorism.*

This next one, **He that is suffered more than is fitting, will do more than is lawful,** is simply a realistic explanation. If taken as a call to a plan, one gets the idea to attempt to eliminate the suffering, from which it is a simple progression to the idea of the standard solution of a Palestinian State. From there, using tweaking rule T10:

T10: Rather than the obvious object, change the obvious into another object that also satisfies the rule.

we can come up with many reasons why they may be suffering: poor housing, lack of sanitary conditions, etc. Any one of those would produce some suggestions, for example, perhaps *we should build a luxury housing development for them to end their suffering.*

From **Pouring oil on the fire is not the way to prevent it** we get the idea that it is the intention of the leaders of the terrorists, not to prevent troubles, but to fuel them. Now we need a reason why they would want a constant state of troubles. This is actually quite close to the heart of the matter in reality, and many XPs come to mind, including an XP from the 60s that I recall, namely: **Social Unrest Brings Revolution.** There is also another old standard here: **Little Man Benefits From War between Two Big Men.** These are not creative explanations of course, just realistic ones.

Next, we have two attempts to explain the theory that terrorists operate under. The first, **It is better to be the hammer than the anvil,** giving a philosophy of life of down-trodden people and the second, **Cities are taken by the ears,** giving the operating philosophy that underlies propaganda warfare. Again, suggested solutions must be directed to the heart of these issues. In the first, one might think of *ways to make the Palestinians more proud of their own positive achievements.* In the second, *one might decide to fight a war of words in Lebanon, using stronger methods than are now used.* This latter, which one might call the **1984 XP,** is often used as a rationale for creating a totalitarian state.

The proverbs in the next set all deal with who is behind it all. The first, **No penny, no paternoster** suggests that *the clergy is behind it all and that they can be paid off in money.* The second, **He who squeezes in between the onion and its peel picks up the stink** suggests that *the people surrounding the terrorists are so corrupt that one must get them first.* Here that might mean Syria, Khaddafi, or the PLO leaders. The third, **Fish begin to stink at the head,** says exactly that.

The next, **The more one knows the less one believes,** suggests that the problem with the terrorists is primarily that they are *true believers,* and that there is a standard remedy for that, namely education. So, *perhaps we should open a free university for them, or else give them all scholarships to come to the U.S.*

Tis action makes the hero suggests that the terrorists need to be heroes. Thus, one solution would be to give them another opportunity to be heroes. Using the XP that **Opportunity makes heroes,** we must provide the opportunity. *Perhaps we should start a war that they all could fight and be heroes in.* Or, on the other hand, using the proverb indexed under EQ14,

Some have been thought brave because they were afraid to run away, we have the suggestion that the terrorists would really just like to run **away,** and that therefore *maybe we should launch a rescue operation to retrieve them from their leaders.* This idea gains further credence when one reads the article reprinted in Chapter 8.

And, finally, we have two rather realistic commentaries on it all. The first, **You may play with the bull until you get his horn in your eye,** suggests that it will all go away of its own accord, and the second, **Danger makes men devout,** suggests that there is no way to prevent religious fanaticism as long as people feel themselves to be in danger.

COLLECTING PATTERNS

In order for people or computers to be creative, they must have many explanation patterns available to them. These would come in two ways—by being fed them directly, something most people are quite willing to do for other people, either as parents, teachers, or friends, and by learning new ones through creative misapplication.

Thus, if we are interested in creativity by computer, it is not unreasonable to attempt to understand how one might go about making an exhaustive list of the XPs with which a creative computer could function. In order to get started on this enterprise, let's first look at some newspaper stories that are, one way or another, about explanation and explanation patterns. The first is from the New York Post Sports Section:

St. Louis boos get under Keith's skin

WHAT'S GOING ON HERE?

NEWS ITEM: *Card fans boo Hernandez*

IT WAS A STRANGE tableau. Keith Hernandez stood at the batter's box. The Cardinal pitcher stood poised on the mound, ready to pitch. The boos cascaded in a roar from the stands. Booo.... booo.... booo, unceasingly, for maybe 20 or 30 seconds. That is an eon when you are being booed.

My first impression was weird. I saw John Tudor frozen on the mound, hands together, refusing to throw the ball, prolonging the wrath of the crowd, punishing Hernandez. That couldn't be. No one is that sadistic.

And then I noticed that it was Keith Hernandez who was prolonging the punishment. He hadn't stepped into the box. Tudor couldn't throw the ball until Hernandez stepped in, and

Keith wasn't stepping in. He was standing there, just outside the line, holding his bat erect, squeezing the handle, as if saying to himself, *"Go ahead, get it out of your system. Get it all out."*

"No," he said afterward. *"That isn't what I was doing. I was trying to collect my wits."* He was shaken. He needed time to get himself together and he took it, even though it prolonged the booing.

"Half the reason," he said, *"is that I am the enemy to them."*

He took for granted that the newsmen would assume the other half, that he had admitted to using cocaine while a member of the Cardinals.

His analysis is accurate but a step short. There was yet another reason. The St. Louis fans were booing the New York fans.

This is mid-USA. They had heard here of the standing O given Keith Hernandez upon his first trip to the plate at Shea following his self-incriminating testimony at the drug trial, and they resented it. This was their reverse standing O for his.

The people are not waiting for commissioner Ueberroth to mete out punishment. At the start of the game, a large banner hung from the upper deck in right-center:
Keith says "Coke Is It"

There are a great many explanations and XPs referred to, and used by, this story, so it is a good place to start. Lets look at the story again, this time with the sentences that refer to XPs in bold and the XPs they refer to listed below them:

St. Louis boos get under Keith's skin

WHAT'S GOING ON HERE?

NEWS ITEM: *Card fans boo Hernandez*

IT WAS A STRANGE tableau. Keith Hernandez stood at the batter's box. The Cardinal pitcher stood poised on the mound, ready to pitch. The boos cascaded in a roar from the stands. Booo. . . . booo. . . . booo, unceasingly, for maybe 20 or 30 seconds. That is an eon when you are being booed.

My first impression was weird. **I saw John Tudor frozen on the mound, hands together, refusing to throw the ball, prolonging the wrath of the crowd, punishing Hernandez.** That couldn't be. **No one is that sadistic.**

1. **People prolong the agony of others in order to punish them.**
2. **People don't punish people in front of millions of people unless they are incredibly sadistic.**

And then I noticed that it was Keith Hernandez who was prolonging the punishment. He hadn't stepped into the box. Tudor couldn't throw the ball until Hernandez stepped in, and Keith wasn't stepping in. He was standing there, just outside the line, holding his bat erect, squeezing the handle, as if saying to himself, *"Go ahead, get it out of your system. Get it all out."*

"No," he said afterward. *"That isn't what I was doing. I was trying to collect my wits."* He was shaken. **He needed time to get himself together and he took it, even though it prolonged the booing.**

3. **To stop punishment, one can prolong it until it gets boring.**
4. **When you are upset, but need to perform, you can calm yourself by waiting a while before starting.**
5. **Sometimes one must accept more pain in order to accomplish what one wants.**

"Half the reason," he said, *"is that I am the enemy to them."*

He took for granted that the newsmen would assume the other half, that he had admitted to using cocaine while a member of the Cardinals.

6. **People feel justified in torturing their enemies.**
7. **Sports heroes are not permitted any human failings by their fans.**

His analysis is accurate but a step short. There was yet another reason. **The St. Louis fans were booing the New York fans.**

This is mid-USA. **They had heard here of the standing O given Keith Hernandez upon his first trip to the plate at Shea following his self-incriminating testimony at the drug trial, and they resented it.** This was their reverse standing O for his.

The people are not waiting for commissioner Ueberroth to mete out punishment. At the start of the game, a large banner hung from the upper deck in right-center: *Keith says "Coke Is It"*

8. **People in the Midwest have different social views than people in New York.**
9. **People dislike people who see the world differently than they do.**
10. **Some people feel called upon to support their heroes when they are in difficulties, while others criticize them.**

11. **People get tired of waiting for authorities to act and take justice into their own hands.**

These eleven XPs span a large range of domains and goals. To be useful, an XP shouldn't be too specific to a given domain, but quite often they can get very specific. Also, an XP can be implicitly referred to in both a specific and a general way. Look at the following story, in which I have again marked the implicit XPs:

City SATs climbing slowly

The College Board test scores of public high school seniors went up this year—but they were far behind the national average, Schools Chancellor Nathan Quinones said yesterday.

The city's high school seniors who graduated in June scored five points higher on Scholastic Aptitude Tests in 1984–85 than their counterparts the previous year.

On the verbal section of the test, the score of 20,581 public school seniors went up four points to 381. The math scores crept up only one point to 430.

SAT exams are graded on a scale of 200 to 800.

However, the city's combined score of 811 was behind the national average of 906 announced last week by the College Board.

While Quinones acknowledged the gap, he pointed out that students locally were keeping pace with the rate of improvement seen on the national level. Quinones said that over the past two years city scores have climbed 12 points while the national score went up 13 points.

"This is another indicator in the positive trend of student achievement, he said."

Traditionally, the city average has been lower than the national average because of the higher number of poor and minority students, who tend to have lower scores.

Quinones said that while only 20 percent of the nation's seniors who took the test were minorities, the percentage was 67.7 percent here.

12. **A problem is not a problem if everybody else has the same problem.**
13. **Things are improving because the system is in good shape.**

14. The leader of a system in which good results have occurred is responsible for those results.

15. One needn't fix a problem if one can explain it.

The four XPs given above are very general and can be used anytime, anywhere, since they are about explanation itself. Below, we have some XPs that are used all the time in a very specific domain, *sports betting*. They are also used elsewhere, but their ubiquity in sports, and their faithful application by millions of betters trying to make a prediction of an outcome, make them interesting XPs to study:

Gallo's College football analysis

By Greg Gallo
Boston College (2-3) at Rutgers (0-2-1)

> **Early season grind—BYU, Temple, Maryland, Pitt, Miami in succession—has exhausted Eagles on verge of collapse. Winless Scarlet Knights, who scared Florida and Penn State, can wade in and deliver KO punch at Meadowlands. Go Rutgers.**

The explanation used here is that teams get tired from playing tough games and teams that don't win but come close against good teams will win against weaker teams. This XP is:

16. Improvement beats exhaustion.

It has a counterpart in life outside of football betting namely:

17. Hopefulness sustains while exhaustion weakens.

Such a pattern can be used to explain why certain people can continue against all odds while others tend to quit.

South Carolina (2-2) at Pittsburgh (1-2-1)

> Gamecocks, a pre-season Top-20 club, have come unglued. Joe Morrison's D vs Georgia was a sieve, allowing low-scoring Dawgs 35 points! Watch hot and cold QB Congemi burn Carolina for last year's 45–21 pasting at Columbia. Give the points.

The Gamecocks (South Carolina) have lost after they were expected to win. Thus, they are likely to lose because:

18. Failing people's expectations can be devastating.

Furthermore, it is also the case that:

> **19. If your expectations are too high you are bound to be disappointed.**

In the analysis of the game itself, the author refers to revenge for last year's defeat. This is a big factor used by bettors. The XPs being used are:

20. People who were humiliated want revenge.

21. The motive of revenge can enable a weaker combatant to beat a stronger one.

22. Motivation is a stronger factor than ability in a battle.
Princeton (1-1) at Brown (1-1)
One point loss to Yale in opener makes this one a must for Bruins if they want to make run at Ivy crown. Brownies offensive wallop too much for Princetonians. Give.

This prediction refers to the XP we labeled 22 above. It relies upon:

23. People perform better than they otherwise might when they see disaster if they don't. (Known popularly as: *Their backs were against the wall.*)
North Carolina (2-1)
at Georgia Tech (2-1)
John Dewberry-Kevin Anothony QB duel should keep scoreboard blinking like pinball machine. Improved Tar Heels can take Yellow Jackets to wire. Take.

These next two refer to the betting spread in football. It is not my intention here to teach football betting, so suffice it is say that *take* means *bet on the underdog,* and *give* means *bet on the favorite.* When a game is expected to be unevenly matched, bookies add points to the total of the underdog to even things out. Thus, this last prediction uses an XP that is entirely domain-specific with respect to football betting, namely: **When teams are evenly matched and the bookies think they aren't that is a good reason to bet on the underdog because you get extra points from the bookie.**
This XP, does have its counterparts in the rest of the world, namely:

24. When you are offered something for nothing, take it.
(Never look a gift horse in the mouth.)

25. Experts don't really know all that much.

Part of the point here is that there really aren't any totally domain-dependent XPs after all. That is, since XPs are all derived from each other in the sense that their origin is to be found in the tweaking of old patterns creatively, even advice to bettors is grounded in some pretty clichéd stuff with which any non-bettor would be familiar. The significance of this is easy to underestimate. The point is simple enough: their ought to exist a basic set of XPs from which all others have been, or will be, derived.

Clemson (1-2) at Kentucky (2-1)
Wildcats very tough on Lexington turf at night. Wimpy Tiger offense (16 points in two straight home losses to Georgia and Georgia Tech) has Danny Ford worried. 'Cats QB Ransdell sparks UK victory. Give.

In this one, previous patterns are relied upon heavily. The two in use here are:

26. Previous patterns of action tend to repeat themselves.

27. A bad record is a harbinger of things to come.

Florida (2-0-1)
at Louisiana State (2-0)
Arnsparger wisely scheduled off-week to better prepare for Galen's Gators. Bengals battled Florida to 21-21 deadlock in Gainesville last year, can surprise under lights in bayou. Take.

There are some rather football-specific remarks in this one, but translated back to the original XPs from whence they came, we have the following:

28. Preparation and rest prepare one to meet challanges.

29. People perform better when they are comfortable. *(Home is where the heart is.)*

30. Even slight changes can alter contests between evenly matched contestants.
Mississippi (2-1-1)
at Auburn (2-1)
Tigers got butts kicked by Vols in Knoxville and took severe tumble in national polls. Pat Dye will have fire in his eye, looking to run it up on Rebs, who proved testy foe last year at Oxford, losing 17-13. Bo plays hurt. It's a give.

31. Beware of opponents who are angry.
Wisconsin (3-0) at Michigan (3-0)
Looks like another walkover for shockingly efficient Wolverines, who have now shipped Notre Dame, South Carolina and Maryland without giving up a TD. Badgers' spotless mark has come against little N. Illinois, UNLV, Wyoming. Better to stick with Bo's Terminators until they show sign of being mortal. Lay the wood.

32. Beware of opponents who are invincible.

33. Don't go against the odds.
Michigan State (2-1) at Iowa (3-0)
Hayden Fry's No. 1 Hawkeyes haven't forgotten last year's 17-16 loss (as 12-point favorite) to Spartans in Iowa City. The defeat put Hawks into tailspin that eventually cost them Rose Bowl berth. Won't matter that Yarema returns at quarterback for MSU. QB Chuck Long and Bayside's RB supreme Ronnie Harmon trigger Iowa's fourth-straight rout. Give.

There really is nothing new in this one, since yet again the author relies on the **revenge** XP, which is obviously one of his favorites. The interesting point here is that he was quite wrong about this one. Michigan State almost won the game, and in any case came close enough to make the people who bet on them winners. Any bettor, when asked about why that happened when Iowa seemed the better team, would have responded with two standard XPs:

34. Sometimes it is easier to do well when no one expects you to. (*The pressure was off.*)

35. People play up to the level of their competition. In football parlance, *they were up for the game,* and, *everyone wants to knock off number one.*

A LITTLE SYSTEMATICITY

What shall we make of the above 35 patterns? They were chosen pretty randomly, from a set of stories that I happened to read in the newspaper one day. It would, of course, be nice to know where they come from. We shall return to them shortly. First, we must set the stage.

In order to provide some systematicity here, recall that we have already discussed that there are basically seven goals that serve as the reason for attempting to explain something. However, some of these goals do not have specific XPs associated with them. For example, there is no operational difference between the goal of finding a new truth or of finding a pattern that someone else has successfully used. Both, from the perspective of the XPs that they control, have the intent of adding new XPs to one's personal data base when one find them. This is true of goal number 5 below as well. It is also true of predictive rules, which are, after all, just universal truths turned around to be used before the fact. In other words, one may be seeking to predict, or to explain post-hoc, but the same rule would be used in any case. Also, finding if an actor is crazy or not, just means having successfully located an XP. Thus, the original seven goals, which are quite different from each other in intent, reduce to four basic goals from the perspective of the control of XPs unique to them. The original goals from Chapter 3 were:

1. To establish if the actor has something coherent in mind when all signs are to the contrary.
2. To find the natural context for a given event in the belief-action chain.
3. To find new predictive rules for the behavior of a given individual.
4. To find new predictive rules that hold for a group.
5. To add new facts to one's personal data base.
6. To get new rules for operating in the world by copying those of others that seem to work.
7. To find universal truths that hold across wide ranges of phenomena.

But, these reduce as follows:

A. To find the natural context for a given event in the belief-goal-plan-action chain.
B. To find new rules relating physical causes and effects.
C. To find new rules relating social causes and effects.
D. To find universal truths that hold across wide ranges of phenomena.

To make recall a bit easier, I will give these names as follows:

A. reason
B. physical cause
C. social cause
D. truths

In addition to these explanation goals, there are eleven types of explanations. Often, more than one type of explanation may be sought, and an XP may relate to more than one type. Recall that the explanation types we presented were:

1. Alternative Beliefs
2. Laws of Physics
3. Institutional Rules
4. Rules of Thumb
5. New Facts
6. Plans and Goals
7. Thematic
8. Scripts
9. Delta Agency
10. Lack of Alternative Plan

11. Laws of the Universe

In addition, of great relevance for any XP, is the goal that the XP is operating under. That is, an XP can be viewed as a little story about how certain goals are typically achieved. Thus, XPs tend to relate to particular goal types. In Schank and Abelson (1977), we presented a classification of goals that is quite useful here. There, we delineated the following types of goals:

Goal Types (from Schank & Abelson, 1977)

Satisfaction   **(S-goals)**
Enjoyment   **(E-goals)**
Achievement   **(A-goals)**
Preservation   **(P-goals)**
Crisis   **(C-goals)**
Instrumental   **(I-goals)**
Delta   **(D-goals)**

In that book, we presented a number of rules for how these goals functioned, together with many examples of particular forms of each goal. Thus, there is no reason to reproduce that here.

Now, we can assume that all combinations of these three classifications are possible in describing a potential XP. Further, each possibility in principle, can, quite naturally, possibly exist in only one domain of inquiry. Of course, we would expect that some XPs would be domain-free in that they had application in any domain. Nevertheless, there are, in principle, 4 × 11 × 7, or 308 possible types of XPs. But, this is an uninteresting number, because there are a great many different types of goals within each group of goals. Undoubtedly some of the possible combinations would be too stupid, irrelevant, or particular, to actually exist as useful XPs.

As a point of departure for examining those that do exist, lets begin by considering some of the XPs we have found used so far with respect to the possible types of XPs that there should be, in principle. The ones we consider are: **Killed For The Insurance; Early Success Leads To Life in Fast Lane, Drugs, and Death** (the Janis Joplin Memorial Reminding); **Revenge; Poverty is the Mother of Crime; Faith Will Move Mountains; Cities are Taken by The Ears; Fish Begin to Stink at The Head; Danger Makes Men Devout; Divine Retribution; Violence Brings Repression which Brings Revolution; To Punish Someone Prolong Their Agony; People Dislike Those Who Differ From Them; High Expectations Bring Disappointment; Hopefulness Sustains While Exhaustion Weakens; Motivation Is More Important Than Ability; Previous Patterns of Actions Tend to Repeat Themselves; and, Beware Opponents Who Are Invincible.**

Thus, the first problem is to see where the XPs we have chosen to analyze would fit in the 308 possible slots:

XP	Failure	Type	Under Goal
Killed Insurance	reason	plan-goal	A-money
Fast Lane	truths	theme	A-success
Revenge	reason	plan-goal	any
Mother of Crime	truths	theme	A-money
Faith Moves Mountains	truths	law	any
Cities Taken By Ears	truths	plan-goal	D-control
Fish Stink at Head	truths	inst rule	A-know
Danger Makes Devout	truths	thumb	A-know
Divine Retribution	truths	law	A-success
Violence-Revolution	soc-cause	plan-goal	D-control
To Punish-Prolong Pain	reason	plan-goal	S-power
Dislike For Differences	reason	theme	P-status quo
Expectations-Disappoint	predict	law	A-know
Hopefulness Sustains	truths	thumb	A-money
Motivation-Ability	truths	law	A-money
Patterns Repeat	truths	scripts	A-money
Beware Invincible	truths	lack	A-money

From a glance at this chart, we can see that, because of the examples we have been using, the types of patterns that we have been seeing fall into a few basic classes. For example, the last five on the chart were taken from the information we gave about football betting. Therefore, they are all about how to get money by making an accurate prediction based on a general law of the world, or, at least based upon a rule of thumb that seems to work. In general, we expect that rules of thumb pertain more to particular domains, while universal laws, which behave in much the same way with respect to prediction, should be more applicable across domains. Needless to say, there are many different, and often conflicting XPs in the domain of football betting. And, also, many of the XPs that one can find in football betting pertain to other domains and can be used for goals other than A-money.

Another group that stands out, in the chart, is the group of XPs derived from proverbs. Proverbs, as well as predictions in betting, tend to be of the *universal truth* type of explanation and thus we have a large percentage of such XPs in the chart. Proverbs have a wide range of goals over which they apply, of course, so we see much variation in that respect.

In general, XPs group themselves unequally. We would expect that there would be many XPs about planning, about universal laws, about themes, and about rules of thumb, for example. Similarly, we would expect many XPs to be attempts to satisfy A-money, or A-success, or A-control. We would not expect there to exist XPs for every possible combination, as I said, but it is not unreasonable to expect to find them across a great spectrum of combinations. In particular, **for the three failure-types** (excluding physical rules, which certainly exist but not so much in this form), **five principal explanation types (institutional rules; rules of thumb; plans; themes; and universal laws),** and the most **important goals (for example, S-hunger; A-possessions; A-power; A-social relationships; P-health; D-know),** we might expect XPs to quite commonly exist at their confluence. To see if they do, we now take a look at the 90 possible types of XPs that would result from all possible combinations of these.

A LOOK AT 90 POSSIBLE XP TYPES

To begin, let's list the 15 possible combinations of failure needs and explanation types that we have selected, irrespective of the 6 goals that they serve.

combination of type + failure		this would mean an XP such as:
inst-rules	**reason**	This would obviously be a rule about why institutions do what they do. Under A-control, we would expect an XP about how governments stay in power for example, under D-know about their methods of gathering information. Thus, we have the proverb: **It is ill putting a sword in a madman's hand,** which refers to the problems under A-control when reasons aren't present. And, of course, we have the well-known proverb: **Power corrupts and absolute power corrupts absolutely,** under A-power in this category.
	soc-cause	Here, rules about the social causes of institution's actions. Of course, many XPs transcend particular groups. Thus, for example, the proverb **Who keeps company with the wolf will learn to howl,** applies equally well to institutions and individuals. Also, such an XP is intended to work under any goal.
	truths	Here, XPs about the truths that hold for

an institution with respect to various goals. For example, under the goal P-power, we have the proverb: **He that has a fellow ruler has an over-ruler.** This XP is intended to explain the particular problem of shared power. Thus, it is explaining how to (or how not to) preserve the power one has over an institution. It is an XP that can be used predictively as well, of course.

rules of thumb

reason   The rules listed here, being general rules of thumb, can pertain anywhere, so we need to consider some of the goals at the same time. For example, under S-hunger we have: **Hunger is stronger than love.** Under S-shelter, we have: **If a man receives no guests at home, when abroad he will have no hosts.** This last one is essentially a plan for satisfying S-shelter under certain circumstances.

soc-cause   The proverb: **When bees are old they yield no honey** refers to the social causes behind the difficulties in getting A-possessions, or A-success when you are old. Naturally, such an XP would also be indexed under *old age*. Such indices are helpful for finding XPs, of course.

truths   Here we are looking for a universal truth that is a rule of thumb for some goal. For E-life, we have: **Happy is he that is happy in his children.** For P-health, there is: **Temperance is the best physic.**

plans

reason   Any XP listed here must comment on the use, effectiveness, or selection of plans. Naturally, there are many of these, and we shall see quite a few of these in Chapter 7. For example, under A-possessions, we have: **With honey you catch more flies than with vinegar.** And, under

A-social relations: **With nets you catch birds, with presents—girls.**

soc-cause   Here, XPs must relate to the social causes that underlie the selection of plans. Under A-social relations, we have: **Poverty is an enemy to good manners.**

truths   Truths having to with plans are of a more general nature, of course. The proverb, **A man is known to be mortal by two things, sleep and lust,** refers to plans that will always be extant and thus need no reasoning or explanation of external social factors.

themes

reason   Themes are about one's choice of goals, so here we would expect to find the context or reasons under which certain themes are likely to be extant, or, we might look for the thematic explanation of certain plans or goals. For example, under the goal A-happiness, we find: **Better be an old man's darling than a young man's slave.**

soc-cause   Here we would expect to find XPs that say why certain themes are extant. Under A-know, we have: **Under a ragged coat lies wisdom.** Under S-hunger: **Hunger finds no fault with the cookery.**

truths   The truths that relate here would be about why certain themes exist. For example, under A-money we have: **Gold dust blinds all eyes.** Or, we have as a general explanation at this level: **Blood is thicker than water.**

universal laws

reason   Here we expect universal laws about how people reason in a given domain, for example. Thus under P-health (or P-power) we find: **Rats desert a sinking ship.** Under A-success, we have: **Fools bite one another but wise men agree together.**

soc-cause Here we find XPs concerning universal laws about social phenomena under various goals. For example, as a general explanation of why goals occur we have: **Man cannot live by bread alone.**

truths Truths about laws are common enough. My favorite is: **No generalization is worth a damn, including this one.** Some other examples: under P-goals and C-goals in general we have: **What's done cannot be undone.** Under S-sleep and P-health, we have: **Sleep is better than medicine.**

What exactly have we done here? We have looked at a few of the possible types of XPs that might exist. Naturally, there are thousands, maybe even hundreds of thousands of XPs in existence. Here, I am not talking about proverbs, exactly. I used proverbs here because they can be found in books, and because my private XPs would need a fair amount of explanation, and explaining my own personal view of the world is hardly the point of this book. But, the fact that XPs do express one's view of the world is one of the points of this book.

XPs have, as their primary role, the intention of rendering comprehensible what is initially incomprehensible. They have also, as a secondary role, the ability to be brought to mind inappropriately, in such a way as to serve as fodder for creative explanations. The XPs given here are universal in the sense that they are to be found as wisdom from books. Thus, they are not quite expressive of what XPs are really like. Nevertheless, they are useful for illustrative purposes.

Of course, the intent here was not to produce a method by which types of XPs could be generated. One would expect to find XPs that relate to each combination of category presented, but the fact that that is the case is beside the point. People, by and large, do not generate very many XPs for themselves. On occasion, they see many examples of the same phenomena and find that an explanation will work over and over again, thus creating an XP. But, the average person uses other people's XPs, ones he was told, or taught, or read about somewhere.

I mention this because while it is perfectly fine to go after the problem of finding out how we can create XPs, there is a much more serious problem to be attacked first. Our computers are not at the level of the average person, by any means, so it makes little sense to have them attempt to create their own XPs. That having been said, why then have we focused upon issues of creativity here?

Essentially, the two problems are inextricably tied together. One cannot understand without applying XPs, and one cannot explain something new without misapplying an XP to some extent. Thus, my point is that creativity, in the sense of explanation of new phenomena by the intentional misapplication of an XP, is not as sophisticated a phenomenon as one might think. Rather, it is easier than the intentional invention of an explanation, starting from scratch. Thus, one method of explanation, the application of an XP, is so much easier than the other, the invention of a new XP, that it is both clear which should be studied first, and which is the first subject to worry about with respect to AI. Now, as it happens, during the normal use of XPs, they are necessarily misapplied and thus create new XPs. This is not the same thing as attempting to create a new explanation from scratch. My claim is that it is the method that people use for explanation and creativity, and thus, ought to be the method that machines use.

PROVERBIAL CREATIVITY

To come up with new ideas, use old ideas as a basis. This is straightforward enough, and seems hardly worth remarking upon. However, as I noted in the beginning of this chapter, once one uses the word *creativity* in the same breath that one says *computers,* all kinds of ire is aroused. My point then, is rather simple. **Creativity is not such a mysterious process. It depends upon having a stock set of explanations and some heuristics for finding them at the right time, and for tweaking them after they have been found.** These last two steps should not be denigrated with respect to their complexity. **Search and adaptation of patterns are two of the biggest problems facing AI.** I have not attempted to talk about either of them much, because any attempt to do so, in a work devoted to another issue, would be rather superficial. They are major problems in their own right.

However, they are not problems of creativity. At least they don't seem so on the surface. We don't think of search, or of adaptation of old patterns to new situations, as being very creative. Surely there is nothing mystical about *those* processes. Surely creativity lies elsewhere. But, I don't believe this to be the case.

The mechanistic ease with which creative solutions and creative explanations can be found, that is the point of this chapter. Creativity does not lie elsewhere. It is not mystical. It lies within the provinces of search and adaptation, and is heavily dependent upon reminding. And, most importantly, it should be possible to design mechanisms whose output is creative. Creative machines are quite possible, in principle. This ought not trouble any humanist. Rather, any further understanding of humans, including demystification, ought to be quite welcome.

7
Question-Driven Understanding

INTO THE HEART OF CREATIVITY

Creativity depends upon the ability to formulate the right question at the right time. When we explain, we must find an XP, possibly even an inapplicable one, in order to have a starting point for our efforts. The first step in explanation is the formulation of a question about an event that one does not understand. The second step involves the transformation of that question into a standard explanation question. Then, we must inquire about what XP might work best as an answer to the EQ. The formulation of questions, rather than the answering of questions, is at the heart of creativity.

If questions are at the heart of creating new knowledge structures, then it follows that they are also at the heart of understanding in general. We have been working on programs that understand natural language text for many years now in our laboratory at Yale and at the Stanford AI lab before that. In general, the paradigm used in that work was to attempt to match an input string to some pre-existing framework. In the early days that framework was Conceptual Dependency (Schank, 1972, 1973). Later we began to develop static knowledge structures and mapped sentences into those structures.

When the transition to dynamically-modified memory structures was made in the early 1980s, I was fond of mentioning, in public lectures, that one of the main problems with FRUMP (DeJong, 1979), to take a typical example, was that it never got bored. One could feed it the same earth-quake story, day after day, and it would never complain. In fact, it never even noticed! It would, of course, be fairly easy to fix this state of affairs in

178

a rather *ad hoc* fashion. But, to fix it in a principled fashion, in other words, to have it actually get bored or at least begin to wonder why it kept hearing about so many identical earthquakes, required a *dynamic memory.*

We have, over the last few years, begun to invent programs that embodied a dynamic memory to some extent, but Lebowitz's and Kolodner's programs were the last ones that were concerned with reading text (and even those had memory as their primary concern). The reasons that we stopped working on natural language processing per se are complex and irrelevant for our purposes here. The point of this chapter is to attempt to take the next logical question in the progression of our work on text understanding. It was reasonable to ask how a program could be said to be understanding if it failed to recognize that it had seen a given story before, because a program that did not learn from its experiences could not reasonably be said to understand. Similarly therefore, and in view of what has come before in this book, it seems obvious that a program cannot reasonably claim to understand if it does not, on occasion, wonder about what it has read.

To put this another way, understanding is most assuredly not an all or none affair. Understanding is gradual, on occasion partial, and most important, subject to wide variation depending upon one's interest in what one is reading. The sum of this state of affairs is that **understanding must be a mixed-mode process,** one that involves understanding a portion of what one is reading, mulling on that portion, wondering about it, and then returning to the text with new ideas and questions that will serve to control the subsequent understanding of the remaining text. **Understanding depends upon explanation, and explanation depends upon the ability to formulate questions.** Therefore, understanding ought to be considered to be question-driven.

That having been said, we can now reconsider what a language understanding program ought to look like in light of the work on explanation questions and explanation patterns presented so far in this book. IPP (Lebowitz, 1980) was a computer program that we can use as the starting point from which to reconsider the general topic of the processing of natural language texts. IPP was originally designed to work on a text that I found in the *New York Times* one day:

An Arabic-speaking gunman shot his way into the Iraqi Embassy here [Paris] yesterday morning, held hostages through most of the day before surrendering to French policeman, and then was shot by Iraqi security officials as he was led away by the French officers.

When I originally read this story, I wondered how we could get a computer to have the same kind of reaction to it that I had had. I found myself thinking that it was rather strange that the Iraqi security guards had shot the terrorist *after* he had been captured by French police. I expected no such thing. The problem was: first, how to get the computer to know enough to be able to read the story and understand it up to the point where the unexpected event occurs; and second, how to get this program to be amazed and surprised by the subsequent events. To do this, we needed a theory of expectation-based, top-down processing that could, in some sense, turn around and be bottom-up in attempting to understand something for which it could not have had expectations. IPP was an attempt to implement a theory about how this might be accomplished, which also attempted to integrate parsing and memory operations. The idea was that if we knew enough about terrorism we would know how to quickly process common, everyday, events that were expected and we could attempt to learn something new from items that were different by virtue of being unexpected, by storing them and comparing them to other expectation violations of a similar type.

That was the intention behind IPP. It succeeded to some extent, but that is not what I am interested in discussing here. In light of the problems of explanation discussed so far, another problem arises that, if considered seriously, would have a profound effect on the flow of control extant in any natural language processing system. It is a problem that comes from the work that has followed the development of IPP and that has made me go back and think about that program again.

It became clear to us, while we were working on problems of language understanding, that memory phenomena had to be considered as a natural part of any natural language understanding system. After all, people do not understand things in a vacuum. They relate what they know to what they are trying to find out. One way in which they exhibit their ability to do this is expressed by their capacity to be reminded.

The principle of dynamic memory illustrated by the phenomenon of reminding is that, in the process of understanding, we are changed by what we have understood. Understanding is, in essence, a learning process.

Work in reminding and dynamic memory systems that change as they understand, led naturally into our current work on explanation. Not only do failed expectations match across remindings, but the explanations of why the expectations failed also matched. Thus, the explanation in the *Steak and the Haircut* story is the same for the remindee and the remindand, namely, *the person in the service role must have believed that what was requested was too extreme to actually do.*

Because of this we embarked on a series of projects whose intent was to expand our understanding of the human ability to construct explanations. When a football coach uses a play and it doesn't work, he must construct an explanation of why it didn't work. Similarly, when a chef creates a new recipe that doesn't work, or when a predictor of the stock market makes a prediction that is wrong, he must revise his current theory. In each case, what is required is an explanation of why what he thought before did not work.

Explanations and remindings are, in part, goal-based. But, most of our understanding programs failed to have any real goals of their own. Or, to put this another way, what is it that IPP was trying to find out when it was reading about terrorists? Or perhaps more interestingly, what was I trying to find out when I read about *the Arabic-speaking gunman in Paris?*

CYRUS

Now I would like to digress for a moment and talk about CYRUS, a program that was done at the same time as IPP, whose underlying philosophy is fairly similar.

CYRUS was an attempt to model one particular individual's memory, to the extent that that could be done. It got its data from news stories about Cyrus Vance and then attempted to place these stories in a dynamic memory structure that would enable them to be found again. CYRUS was not an understanding program because the stories had already been processed for it (either by hand or by FRUMP, another of our text understanding programs, DeJong, 1979.) Rather, it was a new kind of storage and retrival program, one that employed a dynamic memory similar in philosophy to that used in IPP.

One area of particular interest in CYRUS was how it answered questions. Its job was to answer questions about the experiences of Cyrus Vance as he traveled around the world in his role as Secretary of State. To do this, the program had to invent and re-invent categories in memory in which to place new stories as they became available. Since one could not easily anticipate everything that Cyrus Vance might ever experience, these categories had to be created dynamically as new stories were received.

Consequently, when answering a question about Cyrus Vance, CYRUS had to be able to re-formulate the question in its own terms. That is, CYRUS knew where it had stored given stories and if it was asked about one of them it had to determine exactly which story it knew about was germane to the answer and where it might find that story in its memory.

Because of this, CYRUS wound up doing something quite interesting. The question-answering module in CYRUS had to be written in such a way as to enable it to take a question, determine whether it could answer that question directly, and if it could not, it would have to re-interpret that question as a question that it believed that it could answer. This *question transformation process,* which we saw earlier when we discussed adapting XPs, is a crucial aspect of understanding.

To illustrate what I am talking about, consider the following I/O from CYRUS:

> **Has Vance's wife ever met Mrs. Begin?**

YES, MOST RECENTLY AT A STATE DINNER IN ISRAEL IN JAN 1980

The question is, how did CYRUS answer this question? In fact, CYRUS did not have the information contained in its answer in its memory in any way. Nevertheless it was able to answer the question. It did so by transforming the question into a series of questions, as follows:

Q1: Did your wife ever meet Mrs. Begin?

Q2: Where would they have met?

Q3: Under what circumstances do diplomat's wives meet?

Q4: Under what circumstances do diplomats meet?

A4: On state visits to each other's countries.

At international conferences.

A3: When they accompany their husband's on these visits.

Q3a:When did Vance go to Israel?

Q3b:When did Begin go to the U.S.?

A3a/A3b: various dates can now be retrieved from memory

Q3c:Did their wives accompany them on any of these trips?

A3c: a trip where this happened is found

Q2a: During what part of a trip would wives meet?

A2a: during a state dinner

Final revised question: **Was there a state dinner on May 24, 1977 during the diplomatic visit that Vance made to Israel with his wife?**

Answer (A1): **Probably on May 24, 1977, in Jerusalem at a state dinner in which they were both present.**

The point here is that the question transformation process is a way of getting an answerable question from an unanswerable one. The original question is unanswerable because it gives no help as to where in memory we might search for the relevant facts. Through a series of transformations, this original question is changed into one about the dates of diplomatic visits and state dinners, both of which the program knows were used as categories in which to store information.

CYRUS seems smart because it can answer questions. Now this may seem like an obvious thing that most AI understanding programs can do. And, in fact, it is fairly easy to get a program to retrieve facts from a data base and thus answer questions. Actually, any intelligence attributed to CYRUS should be because it can *ask* questions. As we saw in Chapter 6, posing the right questions can lead to important results. **Asking questions is at the heart of intelligence.**

IPP REVISITED

How does CYRUS compare to IPP? CYRUS is, in some sense, a far more interesting program because it knows more about what it knows and it can ask about what it does not know. The problem with IPP (or any currently extant understanding program for that matter) is that it doesn't *ask* in any profound way. CYRUS doesn't ask all that much, but it was capable of posing answerable questions to replace unanswerable ones. Thus, it seemed to want to know things more than IPP does.

The major problem with IPP is that it never was actually astonished by the shooting of the Iraqi gunman after he had been captured by the French police. IPP was able to produce a sentence that voiced its *surprise* saying essentially that it didn't have any expectations or knowledge structures available for interpreting this part of the event. Thus an expectation violation had occurred.

An expectation failure occurs when something that is expected fails to appear or when something occurs that was not anticipated. Either way, the terrorism MOP (the memory and storage structures used by both IPP and CYRUS are called MOPs) can be altered with a notation that a gunman had been shot by his own people, so that next time the program would be able to be reminded of this by a similar kind of experience, thus allowing the program to alter its terrorism MOP accordingly.

In essence, what IPP was capable of doing was to characterize an odd circumstance in such a way that it was possible to find it again when a similar circumstance arose. This is the indexing problem and is the significant accomplishment in IPP.

Recently I read the same *Arabic-speaking gunman story* to someone who was reminded of how Israelis attempt to shoot Palestinian terrorists in similar situations on the grounds that if they were captured by the French, for example, the French would more than likely be too nice to them (from the Israeli point of view). It is possible to be reminded of such a fact and to determine that in this case it's not too relevant.

The issue here however is that, in the absence of the type of reminding mentioned above, a reader has an uneasy feeling about this story. Certainly I was quite fascinated by it when I read it. I wanted to know why the gunman was shot. It is true that I was surprised by the ending of the story, but that is really not what is so interesting about it. After reading it I found myself speculating about it. I wondered why they did that.

I began to create hypotheses:

Maybe the French intended to release the Iraqi. (This is the Palestinian reminding case.)

Maybe the Iraqis were afraid that this guy would say something damaging to them.

Maybe they were afraid that he would be used as a *cause célèbre* by some dissident group.

No matter what the true answer, there is reason to believe that the Iraqi security guards had some underlying motive. That is, some explanation of this story is needed.

When we see something in a story that we could not have anticipated, we can safely assume that the event under consideration had some justification or purpose. We do not simply assume that expectation failures are random events not to be further bothered about. We assume, especially when the unexpected event involves a plan on the part of other people, that they had some motives and intentions and we wonder about what they were. Thus, a great deal of what understanding is about, in principle, is our ability to comprehend an unexpected event by constructing a hypothesis that accounts for how and why that event happened.

But this is very different from what IPP was doing. IPP was attempting to account for what was happening by finding previous events that were like the current one and comparing the two. This is, of course, a method that is quite useful. It forms the basis for dynamic memory as proposed in Schank (1982). The idea is simply that by being reminded of one experience by a like experience, we can compare the two experiences and see what they have in common, thus allowing us to create better expectations in the future.

But we are capable of creating explanations de novo. We can come up with an explanation without coming up with an initial reminding. As we noted earlier, reminding often serves as a *verification* of an explanation. It seems obvious that we do come up with explanations just by looking at the facts, utilizing whatever principles are relevant to that process.

A program that purports to understand has to, in some sense, have a healthy curiousity. It has to want to know about things. In this instance, it has to care about the motives of people and the specific plans used by terrorists, police, governments, and so on. It has to care about these things in some non-artificial sense.

What we are talking about here is justifying actions of characters that we are hearing about by having a hypothesis for what motivates them. Having a sense of understanding of why a character in a given role does what he does is critical to understanding. In IPP this sense of the plans for characters it knew about was rather superficial, enough so that when a character acted differently from the norm it had no ability to question it. An understanding program should have a series of questions that are always ready to go. For example:

Why is this character doing what he's doing?

What are his motivations?

What are his plans?

What's his intention?

IPP should have wanted to know why the Iraqi gunman was shot. And, in wondering about it, it should have begun to speculate about it, to hazard some guesses. Now, it should not have to ask that about every action that occurs in a story. It should not be wondering why a terrorist was armed because it would already have explained such things to itself after encountering its first terrorism story.

In essence, what we have been saying up until this point is that when we say that we have understood something we mean that we have been able to either find an explanation that we have previously stored (either gotten whole from someone else or constructed on our own), or that we have successfully constructed an explanation of an event for which we had no relevant prior experience.

Thus, to understand something means to be able to *re-cognize* it as something that has been *cognized* before. In a sense, we are saying that, yes, I have already explained this before, so I won't have to explain it again. Understanding means having already explained it, and being able to access that explanation. In the case where one hasn't already explained an event like it, when something is novel in that sense, the issue becomes:

What questions are extant in my memory and how do those questions relate to the depth of the explanation that is required in this case?

Understanders, on occasion, can look for complicated, in-depth explanations. However, in order to get in-depth explanations one has to have been asking in-depth questions. The question of why the security guards did what they did can be answered at a rather simplistic level. But, of course, the issue in enhancing computers with a real understanding capability is to get them to ask questions of a much greater complexity.

For example, we might wonder about what this event tells us about the nature of security guards, or about the nature of the political relationship between Iraq and France. We might wonder about the increasing acceptability of terrorism in embassies throughout the world, or about the feelings and attitudes of people who have been held hostage. Each of these questions, once posed, causes us to construct an explanation that has that question at its base. That is, the question, once posed, biases the answer. **When there is a difficulty in understanding, the questions that are already present in our minds will direct the explanation process.**

Suppose, for example, that the Iraqi security guards who did the shooting were the ones held hostage by the gunman. Then, certainly, retribution would have been a reasonable explanation of the subsequent shooting. So, it seems fairly important to pose the question of whether or not that had been the case before deciding upon an explanation of the event. Issues such as what the actors may have been feeling, or what the gunman's fellow travelers might have done to relatives of the guards are relevant here. In other words, in order to understand fully, we have to call to mind knowledge of what revenge is about. Or, we have to be able to speculate that the action by the guards might be viewed as a heroic action within the Iraqi culture. Perhaps when guards behave in this fashion they are considered to be "heroes of the revolution."

As we have noted, in order to make interesting explanations it is necessary to have the capability of asking interesting questions. The explanations that you create for yourself depend upon the questions that you ask. It is the question that is key here, not the answer. So, the question for us, in this example, is: how do you pose the question, *could retribution have been a factor?* Unfortunately, we seem to have a vicious cycle here. The only way one could possibly pose a question about whether retribution might have been a factor is to somehow have had access to the idea that retribution might be a possible explanation. Which comes first?

THE RELEVANCE OF EXPLANATION PATTERNS

The basic cycle that I have in mind here is:

BASIC OPERATING QUESTIONS

EXPLANATION QUESTIONS

EXPLANATION PATTERNS

SPECIFIC QUESTIONS

EXPLANATIONS

Basic operating questions follow the course of the story. They include questions about who is going where, when he got there, what he intented to do there, and so on. Explanation questions come into play when the expectations generating the normal run-of-the-mill questions begin to break down. These questions link to explanation patterns, as we have seen. Then, the XPs get turned into specific questions whose answers produce actual explanations.

Let's see what this would look like in the *Arabic-speaking gunman* story: The **basic operating questions** of a standard language understanding program might be, for example:

Who is the gunman?

What does he hope to accomplish?

What group does he represent?

The **explanation question** would be:

Why did the security guards break the rules of the capture script?

At this point **XPs** indexed off that question come to mind (i.e., the retribution pattern).

Next, we attempt to see if we can re-consider the event in question to see if indeed the old retribution pattern can be made to fit. This means generating one or more **specific questions** about *what events the gunman might have been involved in previously, what the guards were like, who payed them, what instructions were given to them,* and so on.

All of these questions are derived from the specifications of the old pattern as it applies to the new situation. Thus if, in order for there to be retribution, a prior evil had to be committed, we must ask if the hostage-taking qualified as such an act, or if there were some even more dastardly act in the gunman's past. A great many questions are thus generated in this fashion, each from the combination of a different explanation question and the explanation pattern that is fired off from it, together with the aspect of that pattern that is being called into question.

The role of the explanation questions and explanation patterns therefore is to generate new questions. The task is to make the program or the person look at the situation and ask if this could be an example of retribution. Then, many specific questions are generated by accessing the explanation pattern and treating it as a hypothetical explanation, which is then used to match against the current situation. To the extent that it matches, that match generates questions about whether the match is appropriate; whether the circumstances are very different; or whether some other explanation pattern should be sought.

THE UNDERSTANDING CYCLE

Returning to IPP for a moment, it is clear that IPP was missing what we can now term *the basic understanding cycle.* That is, to really understand we must be able to ask questions; in other words, to wonder about the things we are reading or hearing about. We must be able to take phenomena that are out of the domain of our prior experiences and find remindings of two types. First, and best, we must be able to find remindings that are quite close in spirit to the experience that we are currently processing. When this is not possible, that is, when there does not exist a specific relevant memory, indexed under an explanation of an expectation failure that we construct in an ad hoc manner, or we cannot find that memory, we must be able to take more neutral (that is, less specific), standard explanation patterns and derive a set of questions from them.

In a sense, the first kind of reminding is a shortcut, an easy method of processing a new situation by finding a very closely related old experience to contrast against the current one. When that path is not open to us, usually because such a memory simply fails to come to mind, then we must take a more active role. We must find related explanation patterns that we allow to drive the questioning process. Or, to put this another way, we must *try* to get reminded.

The essence of my hypothesis here is that it is through the creation of these questions that we understand. IPP, or any understanding program, has to be operating under a set of questions. Its driving force, so to speak, has to be the desire to know the answers to questions that are generated during the process of understanding. That means that if you are going to read a terrorism story, you must have some questions that are driving the process. In other words, there has to be some reason why you have begun to read this story in the first place.

Why *does* one read a story in the newspaper? This may seem like a whimsical question, but a program that is intended to understand a story at anything more than a superficial level must have some idea about what it wants to know. When one reads a story like the one about the *Arabic-speaking gunman,* one is not just reading it to find out what happened in the Iraqi embassy in Paris, one is reading it for some set of personal reasons having to do with one's cares and concerns about the world. Otherwise there's no reason to read the story.

So, when the story about terrorism comes by, you have to have had a question in mind such as *I wonder why there's so much terrorism today?* or

What's going on in Paris? or *I wonder if I can find some new material for a joke in tonight's monologue?* or *How can I better come to understand the world situation by seeing what is going on with terrorism?* or even *I feel the need to know about blood and gore, give me all the details so I will know how to act if it happens to me.* There are all kinds of reasons to read a newspaper story.

It might seem, at first glance, that a person can pick up a newspaper and just read the articles to kill the time, or amuse oneself, or whatever. What happens then? Actually what is going on there is that you are letting your background questions take over. There are things you always want to know or always are curious about; hundreds of them, maybe thousands. You don't have to be thinking of them explicitly when you pick up the newspaper. They are there all the time, ready to be answered.

In other words, we cannot expect to build an understanding program that has no reason to read. It can have specific information it wants to find out, but then it won't find out anything else. I don't think that it is really possible to build a newspaper reader that doesn't have some questions it's trying to answer that are at a level greater than that of the specific article it is considering at any given time. Such a program would fail to make use of anything at all unusual in what it read.

Any new understanding program ought to be driven by the issue of how to approach a situation with a set of questions. Now this may remind you to some extent of FRUMP (DeJong, 1979) which, I believe, was methodologically correct as a program in the sense that it did have questions. These questions were not posed in the form of questions. They were posed as requests or conditions. The requests, translated into English questions, were *What was the Richter scale reading in the earthquake?* or *How much damage did it cause?;* or *How many people died?* Thus the questions in FRUMP were solely what I have termed *the basic operating questions.* I don't think people who read earthquake stories really spend their time asking about Richter scale readings in any significant sense. We may have a bottom up routine that says *if it's over 7 take note and recall the San Francisco Earthquake or the Mexico City Earthquake.* One of FRUMP's problems was that it worked on dull stories.

If we were to attempt to make FRUMP work on interesting stories, or if we were going to attempt to understand earthquake stories in an interesting way, we'd want to be able to start the understanding process with a hypothesis. **The next generation of newspaper reading programs will have to have a set of questions at their heart that drives the understanding process.** They would be, in essence, the reason that the program is reading the story. These questions would have to be more profound than *How many people died?* or *What's the latest news, I want to summarize it.* Such an attitude is all right for transmitting information but it's not good for absorbing information. **The difference in processing depth required for the task of transmitting information as opposed to the task of absorbing information is profound.**

Any program has to have a set of questions that constitute its starting point. They would have been generated as the result of previous experiences (other news stories perhaps) that raised these questions but failed to answer them. In some sense then, **the input to the understanding process is the story** *and* **a set of questions.** And **the output is another set of questions. If the processing of natural language texts is done correctly, it ought to answer some questions and raise others.** This is not an infinite loop because, presumably, the questions that are being raised are somewhat more sophisticated than those that are being answered.

Thus, what we need to achieve real understanding is what I call *question-driven understanding.* Questions can come from all kinds of areas. For example, they can come from old stories, that is, old remindings, with incompletely understood parts, which you wonder about. The *Arabic-speaking gunman* story, if no certain explanation were arrived at, would become a set of questions which may drive the understanding of another story related to those issues. That is what reminding is really all about. The question in that case, is: *are there any other instances of this bizzare behavior that might help me to better understand that story?* That kind of question might lay around passively, for years, waiting for an answer. Questions such as this wait, under the surface, looking for an answer. And, of course, there are questions that lie right at the surface, questions that we explicitly and consciously worry about. Lastly, there are underlying thematic questions that one is always looking for the answer to consciously in the sense that one knows one is looking for them, but unconsciously in the sense that there are not on one's mind all the time. The distinction between these types of questions and the specific embodiment of each of them is necessary in any understanding program we might develop.

SOME QUESTIONS

Viewing IPP in terms of the questions that it could ask (and therefore could answer), we can see that IPP functioned at what we might call the *journalist level*. It asked *who, what, where, and when* questions. This is not terribly surprising—after all, it was reading newspaper stories. These journalist-level questions were programmed as expectations (or requests) and they were part of an overall system that also had the task of doing the basic language analysis.

It seems safe to say that people do have these journalist-level questions in mind when they read a story. (That is why journalists seek to answer them in their pieces, after all.) When one hears a story that does not present all the above information, one is very likely to attempt to fill in the roles and slots either by inference or by specifically asking (in the case of an interactive situation) so that one can know who did what, when, and where. The major problem, from one point of view, with IPP, is that these questions were not self-generated. In other words, IPP didn't *want* to know these things. Rather, it was told to ask about them (by the programmer). Quite naturally, this is true about all our programs. Such questions are put in the program (although not always in the form of questions), before the program actually attempts to read a story. We inform the program that reading means attempting to answer these questions. But what we don't do is tell the program to inquire about what it needs to know. Now, there's a subtle difference between these two things. Asking a question comes from a need to know. It comes from wondering about something, or being interested in some aspect of something. The argument here is that you really can't get a program to understand in any deep sense unless it's interested in what it's reading about.

You can say the same thing about people. It's not really possible for a person to really understand what they are reading unless they are really interested in it. A good example of this is a typist who is typing something from a dictaphone or tape recorder. The typist needs to hear the words but does not need to understand in any deep sense. The typist isn't expected to understand what is being typed, and won't, unless the typist happens to be interested in the subject matter. The typist is unlikely to even try to understand it. As I have said, interest is derived from having a set of questions.

One of the reasons why a typist or a translator (this is another example of the same phenomenon) is unlikely to really understand what they are typing or translating is because it's likely they're not interested in it. Translators at the UN might be interested in international events to some extent, but in pursuit of their jobs as translators there is some question as to whether they can even *try* to understand what they are translating. It goes by too fast, and they have too much to do, to consider allowing their minds to begin to question what they are hearing.

Thus, what happens is that they really don't understand what they are hearing or reading. Now, I am not suggesting that they couldn't tell you a little about what was said or answer a few questions. Rather, they would not naturally be able to ask questions. The asking is of paramount importance. Now, of course, IPP could be reformulated so that it was capable of asking questions. The problem would be whether or not those questions would be heart-felt. That is, would it really want to know the answers?

This may seem a little silly, since it is difficult to establish the true feelings of a machine, and one is inclined to assume that the default answer is that there aren't any feelings there at all. The more sensible thing to demand is that the questions be self-generated. That is, were the questions there prior to seeing the story or after seeing the story?

Instead of demanding *Does the program **really** want to know the answer,* we can investigate *How did the program come to want to ask the question?* If it were just told to ask the question, that might be a nice simulation, but it would somehow be different from having generated the question on its own. We can tell a child, or a student, or a reporter, what questions to ask, but it is when they ask them on their own that we feel we have accomplished something. The program has to really want to know; it must generate its own questions. How would a program get to *genuinely want to know?*

In order to want to know, you must have a set of goals. There must be something driving the system so that there is some end that's in mind. In a sense, I'm arguing that what was really wrong with IPP was that IPP (or FRUMP or SAM) had a base of questions (to the extent that we can construe the situation such that they had questions at all) that were no more than the set of BASIC OPERATING QUESTIONS which they needed to answer. All their questions were very specific to their domains. They didn't have a set of hypotheses that were driving them. (This is not a criticism of these works, of course, but merely an expansion of them. The goals of the designers of these programs were to test out basic ideas for the first pass at automated story understanding. All I am saying is that now it is time for a second pass.) Of course, one could simply give IPP a set of hypotheses. One can attempt to develop a theory of terrorists—who they are, what they do, why they do it—and we can attempt to predict how a given terrorist will act, or where terrorism might be likely to occur.

In that case, such a program might not pay attention to the article we are considering—being shot by the Iraqi security guards. It might not find it interesting with respect to an overall hypothesis about terrorism on which it was working. On the other hand, maybe it would be. Maybe what we really want to do in a hypothesis-driven system is to be able to generate any possibly relevant question every time. We might find a program saying, of each event, *Is this of interest to my goals? How can I relate this to my goals?* If the goal is to track terrorists, to make predictions about terrorists, then the issue is, for any given action involving a terrorist, the extent to which that action relates to the overall theory.

The issue then is, what kinds of questions should we be asking? Journalistic-level questions are really the lowest level of questions to ask. The second level of questions, again at a very low level in the sense that they are fairly primitive to the concept of understanding, are those such as:

How does this action affect me?

How does the action affect my goals? How is the action related to my goals?

The goals we are talking about here are those of the reader, so the argument here is simply this: you cannot write a very effective language-understanding program unless it has goals or interests of its own that cause it to question what it reads with respect to those goals or interests. Thus, the result of our revisting natural language processing is this: in order to be effective, a language understanding program must have goals of its own and be able to create and follow up questions that arise from the interaction of new information that is being processed with the goals and memory of the program. **The ultimate driving force of understanding must be the need to know more.**

TYPES OF QUESTIONS

We ask all kinds of questions all the time. To teach machines to ask these questions, we need to have a good sense of the kinds of questions that there are to ask. Since questions arise naturally from the goals that one has, it follows that the explanation goals that we discussed in Chapter 3 must relate strongly to the questions that ought to be generated while understanding a text. These goals generate different types of questions depending upon the level of understanding that one seeks. I have divided up the questions that I believe to be of significance to a creative and analytical understanding system into four broad levels that reflect levels of understanding in conjunction with standard explanation goals. The levels of understanding that I consider are: **self-centered; factual; theoretical;** and **creative.** These correspond to the basic idea that one can want to know only about things as they directly pertain to oneself; or, one can want to attain a basic grasp of the facts of the world; or, one can look to attain a theoretical understanding of how and why the world functions as it does; or one can be looking for new perspectives on things, with the intent of being creative.

Questions–Level One: Self-Centered

The first type of questions, which I call **level one questions,** are the type that no one needs to be taught to ask (except maybe a machine). By and large they are the kind of questions that programs such as IPP have, implicitly or explicitly, been asking all along. Any planning system must ask them as well. They reflect an attempt to understand with a self-centered orientation.

Recall that the explanation goals were:

1. **To establish if the actor has something coherent in mind when all signs are to the contrary.**

2. To find the natural context for a given event in the belief-action chain.
3. To find new predictive rules for the behavior of a given individual.
4. To find new predictive rules that hold for a group.
5. To get new rules for operating in the world by copying those of others that seem to work.
6. To add new facts to one's personal data base.
7. To find universal truths that hold across wide ranges of phenomena.

We can summarize these to make things simpler here as:

plan coherency

contextual place

individual prediction

group prediction

new facts

rule copying

truths

These seven goals, when combined with a general interest in self-centered issues, generate questions that one asks naturally, that are essential to being alive. Young children ask them all the time, but less so as they get older. Machines will have to learn to ask them too, but these are the least of the problem in asking questions because they are the simplest questions to ask.

plan coherency Why did he do that? (What's in it for him?)

contextual place What are his intentions towards me?

individual prediction Why does this matter to me?

group prediction Is this actor a member of a class of actors who will treat me this way?

new facts What did he do exactly?

rule copying Can I learn to do that?

truths Is this going to happen again in the same way?

Questions–Level Two: Factual

The second level of questions, factual questions, are those one is taught to ask in the normal course of a standard education. Not everyone learns to ask these questions because not everyone gets a decent education. However, learning to ask these questions is what a basic education is all about. We learn to ask them over a range of different subjects. We learn about how to acquire facts at a very basic level (Journalistic level), and thus apply our interests in fact acquisition in terms of explanation goals that we already have. Also, we learn to judge the coherency of the arguments of others (Argumentation/Rhetoric), this time by applying our explanatory goals with the aim of establishing the clarity of a line of reasoning. In other words, we can gather facts, and we can gain an understanding about how facts are connected:

Second-level questions: Journalism

plan coherency	Why did he do it?
contextual place	Who did it?
	Where did he do it?
	When did he do it?
	What did he do?
individual prediction	What is the past history of this actor that accounts for his action?
group prediction	Does he belong to a group that acts this way?
new facts	What new trends are there in the world?
rule copying	Is this a start of something we will see again?
truth	What is overall intention or ideology is behind his action?

Second-level questions: Argumentation/Rhetoric

plan coherency	What evidence would support that argument?
contextual place	What counterexamples are there to that premise?
individual prediction	What would have to be true in order for that to follow?
group prediction	What other generalizations like this are there?
new facts	What other facts must be true if the premise is true?
rule copying	What analogous arguments might there be?
truth	What follows in general if all that he says is true

Questions–Level Three: Theories

Third level questions are ones that people are rarely taught to ask. The fact that machines should be taught to ask them might seem questionable in that case. But, in some sense, we are demanding that machines reach a level of understanding that is fairly complex. Many people have failed to achieve this level of understanding. These questions form the basis of a fundamental analytical mind. Scientists and scholars learn to ask these questions, but they often so engross themselves in the answer to any one of them that they forget to continue asking more of them. Machines, if they are to be good thinkers, must learn to ask them too. Third level questions inquire into the theory behind an event, and can be quite general, or can express the point of view of a particular field of inquiry.

Third-level questions: Understanding/Coherence

plan coherency	What information am I missing that would make these events coherent?
	What plan was being pursued that, had I known it, would have made a given action predictable?
	Why would someone do something one way when another way seems better?
	Why was any given planned state of the world planned the way it was?
contextual place	What other event do I have in memory that is like the current one?
	How do we determine the ultimate cost and benefits of an action?
	How can someone who has asserted a fact have come to have known that fact?
	Who would they have to have known in order to have known that?
	How could they possibly be in a position to have come to know that?
	Where were they when they found that out?
	What kind of analysis could they have used in order to be able to figure out that kind of thing?
individual prediction	What theory of that event would I have needed in order to correctly anticipate that outcome?

What results normally follow from a given action?

What do various states of the planned world tell us about the people who did the planning?

What do the various states of the physical world tell us about the rules that govern our lives?

group prediction   What other events like the current one would cause me to rethink a basic hypothesis?

new facts   What would make me believe that a given action makes sense (when it doesn't seem to right now)?

What states of the world would have had to have been the case in order for a given event to have followed naturally from them?

rule copying   What else would be different if this were true?

What good strategies can be copied from a given event?

truths   What else in the world is like this?

Questions–Level Four: Creativity

Fourth level questions are really ones upon which the essence of creativity hinges. These can be very basic or very obtuse. They often differ in different fields of inquiry, sometimes bringing one field of inquiry's standard set of questions to another field of inquiry to which they are not ordinarily applied. Machines will have to learn to ask these kinds of questions to be creative.

plan coherency   How can we cast a given action in such a way that it appears to be something other than what it is?

How can we get someone to support something that they otherwise would not?

How can I devise a plan that would help fix an errant plan that I have observed?

contextual place   What other situations can I set up, that have the properties of the one under consideration, so that I can stress the absurdity of the original?

What other situations can I set up, that have the properties of the one under consideration, so that I can stress the validity of the original?

What other situations can I set up, that have the properties of the one under consideration, so that I can find the generalizations that hold between the two?

What would happen if I juxtaposed the contextual place for one thing with that of another?

individual prediction

What evidence can be ignored in attempting to create a theory of what someone will do next?

How can I see one person I don't understand as an instance of someone who I do understand?

group prediction

What categories for groupings that are used by most people can be seen to be ineffective and in need of change?

How can a grouping be formed that will have more predictive power than we now have for present groupings?

new facts

What cherished assumptions, held by many people, ought to be re-examined?

How can a question that is unanswerable be re-cast in answerable form?

rule copying

How do certain people build up successful rules for coping with the world?

How and why do other people avoid those rules? Do they succeed as well? How can you know which rules of the world to copy and which to rewrite?

truths

Are there any truths in the world?

How does one go about proving ultimate truths?

What is the value of a temporarily-held generalization?

TRIGGERS

If we went through every one of these questions every time we perceived an event, we probably would never get through processing that event.

Applying all these questions to an event, and to our inferences about the causes and effects of that event, would cause a combinatorial explosion. So, one important issue is what exactly **triggers** a question. What causes one or more of these questions to be brought into consciousness? Just when should we consider what?

There are three different types of triggers that we shall talk about here. The first, which I shall label **TRIG-0,** are those which one need not learn about in any complex way. These triggers are either innate (it's not necessary to teach a child to be frightened), or else are learned quite easily in the first years of life. Of course, their nature is still quite important to determine, and they must be taught to a machine if it is to attempt to understand people and if it is to have any conscious life of its own.

The level of a trigger is unrelated to the question levels. A creative person may generate a level four question from a TRIG-0 trigger. TRIG-0 triggers are simply triggers for events that have great immediacy; they relate to expectation failures arising from processing an action while it is under observation.

The second level, which I shall label **TRIG-1,** are those we learn fairly early on in life, but which might not have been learned by everyone. Often these are rules of thumb that are taught in school. For example, a child may learn to trigger *did I misbehave?* when adults start talking about his actions. TRIG-1 triggers tend to relate to events that are being processed after the fact, and often with those where there was no firsthand observation.

The third I shall label **TRIG-TBL** (for To Be Learned). If, in order to be smart, as we have claimed, it is necessary to constantly be asking questions, then the triggers that one learns are an important part of that process. Learning to trigger questions at the right times is at the foundation of learning; both people and machines need to learn how to trigger new questions. But, learning takes place in one's own personal context, so TRIG-TBLs tend to be triggered by unusual situations that are perceived as important to the understander's goals. For example, a hypochondriac might have a TRIG-TBL fire when he hears someone complementing his health, so that he can look for reasons the good signs were misleading and make more convincing arguments about his infirmity.

Initially, of course, one can simply be taught the appropriate triggers. Using them at the right time is a matter of experience. Thus, it is the compilation of information about the appropriate use of triggers that is the significant part of learning from experience.

So, for example, the first level questions have the following triggers:

First-level questions: Self-Centered

Why does this matter to me?

TRIG-0: observing a physical action headed your way (basically innate)

TRIG-1: being told about an event (because there is the implication that the teller is telling it to you because he thinks it matters to you)

TRIG–TBL: observational (because observations may matter that do not appear to matter at first glance)

In other words, every animal knows TRIG-0. Over time, his knowledge must be refined on the basis of experience. This means knowing the answer to the specific question generated by the general question that has been triggered. The process has the trigger causing the general question:

Why does this matter to me?

to be generated. This question is then transformed into a specific question, i.e.,:

Why does this wild animal heading towards me matter to me?

The answer to the specific question would presumably be encoded in such a way as to include an action that has worked before in preventing any danger that might be assumed to be a potential result of the on-going action. For TRIG-1, the situation is a bit more complicated. When we are told about an event as a child, it is precisely because this event had direct relevance to us. As we get older, information gets imparted to us that is only indirectly relevant. TRIG-1 causes us to trigger the question:

Why does it matter to me?

and then decide whether to pursue thinking on that question until some personal relevance is gathered.

For example, if you hear, on the news, that the Cardinals beat the Phillies 5–3, you would ask yourself, in some sense, whether or not you cared about that. You would if you were a Cardinal or Phillie fan. You would not if you were not a baseball fan, unless of course, you knew someone who was and cared about them in general, or had some specific reason (like an impending visit to a Phillie fan) to care at this time. If you were a Met fan, for example, you might care about this news if the Mets were tied in the standings with one or the other of these teams, or were about to face one of them, and so on.

The point is that for any given input received in this way (i.e. passively), we attempt to determine its relevance. Through the process of question transformation that we saw with CYRUS, the task is to convert the triggered question:

Why does it matter to me?

to one that is directly answerable, such as:

Will the result of that game affect a team I care about?
Will the result of that game affect a person I care about?
Generating this question is of key significance. To do this, it is necessary to use one of many **question-transformation rules (Q-T rules)**. For example the Q-T rule applicable here is:

Q-T1: For TRIG-1 with respect to the results of an athletic contest:

transform initial TRIG-1 question into
question about the possible relationship to the results of other athletic contests
or
question about affective states of individuals associated with the teams in the contest.

Notice that the rule here is rather specific. We would expect to find rather specific rules because once we learn to know what we care about in a given context, we can easily get to that issue. In essence what we are saying here is that for any new event one transforms general questions about personal relevance into specific questions that one has learned to ask about that kind of situation.

Now, lets consider what happens when the information that causes TRIG-1 to fire is told directly to you. That is, suppose that someone walks over to you and says something to you. Lets assume that he either tells you a fact about himself or about something not directly related to either of you. For example, assume he has said either:
My wife woke up sick this morning.
or
The Iranians have bombed Baghdad.

The problem is to figure out what the relevance of these remarks is to you. A number of different question-transformation rules apply:

Q-T2: For TRIG-1 with respect to illness:

transform into
a-question about the possible contagion of the illness
b-question about the possible effects of the illness on the individual causing the lack of availability of that individual
c-questions about the possible effects on other individuals upon whom you rely of the difficulties of the ill person

Now, this may seem a rather egocentric set of questions, but recall that that is precisely what *why does it matter to me?* is all about. The problem here is to generate a set of questions from the original question. Not all the question types we have discussed are all active all the time. But, level one questions such as this are always active.

The question transformations for the bombing of Baghdad are:

Q–T3: For TRIG-1 with respect to war in foreign countries:

transform into
a-question about the possible spread of the war to other countries
b-question about the possible effects of the war in terms of the production of commodities used by you

The Q–Ts mentioned above are all rather typical. For a variety of given specific areas of knowledge, we have developed a set of standard ways of determining the relevance of events in those areas to ourselves. Thus we learn to ask certain questions when these events occur. Naturally, these Q–Ts look a great deal like inferences or requests that might have been generated by FRUMP or IPP. That is because they are at the simplest level of understanding. My point has been to attempt to raise the level of understanding by having the machine generate questions that it itself was interested in or at least that it knew to ask.

In general, such questions come about in two different ways. Either they come from the TRIG-TBL, or they come from the higher level questions (levels three and four). To see what I mean, consider the TRIG-TBL for the above first-level question. Even though the first level question *why does this matter to me?* is rather unsophisticated as questions go, there can be a strong learning aspect to that question. When one observes an event that is not overtly threatening, one can still learn quite a bit from the event. TRIG-TBLs cause one to ask of a given event whether it is unusual enough to merit further study. In other words, for TRIG-0 and TRIG-1, we know that there is direct relevance to us. The task is to determine what the relevance is. For events other than those that are coming right at us or those that someone has decided we ought to know about, we have to determine for ourselves how important they may be to us.

To do this, we must compile a complex data base of knowledge about the world that enables us to determine if an event is unusual. Unusualness is actually fairly difficult to determine. If a new building is being constructed near one's home, is that unusual? It may be unusual enough that we would want to consider how it might affect us.

The task for a computer is to learn, by asking about the possible effects of every action that it processes, which actions can potentially affect its goals. Here then, we are again at goals. One cannot determine if an event is worth examining fully unless one has a set of goals in terms of which to examine the event.

GOAL–BASED TRIGGERS

Let us consider an example level-three question and an example level-four question in terms of the triggers that would make those questions fire off and in terms of the goals that would have to be present in order to force those triggers. As examples, let's consider the following:

Third-level question
Why would someone do something one way when another way seems better?

Fourth-level question
How can we cast a given action in such a way that it appears to be something other than what it is?
The triggers for the third-level question are as follows:

TRIG-0: expecting an alternative plan

TRIG-1: being told about an alternative plan

TRIG–TBL: goals: theory of actor, theory of plan selection

Essentially what these say is that when an action fails to fit into an anticipated set of actions in service of a known goal, TRIG-0 fires. Another way to put this is that someone did something towards an end that you expected, but in a way that you did not expect. TRIG-0 causes the third-level question that it indexes to fire. The question might then be subject to some question transformations. The question that fires is:

Why would someone do something one way when another way seems better?
   Q–Ts only can be applied in real contexts, so let's reconsider our example from before:

The Iranians have bombed Baghdad.

   The issue is to get yourself to ask a question that might cause you to think about something, in a creative way, that arises from the new information. TRIG-0 would only fire in this instance if you had some expectation about the event. In other words, interest is reflected in expectations that fire, and further interest is generated by questions that come from the trigger.
   So, in order for TRIG-0 to have fired here, some expectation that the Iranians would not bomb Baghdad would have had to have been around. Thus, the Q–T depends upon the failed expectation.

Q–T4: For TRIG-0 with respect to the actions in a war, when expectations were present that such actions would not be taken:

transform into

a-question about what new goal may be held by the actor that this plan serves

b-question about what conditions changed in the war

c-question about leadership changes that may have occurred

These transformations produce, in this case:

a-*Do the Iranians now believe that Teheran is completely defensible?* (This is based on the assumption that the failed expectation was derived from an assumption that the reason not to bomb Baghdad was so as to prevent an escalation that could harm Iran.)

b-*Are the Iranians getting desperate because they believe they cannot go on much longer?*

c-*Is the Ayatollah Khomeini no longer in full charge of his government?*

My point here has been that it is in the generation of such questions that the answer to learning lies. These questions can either be easily rejected or indexed so they can be tested in future cases. They are, in essence, hypotheses that should be generated by an understander in response to his attempt to process a new event.

For TRIG-1 to fire, it is necessary for the event being processed to be presented together with an alternative. Thus, TRIG-1 fires when two plans are under consideration, and where the one that has been pursued seems to be the less likely of the two. **Q–T5** therefore, transforms

Why would someone do something one way when another way seems better?

into

a-Did the actor believe that plan A was better than plan B?

b-Are there negative side effects of plan B for the actor?

c-Was the actor unable to execute plan B for some reason?

For TRIG–TBL to fire, we need specific goal matches. Our question (*Why would someone do something one way when another way seems better?*)

is transformed into:

a-What properties of the actor make him unlikely to follow the plans I expect him to follow? (This fires when the actor is marked as interesting to the processor.)

b-What properties of the plan in question have I failed to think about? (This fires when the plan is marked as inherently interesting.)

c-Do actors acting under a given goal behave differently for specific goals? (This fires when the goal is marked as inherently interesting.)

The point is that for a processor that has the goal of becoming more knowledgable about a given actor, plan, or goal, questions such as these would fire when the interest matches with a failed expectation about the interest. The intention is to learn more about a subject of interest when one's expectations are unsatisfied.

AT THE FOURTH LEVEL

Now, let's consider the other example in the context of a fourth-level question. The sentence: *My wife woke up sick this morning* can have numerous subplots to it. An interested understander begins to think about these extra issues to the extent that he has reason to believe any of them. We have the following triggers:

TRIG-0: negative effects of action; blame falls on you

TRIG-1: having an action presented to you in the opposite way than you would have expected

TRIG-TBL: goals, rhetorical: need to convince someone of a point of view

TRIG-0 fires when a reason can be inferred whereby the action in question causes potential blame to the hearer. This is a paranoid-type interpretation and should only fire when the processor has some reason to be paranoid.

Thus, you should ask the question:

How can we cast a given action in such a way that it appears to be something other than what it is?

when you have reason to be suspicious that the event under discussion in some way is being related to you. The task before you is to generate a question that enables you to say or do something that turns the situation around.

Q–T6: For TRIG-0 with respect to an event being blamed on you:

   transform into
a-question about how the event is really a positive event
b-question about how to make it appear as if the event in question couldn't have happened
c-question about who else can be blamed

Again, as with most TRIG-0 firings, the questions generated are known to most children. They rarely have to be taught. But, level-four questions, even for TRIG-0, have some creativity to them. The questions actually generated would be, for example:

a-What will the positive effects of this sickness be for the husband? (This could be generated without blame being assigned, of course.)

b-What reasons would his wife have for faking this illness?

c-Who else could have been responsible for this event? (This might be an important question if the sickness were "morning sickness" and this really was an accusation.)

Here again, these questions are only the beginning, but the answers can be easily generated so as to help create good responses to the initial remark if it were found that it was appropriate to do so. We fire TRIG-1 when there is some expectation about the event being discussed, but where the expectation that is violated is about how that information is being presented. In other words, if you knew that the speaker's wife was unhappy and he told you that she was sick, the issue is why the information was presented in this peculiar way.

Q–T7 therefore, transforms the original question into:

a-Why did the speaker decide not to tell me what I thought he would?

b-What actually has happened (as opposed to what I was told)?

c-Why does the speaker perceive the consequences of one event as being more significant than the other?

For TRIG-TBL, the issue is to be able to recast a given event in terms of one's own goals. This would be fired if one's point of view were at odds with a given assertion. Thus the triggers to be learned depend upon one's ability to test a given assertion to see if it is at odds with one's assumptions on the subject. The question:

How can we cast a given action in such a way that it appears to be something other than what it is?

is transformed by Q–T8 when an event is presented that conflicts with one's own viewpoint and one has the opportunity to make a rejoinder.

Q–T8: For TRIG–TBL:

transform into

a-question about how the event could be portrayed as part of a plan to achieve ends opposite from those that are obvious

b-question about how to make it appear as if the negative aspects of the event were really neutral or beneficial

c-question about the evidence behind the basic assumptions of the event, such as who really did the planning, the acting, and so on

CONCLUSION

Creativity means asking questions. If we want a machine to be creative, to think in any significant sense of that term, then it must be aroused by what it perceives so as to wonder about it. Much of this wondering is fairly prescribed. We know what to wonder about at a certain basic level. After that, we are taught what to wonder about. Beyond that there is a level at which we wonder about truly new things. But, whether new or old, we learn certain tricks about how to wonder and at what level to wonder.

My claim is that we must teach machines to wonder too. To do so, they must be given very detailed ideas about what to wonder about in specific domains, as well as a set of algorithms about how to wonder in general. In addition, they must be given personalities of a sort. That is, one tends to wonder idiosyncratically. One wonders about things in a way that reflects one's own personal experiences and knowledge about a domain.

8

Some Final Questions

In the last chapter, we started off with the idea of having another look at the process of newspaper story understanding, and wound up with a detailed set of heuristics pertaining to the transformation of unanswerable questions into answerable ones. The intent of all the question transformations of course, was to enable machines to pose questions for themselves, and to answer those questions. In order to understand how a machine might know which questions to consider while reading a newspaper it is worthwhile to look at exactly how people go about reading a news story. If, as we have claimed, questions are so important for understanding, then one ought to be able to find questions being raised during the course of understanding. To discuss this issue, let's consider a somewhat unusual article that appeared in the *New York Times*, Sunday, April 14, 1985:

Boy Says Lebanese Recruited Him as Car Bomber

JERUSALEM, April 13—A 16-year-old Lebanese was captured by Israeli troops hours before he was supposed to get into an explosive-laden car and go on a suicide bombing mission to blow up the Israeli Army headquarters in Lebanon, according to Israeli officials and an account from the youth himself.

The teenager, Mohammed Mahmoud Burro, was captured by Israeli soldiers in a raid on a southern Lebanese village on February 23. It is believed to be the first time that a trained suicide car-bomber has been seized alive.

Under questioning by the Israelis and in a separate interview with *The New York Times*, he has given an account of his life, of his enlistment for the suicide mission and of the people he was working for. If true, his account would provide the first inside look at the motivation of suicide bomber and the planning and organization behind his operation.

Although there is no independent confirmation of his account, senior Israeli military officials have spent days questioning Mr. Burro, who has curly, light brown hair, has yet to start shaving and looks like any of a thousand Shiite teen-agers walking the streets of West Beirut today. They have also checked many key elements in his narrative through their own covert means, and in each case, they said, they found he was telling the truth or could not have made up what he said.

We are convinced, said a senior military source, *that his story is true.* He added that a formal announcement of his capture and account would be made in Israel on Sunday morning.

Mr. Burro is expected to remain in Israeli custody for some time.

It is unclear whether Mr. Burro's account is typical of those who have been involved in the wave of suicide car bombings in Lebanon and elsewhere in the Middle East over the last few years. Yet three aspects of his account may have an important bearing on an understanding of the suicide bombing phenomenon.

Not a Devout Moslem

What seems most striking about Mr. Burro's account is that although he is a Shiite Moslem, he comes from a secular family background. He spent his free time not in prayer, he said, but riding his motorcycle and playing ball. According to his account, he was not a fanatic who wanted to kill himself in the cause of Islam or anti-Zionism, but was recruited for the suicide mission through another means: blackmail.

Shiite extremist groups in Lebanon and Iran have given the impression that the suicide bomb attacks have been carried out by devoutly religious people eager to become martyrs. Mr. Burro said he was taken to two religious leaders as part of his training for the mission, apparently to instill religious zeal.

Unacquainted with Organizers

Second, Mr. Burro said he did not know beforehand most of the people who recruited him or brought him to the point where the car laden with explosives would be brought to him. His account, if accurate, would seem to reinforce previous speculation that the people who actually drive the suicide cars are carefully recruited from the general public by intelligence officials of Lebanese militias or Middle Eastern Governments. The planning and preparation, it would seem, are carried out by intelligence experts unknown to the driver, and the car is brought to the suicide driver only at the last minute.

Third, Mr. Burro said the men who recruited him were from the Lebanese Shiite militia Amal. This seems noteworthy because Amal is considered the most moderate and mainstream of the Lebanese Shiite organizations, and while its opposition to the Israeli occupation of southern Lebanon is well known, Amal was generally believed to use more conventional means of warfare, leaving the so-called "fanatical" suicide methods to its more extreme rival, the pro-Iranian Party of God.

Mr. Burro's account could indicate that a method of terrorism that once seemed confined to a fanatical fringe may now be emerging as an accepted tool of warfare for more moderate groups and state intelligence organizations.

Ten days ago, at the request of The Times, which had independently learned of Mr. Burro's capture, the Israeli Army approved a 90 minute interview with Mr. Burro in a Tel Aviv office, without any interference but in the presence of military personnel. The interview came at the completion of Mr. Burro's interrogation by the Israelis. On Friday, military censors in Israel released the interview for publication after reading it and deciding that nothing had to be deleted.

Mr. Burro was nervous at the start of the interview, which was conducted entirely in Arabic, but gradually warmed up as time passed and he appeared to speak freely. He is, as Israeli Officials put it, "just a kid."

What follows is his account.

(I have left out his actual account. It is quite interesting, but irrelevant for our purposes.)

MY STUDENTS READ

My premise here is that reading involves the generation of questions. On one occasion, I read this story to a class of graduate students and asked them to voice any question that occured to them while I read. It took over an hour to read just the introduction to the story that the boy tells. Here are the questions that they generated, at the point where they generated them, for that introductory part of the article:

JERUSALEM, April 13—A 16-year-old Lebanese was captured by Israeli troops hours before he was supposed to get into an explosive-laden car and go on a suicide bombing mission to blow up the Israeli Army headquarters in Lebanon, according to Israeli officials and an account from the youth himself.

Why would someone commit suicide if they are not depressed?
Why does the news tell us only about Lebanese truck bombers? Aren't there any Israeli truck bombers?
These kids remind one of Kamikaze pilots in World War II. Are they motivated in the same way?

The teen-ager, Mohammed Mahmoud Burro, was captured by Israeli soldiers in a raid on a southern Lebanese village on Feb. 23.

Why is it that every Arab seems to be named Mohammed?
How do the Israelis know where to make their raids?
How do Lebanese teenagers compare to US teenagers?

It is believed to be the first time that a trained suicide car-bomber has been seized alive.

Why hadn't they been caught alive before?
What do the parents of suicide-bombers think of their children's training for this job?
Is there a political group organizing the kids?
This story reminds one of Oliver Twist. Is there a Lebanese Fagan around who organizes homeless kids into suicide-bombers?

Under questioning by the Israelis and in a separate interview with the New York Times, he has given an account of his life, of his enlistment for the suicide mission and of the people he was working for.

How severe was the Israeli interrogation?
Did the Israelis tell him what to say?
Why did the Israelis let the Times interview him?

If true, his account would provide the first inside look at the motivation of a suicide bomber and the planning and organization behind his operation.

Why did the writer say "If true"?
Why is the Times suddenly so interested in terrorists? Couldn't they have gotten such an inside look long ago?
Don't psychologists in Israel study the motivations of terrorists? Surely they must have a better understanding than we might get from just this one case.
There is plenty of terrorism in Northern Ireland but one never hears of teenage suicide fanatics there. Why not?
Did the kid think he was going to die?

Although there is no independent confirmation of his account, senior Israeli military officials have spent days questioning Mr. Burro, who has curly, light brown hair, has yet to start shaving and looks like any of a thousand Shiite teen-agers walking the streets of West Beirut today.

Why is the Times giving us a physical description at this point?
What do Shiite teenagers look like?

They have also checked many key elements in his narrative through their own covert means, and in each case, they said, they found he was telling the truth or could not have made up what he said.

What are the covert means for checking story?
What did they check?

"We are convinced," said a senior military source, "that his story is true." He added that a formal announcement of his capture and account would be made in Israel on Sunday morning.

What's the value of "knowing" the story is true?
Does the Israeli press know about the story?
Is the Israeli military command interested in this as propaganda?

Mr. Burro is expected to remain in Israeli custody for some time.

What kind of sentence did he get?
Will they trade him for somebody?
Why did the Times understate this so much?
Are the Israelis going to try him as an adult?
Do the Lebanese consider him legally responsible?

It is unclear whether Mr. Burro's account is typical of those who have been involved in the wave of suicide car bombings in Lebanon and

elsewhere in the Middle East over the last few years. Yet three aspects of his account may have an important bearing on an understanding of the suicide bombing phenomenon.

What are the three things?

What seems most striking about Mr. Burro's account is that although he is a Shiite Moslem, he comes from a secular family background.

Why does the Times believe that it is interesting that his background is secular? Does the Times assume all fanaticism is religious?
Why does the Times assume that a secular background prevents religious fanaticism? In India many religious fanatics come from a secular background.

He spent his free time not in prayer, he said, but riding his motorcycle and playing pinball.

Weren't the Weathermen from nice families also?
Does pinball lead to terrorism?

According to his account, he was not a fanatic who wanted to kill himself in the cause of Islam or anti-Zionism, but was recruited for the suicide mission through another means: blackmail.

Are kids easier to blackmail?
Who blackmailed them?
What can a kid do that could lead to blackmail?

Shiite extremist groups in Lebanon and Iran have given the impression that the suicide bomb attacks have been carried out by devoutly religious people eager to become martyrs. Mr. Burro said he was taken to two religious leaders as part of his training for the mission, apparently to instill religious zeal.

How long were the meetings with religious leaders?
Does he now have the right amount of religious zeal?
Why does it seem important for us to know how he was motivated?
Why do the blackmailers care that the bombers appear religious?
If their trainers really are religious fanatics, why don't they do the driving?
Why do torturers demand change before they execute prisoners?
    One is reminded of 1984, where they did the same thing.
Who is it that the blackmailers are trying to deceive?

Second, Mr. Burro said he did not know beforehand most of the people who recruited him or brought him to the point where the car laden with explosives would be brought to him.

If the blackmailers didn't know him, how did they entice him?

His account, if accurate, would seem to reinforce previous speculation that the people who actually drive the suicide cars are carefully recruited from the general public by intelligence official of Lebanese militias or Middle Eastern Governments.

Are the other truck drivers also blackmailed?
Who's been speculating about this?
How does a militia search for victims?
Why did they choose this kid?
Which "Middle Eastern Governments?"

The planning and preparation, it would seem, are carried out by intelligence experts unknown to the driver, and the car is brought to the suicide driver only at the last minute.

Where do they get the car?
What makes a good "bomb-car"?

Third, Mr. Burro said the men who recruited him were from the Lebanese Shiite militia Amal.

One is reminded of the "human mine sweepers" in use in Iran. Do
  Moslems not care about young people at all?
Why aren't there Christian terrorists? Do the Christians place a differ-
  ent value on young lives?

This seems noteworthy because Amal is considered the most moderate and mainstream of the Lebanese Shiite organizations, and while its opposition to the Israeli occupation of southern Lebanon is well known, Amal was generally believed to use more conventional means of warfare, leaving the so-called "Fanatical" suicide methods to its more extreme rival, the pro-Iranian Party of God.

How did Amal get a "conventional" reputation?
Does Amal have control over its own troops?
Is conventional warfare "cleaner" than suicide bombing?
Why is car bombing a good tactic?
What terrible things does the Party of God do?

Mr. Burro's account could indicate that a method of terrorism that once seemed confined to a fanatical fringe may now be emerging as an accepted tool of warfare for more moderate groups and state intelligence organizations.

How quickly do trends in terrorism change?
Are these trends like clothing fashions? Who mandates the changes
  and why?

Why don't they poison reservoirs? What's special about car-bombs? What does it mean for a tool of warfare to be fanatical?

Ten days ago, at the request of The Times, which had independently learned of Mr. Burro's capture, the Israeli Army approved a 90 minute interview with Mr. Burro in a Tel Aviv office, without any interference but in the presence of military personnel. The interview came at the completion of Mr. Burro's interrogation by the Israelis. On Friday, military censors in Israel released the interview for publication after reading it and deciding that nothing had to be deleted.

How did the Times learn of the capture?
Did the presence of the Israeli troops at the interview influence it?
Why were the Israelis there?
Did they make a deal with the Israelis?
Why did the Israelis allow the interview?
To what extent do Israelis censor stuff?
Why did the Times agree to prior censorship?

Mr. Burro was nervous at the start of the interview, which was conducted entirely in Arabic, but gradually warmed up as time passed and he appeared to speak freely. He is, as Israeli officials put it, "just a kid."

One is reminded of a Nicaraguan kid who was interviewed by the
    press. Are kids more sympathetic for these kinds of interviews?
Is this whole story true? One is reminded of the Washington Post
    story about the 12-year-old drug addict that turned out to be
    fiction.
How did they know he was nervous? Why did they say this?
How could they tell he was speaking freely?

I make the assumption that my class, although being brighter and more internationally-oriented than the average newpaper reader, is nevertheless fairly representative of a careful newspaper reader. That is, I feel free to assume that the questions above are fairly typical of those people might generate while reading a newspaper article that they find intriguing. Given that the type of questions shown above is somewhat typical of what one might expect, then the issue is simply:

How do we generate such questions while reading?

How do these questions drive the understanding process?

What is the ultimate purpose of these questions?

QUESTION FORMATION

One way to get a handle on the generation of questions during the understanding process is to attempt to classify the above questions in order to get
a better feeling as to why they got generated in the first place. The
questions given above can be broadly grouped into the following categories:

Data Collection Questions (DCQs)

Bottom-up Reminding/Creativity Questions (REMQs)

Idiosyncratic Concerns for Hypothesis Verification (HVQs)

Expectation Failure/Explanation Questions (EQs).

We consider these one by one:

Data Collection Questions (DCQs) are questions that are either around
before one begins to read a text or that get generated by some mundane
things that happen while one is reading a text. Before one ever begins to
read a story about terrorism, one has some ideas, often quite general, on
the subject. Further, one has ideas about a great many different subjects—
plane travel, embassies, relations between countries, and so on—that one
might in general wonder about from time to time. These questions are
always around, so to speak, and they come up when a topic appears to
which they relate. These are the questions of which MOPs and TOPs are
made. They represent the sum total of one's knowledge about a subject,
with the natural gaps that exist because, after all, one does not know all
there is to know about any given subject. One is always willing to learn
more. These questions represent the subject matter about which one wants
to learn, and from which one tries to learn when a given subject appears in
a text. On occasion, this subject matter is no way consciously available to
the processor. All of a sudden he finds himself noticing something and
wondering about it. At this point he wonders specifically enough to go
back into the text, or into future texts, in order to find more data to enable
himself to answer the question.

Bottom-up Reminding/Creativity Questions (REMQs) are, in contrast,
not there at the start of the reading process. They are things that occur to
us as we read, and are often the expression of our true interests. What
happens is simple to describe if not to duplicate on a computer. One gets
reminded of a past episode by the episode one is currently reading. At that
point, it may seem reasonable to pursue the reminding. Pursuing the
reminding means attempting to learn something from the combination of
the two episodes. Often this involves consciously wondering if the two are
in fact related and if the remindand can give some context in which to
better understand the text being processed. The questions generated by

this process are of the ilk: *I wonder if* x *that occurred in the text I am processing really has occurred for the same reasons as* y *in the episode of which I am reminded.* Questions such as these allow one to learn things that one was not expecting to even think about, but about which one had previously pondered to some extent. Thus, for **DCQs,** one can be said to have *been generally interested in the subject* of the question, whereas for **REMQs** one is, in some sense, *surprised to be wondering about a given subject.*

Idiosyncratic Concerns for Hypothesis Verification (HVQs) are somewhat like some DCQs in that they were around long before one began to read the story, and somewhat like REMQs in that they are elicited by items in the text somewhat like remindings. Often, one has a set of concerns that color everything that one sees. It is possible to see everything in terms of social injustice, race relations, sex, the drive to succeed, or anything else in which one is interested. We view information with respect to our interests. And, if we are interested in proving that X is the case while Y is not the case, we find ourselves capable of seeing many far-ranging details as *yet another example of X* while failing to see evidence for Y that might be equally plausible. This myopia is maintained through HVQs. These questions are, in essence, demands to be reminded, which cause information to be construed and re-construed until it is seen as something which *naturally reminds one of X,* where X just happens to be one's favorite hypothesis. The questions generated are, at that point, just like REMQs in that they are demands for the use of a prior situation to explain the one currently being processed.

Expectation Failure/Explanation Questions (EQs) are, of course, our old friends from Chapter 4. In this context, their role is the still the same. While a text is being processed, it is necessary to relate the events to one's experiences. When one's experiences are not sufficiently broad to help in the comprehension of a piece of text, it is necessary to attempt to explain what one has failed to comprehend. To do this, one generates questions (EQs) whose role it is to bring XPs to mind as potential explanations to be applied in novel situations. EQs are thus bottom-up in the fashion of REMQs. However, in this case one is not reminded of specific instances but rather of general standard explanations. As we have seen, specific questions are generated from the EQs. Thus, the EQs are not answered directly. Rather they generate new questions whose role it is to make comprehensible what is currently incomprehensible.

In summary then, **DCQs** are for everyday issues concerning the general expansion of one's knowledge. **REMQs** are for creative new ideas that one happens to stumble upon regarding the interconnection of various, quite possibly very unrelated, events. **HVQs** are for reinforcing one's beliefs with new data. And, **EQs** have the intent of generating specific questions whose intent it is to make comprehensible what is incomprehensible, the most common method for doing so being the adaptation of an extant XP to a new situation. In other words, the role of these questions is to enable a reader to learn from what he is reading. Thus, learning has four forms:

Type of Learning	corresponding to	Type of Question
data collection		DCQ
creative combination		REMQ
belief amplification		HVQ
creative adaptation of extant structures to new situations.		EQ

With this classification in mind then, let's take a look at some of these questions more carefully. Consider, for example, the first set of questions, generated from the initial sentence in the story:

1-Why would someone commit suicide if they are not depressed?

2-Why does the news tell us only about Lebanese truck bombers? Aren't there any Israeli truck bombers?

3-These kids remind one of Kamikaze pilots in World War II. Are they motivated in the same way?

The claim here is that question 1 (Q1) was generated from an attempt to apply a standard XP about suicide, and after having the entry conditions for that XP fail, an EQ was generated which in turn generated a specific question whose intent it is to attempt to tweak the standard XP.

It is not obvious where Q2 comes from at first glance. After all, we are attempting here to understand something that is rather difficult to get at. As it turns out, this particular questioner generated a great many questions that had a common theme, namely, the biased reporting of the Mid-East situation by the New York Times. Thus, I claim here that Q2 is an HVQ.

Q3 is a rather nice example of a REMQ. The reminding with the Kamikazes occurred to this student, and he began to think about it. The result of such a REMQ is to set up a series of DCQs whose role it will be to collect enough data to attempt to verify the REMQ. (I might note here that at this point the REMQ becomes indistinguishable from an HVQ. The reason for this is that HVQs and REMQs are the same type of question but one's whose origin in memory is quite different.)

In the next set:

4-Why is it that every Arab seems to be named Mohammed?

5-How do the Israelis know where to make their raids?

6-How do Lebanese teenagers compare to US teenagers?

we find some questions that are superficially of a quite different sort. In fact, Q4 is a typical DCQ. It would be stretching a point to say that this question was burning as a hypothesis of this student, yet obviously it crossed his mind. The premise is that in processing the story, the student had to place the information from the story into an appropriate slot in memory. Doing so, he found other similar stories and he noted a superficial similarity which he wondered about causing the DCQ to be generated. Similarly, Q5 and Q6 are also DCQs. Presumably, these were not questions that were around in the mind of the reader beforehand. Thus, they represent a sub-class of DCQs which I call text-amplification DCQs (TA-DCQs). TA-DCQs are functionally identical to other DCQs, but their origin is based solely upon the text. For that reason they tend to be rather ephemeral, with their answers very possibly being forgotten rather quickly. There being no prior context in which to place the answer, they do not represent a very powerful form of learning. They are a kind of *idle curiousity.*
The next set is a little more interesting:

7-Why hadn't they been caught alive before?

8-What do the parents of suicide-bombers think of their children's training for this job?

9-Is there a political group organizing the kids?

10-This story reminds one of Oliver Twist. Is there a Lebanese Fagan around who organizes homeless kids into suicide-bombers?

Q7 is a little silly, in that it is obvious that suicide-bombers can be expected to die. However, the question that underlies it, namely why this one was different and didn't die, is really one of the key questions of the whole story. Thus, this is really an EQ which one can expect to surface from time to time during the course of reading this story. Or to put this another way, certain EQs become, during the course of reading an interesting story, key questions which drive all the others. If we are interested in this story at all, we want to know why this kid didn't die. Or in other words, given the XP **fanatic does suicidal act to promote cause,** we are left wondering throughout this story, where we must modify this XP which seems to have failed in this case. In a sense then, we can define interest in this way: **interest is the necessity to answer a question generated with the intent of correcting a failed expectation.** In this case an entire XP has failed.

Q8, *What do the parents of suicide-bombers think of their children's training for this job?* is actually a very interesting question since it too relates to a failed XP and is itself an EQ. There is an XP called **parents push children out of nest to take first job,** which seems to fail totally here, since the reasons for it are *to make the child ready for standing on his own two feet,* and that seems obviated in this case. It is thus natural to wonder why the parents of this boy have allowed him to become a suicide-bomber. Thus, this question now gets set up as an EQ. That is, one wants to know how this would be possible, and the need for an XP to explain it is set up.

Q9 and Q10 are versions of the same question, both relating to the general problem of what is going on here, in general. Q10 is a bit nicer in this respect in that it is a REMQ and thus, because of the reminding, in essence proposes a solution to the problem. That is, the reminding suggests that perhaps there is an answer to the question of why young children are becoming car-bombers and that the answer is that there is a Fagan-like character rounding them up. In other words, the XP, **Evil man uses needy children for own ends,** which has *Oliver Twist* as an episode attached to it, is proposed as a potential answer to the EQ, *how can the parents allow this to happen?* This proposed XP can then be evaluated in terms of its applicability. But, and this is the important point, unlike the case where we had to evaluate a pattern solely on an internal basis, in the processing of a natural language text, we have a choice. We can postpone further decisions pending the arrival of new sentences in the text. Or, to put this another way, **processing a text can be seen as the awakening of new questions derived from the text, which are answerable by further perusal of the text.** Thus, rather than having a set of arbitrary pre-selected questions governing the reading of a text, questions are selected and pursued dynamically, as the need to make explanations arises and the inability to find XPs that serve as answers becomes clear.

The understanding of a natural language text then, can be seen as a process whereby one attempts to learn from the text by trying to explain what one has read, and when an explanation is unavailable, one constructs a set of questions, which, if answered, would render the text explained, and therefore, understood. In the midst of this process, three other things are occurring. First, **data is being collected** for the general problem of the explansion of one's knowledge base. Second, already extant **hypotheses about a range of issues are being verified** by input as it arrives. And, third, **remindings that occur haphazardly are being pursued** as possible creative ways of drawing conclusions from the text in concert with analogies and generalizations derived from prior experiences.

Understanding, therefore, is a dynamic process, driven by questions, and changed by both the answers to those questions, and by the exigencies of the new input as it arrives.

THE PROCESS OF QUESTION TRANSFORMATION

In a sense therefore, the end of this work must be, in principle, related to the nature of questions, the use of questions in the formation of explanations, and the transformation of questions in the quest for answers. The question we started with was:

How can a machine be said to be understanding?

We transformed that into:

How can people explain what they have understood?

We transformed that into:

Why do people make explanations?

and that in turn into

What types of explanations are there?

Eventually these became:

What is the nature of the explanation process?

Then we asked:

What standard set of questions might begin the explanation process?

and

Is there a standard set of answers linked to those questions?

Then, we added an additional question:

How can the process of explanation produce creative explanations?

From there we generated the question:

How might the ordinary understanding of texts be changed by viewing it as if it were driven by the process of question-generation?

Thus, in essence, this book cycles upon itself. We cannot talk about learning, explanation, and understanding, without constantly transforming the original question, arriving finally at the problem of exactly how questions are transformed.

There is, of course, no *correct,* systematic method for question-transformation. If there were, we could take any question and instantly transform it into a correct, easily answerable, question. Rather, there must be heuristics for how to make a question more answerable by transforming it, when it seems hard to answer. Those, of course, would be totally **internal heuristics,** in that they would transform questions irrespective of outside issues. With respect to the text we have been considering here, it is clear that questions can be transformed by outside circumstances as well. Thus, there must exist **external heuristics** as well, whereby new information helps to transform an extant question into one that is more answerable. Finally, there can be transformations that come from **outside influences,** such as from friends in a conversation, that, without giving one the rules for making a transformation, do serve to transform questions.

These three things, then, can transform a question. To what end? To make a question easier to answer; to make a question more specific; to make a question more general; to make a question more useful, and so on. In other words, questions themselves have goals, and it is these goals that drive the questioning process. The goals of the questions we have been considering here are all to help explain something better, or to explain something in a new way. Thus, whatever question-transformation heuristics we have been providing, have been provided with that end in mind.

In sum, therefore, this book has been about how explanation questions can be transformed into more answerable questions. To that end, we can now take another look at what we have been saying, viewed from that perspective. The following is a review of the rules that are presented in this book, but taken from a slightly different perspective. We are claiming that in order to come up with new ideas, one needs to ask the right question. This is an old idea in science, but a new idea in AI, at least in the way I am presenting it here. That is, I am suggesting that machines must learn how to ask good questions.

An important part of asking the right question is the transformation of an original starting question into one that is more answerable. So, to that end, let's take a look at some of the question-transformation rules that have been presented, implicitly, in this book, together with the goals behind them:

THE GOALS BEHIND QUESTIONS

We have discussed how explanations, are, in principle, intended to be additive. Thus, one kind of goal behind the question-transformation process is the goal to change the question into one whose answer will add information to the data base: This rule we call QT1:

QT1: Change question into one whose answer adds information to the data base.

This is in contrast to QT2, which is intended to make a question go away:

QT2: Change question into one that is very easy to answer by forcing

a fit between the item to be explained and one that is already explained.

From the spectrum of need in Chapter 3, we can see that some question-transforms depend upon the need that drives them. Thus, one type of goal behind a question-transformation is to change the question into one that addresses a current need. Thus, we have QT3 and QT4:

QT3: If the need to empathize exists, transform question into one whose goal it is to find a situation in memory analogous to the one under discussion.

QT4: If the need to make a prediction exists, transform question into one whose goal it is to find a problem like the one under discussion so as to use the solution for the older problem in the new case.

And, in general, we have QT5 and QT6:

QT5: When a problem needs to be explained away, transform question about problem into a request to search memory for a justifying belief about that problem.

QT6: When a problem needs a solution, transform question about problem into a request to search memory for a reminding that will guide a solution by analogy.

In the Chapter 3, we saw that there were really three basic goals operating, and thus there are three basic types of question-transforms that are applicable:

QT7: Transform the original question about why X occurred into: How can I correctly predict the outcome of situations such as X, next time?

QT8: Transform the original question about why X occurred into: How can I correctly predict the occurrence of X by understanding the reasoning of the actor in X?

QT9: Transform the original question about why X occurred into: What would I have had to know in order to predict that X would occur?

Also, we discussed some other goals behind explanations, corresponding to the following question-transformation goals:

QT10: Transform question about why something good happened to X into: how can I get such a good thing to happen to me?

QT11: Transform question about why something bad happened to X into: how can I avoid such a bad thing to happen to me?

We also saw that people know how to, and therefore machines must know how to, transform *why questions* into more ones that address the particulars of the Belief-action chain. Thus we have:

QT12: Transform a *why question* into a question about the *belief* that underlies an action.

QT13: Transform a *why question* into a question about the *goal* that underlies an action.

QT14: Transform a *why question* into a question about the *plan* that underlies an action.

We also discussed planning in Chapter 3. There we saw that questions about creating new plans should be transformed as well:

QT15: If you need a new plan, try to get reminded of an old plan and modify it to fit the new situation.

And, we saw that one can have rather poor transformation rules as well:

QT16: To find a paranoid explanation, transform question into one that relates event to be explained with subject of paranoia.

QT17: To find a quasi-scientific explanation, transform question into one that relates event to be explained with another just like it and make generalization.

In general then, we can see that the above rules relate the goals that one has in making an explanation to the methods available for changing a rather general question into one that is more likely to satisfy the goal. A machine must be supplied with heuristics for transforms of this type, but, of course, to effectuate those heuristics, two things must be added. First, the rules must be much more numerous and specific. Second, they must be directly related to search rules that correspond to the structure of the data base. Thus, the above rules are really rather general, and thus fairly useless. I present them here to give the flavor of the kinds of rules that must be created in order to give machines the ability to question and to explain.

Inherent in the process of explanation are a number of question-transformations as well. For example, the goal to discover an anomaly drives the question transformation process as well:

QT18: To determine if an action is anomalous, change initial question into one whose intent is to find out if the action is one that the actor normally does.

QT19: To determine if an action is anomalous, change initial question into one whose intent is to find out if the action is one that you would do.

QT20: To determine if an action is anomalous, change initial question into one whose intent is to find out if the action is one that is beneficial to the actor.

QT21: To determine if an action is anomalous, change initial question into one whose intent is to find out if the action is one that is part of a coherent plan.

QT22: To determine if a plan is anomalous, change initial question into one whose intent is to find out if the plan is one that is in service of a goal that the actor might have.

QT23: To determine if a goal is anomalous, change initial question into one whose intent is to find out if the goal is governed by a belief that the actor might have.

And, in general, one of the main question-transformation goals is:

QT24: To determine if an action is anomalous, change question into one that will determine what structure in memory would have been expecting this action had there been reason to believe that that structure was active.

The goals that underlie the process of explanation are, quite naturally, also goals that underlie the question-transformation process.

QT25: To find out if an action is anomalous, change the question into one whose intent it is to establish if the actor has something coherent in mind.

QT26: To explain an event, find the natural context for that event in the belief-action chain.

QT27: To explain for the purpose of future understanding, attempt to find new predictive rules for the behavior of a given individual.

QT28: To understand the actions of individuals, attempt to find predictive rules that hold for the groups of which they are members.

QT29: To know better how to operate in the world, find and copy rules of others that seem to work.

In Chapter 4 we presented a set of explanation questions. Seen from the view of a specific question as a transformation, all the explanation questions presented were, in reality, transformations on the original question, namely *what is the explanation for this event?* Thus, that question can be transformed in at least 63 ways, 24 of which were discussed. There is no need to list the EQs again here, so just to give the flavor of what I mean, here are four of them, presented as QTs:

QT30: To explain an event, change the initial question about why someone did something into a question about the goal priorities of the actor in the event.

QT31: To explain an event, find out the reasoning of the person or institution who control the actor in general in events of this type.

QT32: To explain an event, ask about the groups that the actor of the event is a member of, to see if members of the group might frequently participate in this type of event.

QT33: To explain an event, change the question into one that inquires about the beneficial results of the event for the actor.

So far, we can see that QTs are of basically two types. The first type looks like a police detective's handbook about where to search for the perpetrator of a crime. In the end, there continues to be an emphasis, seen in earlier chapters, on the beliefs, goals, and plans that underlie an action, together with advice on how to work backwards by looking at the results of an action. Put in this way, one can see that, in essence, an event has a large structure behind it, and explaining that event means, in reality, filling in the aspects of that structure that one does not already understand. Thus, what we have are heuristics pertaining to where one might find the pieces of information that we seek that would serve to complete the whole picture.

The second type of QT causes one to consider an entirely new question in place of the old that may shed light, by a kind of analogy between them, on the original question. This is especially true of QTs that have to do with tweaking. Tweaking rules are also, of course, question-transformation rules. Thus, we have, for example:

QTG34: To find the answer to a question, relax the set membership constraints and pose a different question.

QTG35: To find a pattern that might apply, ask, if the actor could not have done the action, whether some other actor could have done it.

QTG36: If a rule applies, ask if its opposite also applies.

Of course, there is not a great deal to be learned from listing all the QT rules that one can think of. Many other QT rules like those presented above, must exist. There are numerous detailed rules that people use in their day to day search for information. Many of them have the flavor of advice that one might give to a child about how to think properly. And that, of course, is precisely the point. How could a computer have any intelligence at all without such heuristics? If they are the type of rules that one must *give* to a child, then one must also give those rules to a machine. Helpful hints as to where to search, and how to search, for information are part of what students, librarians, detectives, lawyers, and so on learn in their normal training.

People learn to ask questions in both of the ways that we normally associate with the word *learning.* That is, people learn QTs by *being told them,* and by *discovery.* To get a computer to know these rules, the necessity of which by this time ought to be clear enough, one must both *spoon feed* them to a machine and give the machine *techniques by which it can discover new rules,* and new information, for itself.

Many of these rules concern *folk wisdom* that people have but that, again, *intelligent* machines must have as well. A great many proverbs, for example, package exactly that kind of wisdom into cute phrases intended to help people ask the right question at the right time. Is this just *stuff your grandmother knew?* Of course, it is. But your grandmother had a great deal of knowledge that a computer does not have. And, scientists who study mental processes do not necessarily understand all that well exactly what it is that your grandmother knew or how that knowledge was used. If AI is to be the subject of the process of control of *grandmother knowledge* then so be it. *Grandmother knowledge* is a lot harder than one might think. And, from the point of view of knowing where to look for an explanation, *grandmother knowledge* is probably critical. Perhaps the rules for creative thought are also bound up in *grandmother knowledge* as well. If that is the case, it may not interest linguists and philosophers to compile such knowledge, but it will certainly interest researchers who want to make intelligent machines and it will certainly interest psychologists who want to know the rules from which intelligent behavior is derived.

CONCLUSION

An explanation is considered to be, in common parlance, a set of words that one person can say to another that make something that is incomprehensible in some way into something that is comprehensible. But, we have seen that an explanation is more like a knowledge structure that is in common, everyday use. That is, the role of a knowledge structure such as a script, plan, or MOP, is to find a place for a new input that allows that input to be interpreted by, or made comprehensible by, a set of previously digested events that surround it. Viewed in this way, explanation can be seen to be much the same process as ordinary understanding. A new input is matched to some previously processed inputs and is interpreted by those inputs in either case. The difference is that, in ordinary understanding, our mental processes are not as transparent to us as they are when we are explaining something to ourselves or are having something explained to us.

The process of explanation entails the realization that a ready-made knowledge structure is not available and some extraordinary work will have to be done. It is not interesting to consider what happens when someone else provides an explanation for you. Rather, the interesting case is the one in which we find ourselves capable of initially failing to comprehend something and then being able to construct what we consider to be a fairly plausible explanation that at least momentarily leaves us believing that we have now understood what was at first incomprehensible. In a sense, being told an answer can often be a waste of time. The process of constructing an explanation forces learning to occur by causing certain questions to be generated that may continue to be asked for a long time after an initial answer is supplied. Knowing *the* one and only answer can tend to kill that process.

Thus, to understand the process of learning and understanding the question to ask is how we construct explanations. At first glance it seemed that the process of explanation construction was likely to be very complicated. After all, explanations of incomprehensible events can often be very creative and rather original. Surely such original behavior must be fairly complex. But, why should it be more complicated than understanding itself? The view of understanding we have, recall, is that it is necessary, in order to understand, to access a relevant memory structure and then apply it to the current situation. The complexity in that process is primarily in the accessing of the right structure. The problem is to determine what features and aspects of the current situation are indicative of the correct knowledge structure to access. Cues ranging from utensils that are unique to a given action (consider, for example, the title of a paper by Charniak, 1977, *With fork in hand this must be the eating frame*), to complex juxtapositions of competing goals, can help isolate the right knowledge structure. The issue in understanding is indexing. We must be able to abstract the cues from the situation that we are processing and use those cues to access a knowledge structure that we have previously stored away using those cues.

In order to understand therefore, we must know how to index and how to analyze new situations in terms of those indices. But what about explanation? What must we do in order to explain? Precisely the same process is involved.

Explanation means finding a relevant knowledge structure and utilizing it to help interpret the new input. How then is it different than the process of understanding in general? The difference is rather simple. During understanding, when a knowledge structure is accessed, there is a *right* answer. That is, there exists a best possible fit in terms of an appropriate knowledge structure. When riding a bus, one should access the *riding the bus script* and no other. Any other script would be wrong to use. If one doesn't have a bus script, then maybe a train script will help, but in that case, the train script is a kind of hypothesis in that it is saying, in effect, maybe busses are enough like trains that we can adapt information from one domain into the other. The idea that old explanations can be hypotheses for new situations begins the process of explanation. And, as we have seen, the idea that old explanations can be adapted for new uses, begins the process of creativity.

In other words, **explaining something means trying to get a knowledge structure that isn't quite appropriate to be of use.** In relatively straightforward situations, this means attempting to adapt a previous knowledge structure that seems only somewhat relevant to the current situation so that it will help in processing the current situation. Previously I have discussed this phenomenon, namely reminding. Reminding occurs when what is subconscious becomes conscious. In this situation, that is, when no applicable knowledge structure exists and a next best fit must be tried, reminding occurs when the next best fit isn't really that close. The reason this phenomenon occurs in this case is obvious. If a new structure is going to be adapted to a different situation, it may be that it is inappropriate. The possibility that it might be inappropriate is large enough so that it is important that the mind view this choice consciously. Put another way, reminding causes candidate knowledge structures to be brought into conscious processing when the likelihood exists that the candidate structure is inappropriate.

Viewed this way, it can be seen that explanation is just a much more conscious process wherein one attempts to go through candidates one by one so as to determine their relevance. The claim then is this: there is a continuum between understanding, reminding, and explanation. Explanation means taking a possibly entirely inappropriate knowledge structure and adapting it to serve in the current situation. Explanation then, can be seen to be only more difficult than normal understanding in the following sense: **explanation requires having a procedure whereby candidate knowledge structures can be brought to mind and manipulated so as to see if they will help in the current situation.**

Explanations aren't original really. What is original is the use of an inappropriate knowledge structure in a new situation and the adaptation of that structure such that it will work in the new situation. It is the search for, and the acceptance or rejection of, structures in novel situations that is the difficult part of explanation.

What structures are there then that are peculiar to explanation itself? It would be reasonable to assume that explanations would operate with no structures that are peculiar to them alone. Rather, since explanations are based upon previously used knowledge structures, they should, in principle, require no special structures of their own. But this is not exactly the case. Why not? In principle it is possible to adapt any old structure for a new purpose, but when understanding fails, when we have no usable structure to help us understand, we must resort to adapting some other structure. Since this kind of thing happens all the time, there should exist some structures whose job it is to be used in precisely these situations. That is, since understanding fails frequently, one would expect that some standard methods to deal with such failures would exist.

There exist a standard set of tried and true knowledge structures that have evolved in an individual's knowledge base for precisely this situation. These structures are useful for understanding ordinary events as well as being useful for adaptation for use in difficult to understand situations. Work on establishing just what such explanation patterns are like, how they are learned in the first place, how they are called to mind when needed, how they are indexed and retrieved, and how they are modified to create new explanation patterns, is critical if AI is to ever become a reality. Solving all these problems is critical if computers are ever to be creative, and as I have said, computers that are not creative, computers that do not have access to their own mental processes, computers that do not wonder and pose questions to themselves while wondering, will never be even close to intelligent.

In Chapter 1, we made a distinction between three types of understanding, which we termed **Making Sense, Cognitive Understanding,** and **Complete Empathy.** We claimed that it was possible, now, to enable programs to make sense of what they read. But, for a computer to be able to understand at the intermediate level of Cognitive Understanding, we claimed that computers must be able to explain what they have read, and also, to explain what they have done in any given case, beyond the level of *I did it because you told me to.* In this book, I have tried to make clear what it would mean for a computer, or a person, to explain something. And, we have seen that explanation is really at the heart of learning. Moreover, we have seen that creativity, that mystical process known only to humans, is not really so mystical after all, and that it may well be possible to replicate creative behavior on a machine by transforming standard explanation patterns. From this it follows that the processes of creativity and learning are not so elusive, and may be quite algorithmic in nature after all.

In this chapter, in an attempt to put together what we have been discussing, I have added a slightly different twist to the situation. I am claiming that the ability to question is at the heart of our comprehension processes, explanation included, of course. And, my point is that the ability to question is learned, over time, by the copying or invention of question-transformation rules. In other words, I am claiming that learning and understanding are processes based in the correct application of numerous heuristics, rather than in the mathematics of universal principles that determine the nature of the mind. To build a mind, one must build in numerous heuristics, and processes that control those heuristics. To build comprehension into a machine, one must build in heuristics for the creation of questions, for the answering of those questions internally (introspection) and externally (by looking at a text, for example). Intelligence is, among other things, a function of having heuristics for questioning and heuristics for explanation. Creativity represents more heuristics still, which operate upon the results of the others. It is as simple, and as complex, as that.

Appendix:
SWALE, A Program that Explains

Alex Kass, David Leake, and Christopher Owens

INTRODUCTION

The preceding chapters outlined a theory of explanation-based understanding. An important step in the development of any AI theory is the development of computer programs, because writing programs tests the theory and forces the researcher to confront crucial details that are otherwise all too easy to gloss over. This appendix describes the initial stages of an attempt we are making to build an explanation-based understanding program along the lines outlined in this book.

SWALE is a program that produces novel explanations by retrieving old explanations and modifying them to fit new situations. Thus SWALE is both an understanding program and a learning program. Its actions are driven by the goal of discovering an explanation that will help it understand an anomalous event, and in doing so it learns new explanations, and stores them for future use.

The philosophy behind the system follows the general framework that has been outlined in the previous chapters. Of course, the theory covers more ground than we have covered in our programming efforts. For example, we have not had time to do anything with the problem of forming Explanation Questions, as described in chapter four. On the other hand, the details of several processes, such as explanation verification, XP search and XP tweaking strategies were not discussed in the book but have been attacked by the programming effort. The general algorithm employed by the SWALE program is as follows:

1 **ANOMALY DETECTION (Described in Chapter 2)**
Attempt to fit story into memory.
If successful DONE; otherwise an anomaly has been detected.

2 **XP SEARCH (Partially described in Chapter 5)**
Search for an XP that can be applied to explain the anomaly.

3 **XP ACCEPTING**
Attempt to apply XPs.
If successful then skip to step 5.

4 **XP TWEAKING (Generally introduced in Chapter 6)**
If unable to apply XPs directly then attempt to tweak them into XPs that might apply better.
If successful send these tweaked XPs back to step 3.

5 **XP INTEGRATION AND GENERALIZATION**
If any results accepted, integrate results back into memory making appropriate generalizations.

The steps of the above algorithm have been broken (somewhat arbitrarily) into an overarching control program and two sub-modules. The main program, which we call the **XP ACCEPTER** was written by David Leake and is directly responsible for steps 1, 3 and 5. The **XP SEARCH** (step 2) and corresponding indexing of XPs described later, is handled by a separate module, written by Christopher Owens, and the **XP TWEAKER** (step 4) was written by Alex Kass. The basic communication between modules is summarized by the diagram on page 234.

In this appendix we walk through a few explanations that SWALE produces and discuss how each step of the algorithm is actually implemented in the SWALE program. The idea is to show what some of the ideas presented in the preceding chapters (like XPs) actually look like in practice and how a program that works with XPs can work.

OVERVIEW

We begin by describing some sample input and output from SWALE. At the end of this appendix is a detailed trace of the SWALE program producing some of the explanations below.

The Episode

Swale, a successful 3-year old race horse, was found dead in his stall a week after winning the Belmont Stakes race.

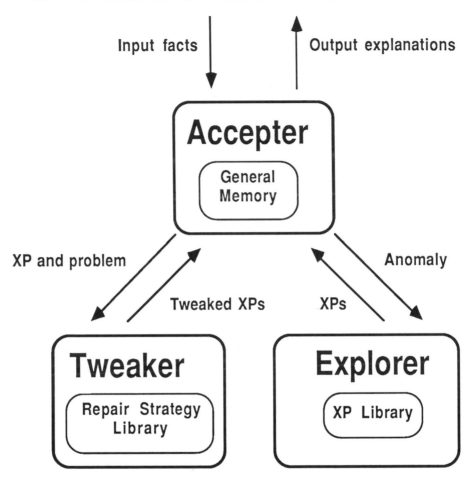

The Explanations

What follows is a list of the explanations that SWALE comes up with.

The Jim Fixx Reminding Explanation:

Swale had a congenital heart defect. The exertion of running in horse races strained his heart and brought out the latent defect. He had a heart attack and died.

The Drug Overdose Explanation:

Swale's owner was giving him drugs to improve his performance. He accidentally gave him an overdose, which killed him.

THE STUD FARM TRILOGY

As is described later, SWALE's processing brings it to consider the idea that thinking about sex too much caused Swale's demise. It then attempts to imagine ways in which this might have occurred and develops the three explanations that follow:

The Sexual Excitement Explanation:

Swale was thinking about his future life on a stud farm. Since he was an excitable creature, thinking about the prospects proved to be too much strain for his heart. He had a heart attack and died.

The Hit-By-A-Bus Explanation:

Swale was thinking about his future life on a stud farm. Being preoccupied with visions of the delightful prospects, he absent-mindedly wandered out into the street and was struck by a bus.

The Despondent Suicide Explanation:

Swale was thinking about his forced chastity during his racing career. He became despondent and killed himself.

The XPs

Following is a summary description of several XPs that SWALE uses in constructing the explanations above.

The Jim Fixx XP <episode-based>:

Joggers jog a lot.

Jogging results in physical exhaustion because jogging is a kind of exertion and exertion results in exhaustion.

Physical exhaustion coupled with a heart defect can cause a heart attack.

A heart attack can cause death.

The Janis Joplin XP <episode-based>:

Being a star performer can result in stress because it is lonely at the top.

Being stressed-out can result in a need to escape and relax.

Needing to escape and relax can result in taking recreational drugs.

Taking recreational drugs can result in an overdose.

A drug overdose can result in death.

The Too-Much-Sex XP <folklore-based>:

Having too much sex can kill you.

The Preoccupation XP <basic causal pattern>:

Being preoccupied about something can cause you to be inattentive.

Being inattentive can result in walking into traffic.

Walking into traffic can result in you being hit by a vehicle.

Being hit by a vehicle can cause death.

The Despondent Suicide XP <basic causal pattern>:

Thinking about something you want but that you don't have can make you despondent.

Being despondent can result in suicide.

THE EXPLANATION PROCESS

1. Detecting Anomalies

When SWALE reads a story, it tries to connect each input to its existing knowledge; a fact is anomalous if it cannot be integrated into memory. There are two ways the program connects input facts to memory. First, it tries to fit each input fact into a relevant memory structure. When later input gives additional information about a fact, the program uses the information to guide placement of the fact in a more specific structure. For example, suppose a racehorse wins an important race. Then the memory token for the horse, which was originally of type *racehorse,* is specified to type *successful racehorse.* (Lytinen, 1984) Storing the token under this type gives access to additional knowledge: *Successful racehorse* carries with it expectations about the horse's high monetary value, excellent physical condition, etc. This knowledge is used to evaluate the reasonableness of later inputs. Once we know that Swale has won an important race, it would be surprising to read that his physical condition is actually poor, and the program would recognize this as anomalous.

The second way of connecting input facts is by linking them with higher-level expectations, such as those which arise from MOPs (Schank, 1982) and from knowledge of actors' current plans, goals, and role themes (Schank & Abelson, 1977). For example, we expect racehorses to race. The program accepts Swale's Belmont win by relating it to the MOP M-race-horse-life, as shown in the following output fragment:

Input: Swale won the Belmont Stakes.
      Represented as:
      [HORSE–RACE
           ACTOR– SWALE
           LOCATION– BELMONT
           TIME– TIME–TOK–131
           OUTCOME– WIN]

Program output:

Integrating SWALE's HORSE–RACE into memory

Trying to link SWALE's HORSE–RACE to SWALE's active scripts.

The fact SWALE's HORSE–RACE will be stored as the HORSE–RACE line in SWALE's RACE–HORSE–LIFE

When the program reads that Swale died, it realizes that his death is premature, since the M-racehorse-life says that a racehorse's death takes place years after his racing career. The program detects the anomaly as follows:

Input: Swale died a week later.
      Represented as:
      [DEATH
           ACTOR– SWALE
           TIME– TIME–TOK-189]
      ; TIME–TOK-189 represents a time occurring within a few weeks
      ; of TIME-TOK-131 above.

The program's output is:

Integrating SWALE's DEATH into memory

Trying to link SWALE's DEATH to SWALE's active scripts.

The fact SWALE's DEATH will be stored as the DEATH line in SWALE's RACE–HORSE–LIFE

Temporal anomaly detected:
      SWALE'S DEATH occurs abnormally early in RACE–HORSE–LIFE

When the program detects an anomaly, it needs to find an XP which can explain how the surprising event is actually reasonable.

2. Finding an XP

The purpose of the Exploratory Searcher is to find candidate Explanation Patterns that might be applicable to an episode. The Exploratory Searcher is quite loose in its idea of what might be applicable; it proposes Explanation Patterns that might or might not be useful and leaves the acceptance decision up to the Accepter and the Tweaker.

Currently, the program tries to find XPs at three levels: **Routine Search, Unusual Features Search** and **Folkloric Explanation.** These levels are presented in order of their specific applicability to the episode being explained.

Routine Search uncovers XPs that are closely indexed to the type of episode being explained. This method of search depends only on the general category of event being explained and not on the specific features of that event. Given a death, for example, Routine Search returns such obvious candidates as Old Age or Sickness. The types of explanation pattern returned by Routine Search are applicable as explanations of non-anomalous, stereotypical events.

If Routine Search fails to come up with a useful explanation pattern, the program must look for some kind of "near miss"—an explanation pattern that, although not directly applicable to the input, is a likely candidate for tweaking. Central to this kind of search is the notion that any explanatory knowledge structure sharing a reasonable number of features with the episode being explained is likely to be useful in constructing an explanation. So, the task can be defined as: Choose some features of the episode that are likely to be useful indices to XPs, and then find the XPs indexed under those selected features.

One XP-finding heuristic is Unusual Features Search, based on the Coordination of Anomalies explanation method discussed earlier in the book. The point of this heuristic is to capture our intuition that people, in constructing an explanation of an event, are likely to consider unusual features of the event before ordinary features. Unusual Features Search requires selecting features of the episode based on how unusual they are relative to normative episodes of the same type, without regard to how likely it is that each of those features will ultimately participate in an explanation of the episode. Features selected because they are unusual are merely to be used as indices to find XPs.

Swale, the central character in the death episode, is compared against normative instances of categories in which he might be a member. Swale, compared with other racehorses, for example, is highly successful and young. The program indexes into its XP memory with "death of the successful young" and finds the Janis Joplin XP. Similarly, racehorses, as compared with other horses, are typically in excellent physical condition.

Indexed under the death of someone in excellent physical condition is the Jim Fixx episode and its associated explanation pattern. XPs such as these can then be examined and possibly tweaked to fit the current episode.

What the program is doing is comparing Swale against generalizations of Swale. But, this search cannot be completely general or it will provide too many answers. We can't compare Swale against all generalizations of Swale, since any reasonable memory would show Swale as belonging to many groups. In addition to Swale belonging to classes against whose normative instances a comparison would be useful, Swale belongs to other classes as well. Swale is a furry-thing, for example. Or a resident of Kentucky. Or a large object. Some of these are realistic categories and some are not. How do we pick a path through the memory net to focus comparisons? We can't depend on memory to provide everything we want via an ISA-type hierarchy. That is just not realistic.

The program overcomes this problem by letting the type of event we are trying to explain focus this search. We are trying to explain a death here, and it makes sense only to use generalizations of Swale that can also fill the Actor slot of Death. The Actor slot of Death is typically filled by a Living Thing. In other words, use concepts that are generalizations of Swale but specializations of Living Thing. This constrains search to a great degree. Here the Exploratory Searcher finds the Jim Fixx XP:

Looking for explanations of SWALE's DEATH
Considering SWALE's DEATH as an instance of a generalized DEATH.

SWALE's NAME is SWALE, while
      a generalized SUCCESSFUL–RACE–HORSE's NAME is
      UNKNOWN.
           Nothing found connecting (NAME SWALE)
           with DEATH

a generalized SUCCESSFUL–RACE–HORSE's HEALTH is HIGH,
      while a generalized RACE–HORSE's HEALTH is UNKNOWN.
           Nothing found connecting (HEALTH HIGH)
           with DEATH

a generalized SUCCESSFUL–RACE–HORSE's PHYSICAL–
      CONDITION is HIGH, while a generalized RACE–HORSE's
      PHYSICAL–CONDITION is UNKNOWN.
           found JIM–FIXX–XP-263 indexed under DEATH
           with index: (PHYSICAL–CONDITION HIGH)

After Unusual Features Search, the program tries Folkloric XP Search. Again, these explanations are not guaranteed to be believable. As currently implemented, Folkloric Explanation returns a list of XPs indexed solely by the type of event being explained. Death, for example, returns the Death-From-Too-Much-Sex XP.

These XP-finding strategies must obviously bear some close relationship to the means by which XPs were originally indexed in memory. Given that we have strategies for selecting features of an episode to use as indices for finding XPs, we must have corresponding strategies to index XPs under the features that will later be used for retrieval. These strategies will be discussed at the end of this chapter.

An important variant of Unusual Features Search depends upon trying to see the event being explained in a different light. What if, for example, we tried to consider Swale's death not as a death but as the destruction of a piece of property. Now we consider the normative slot filler of the destruction of a piece of property (which is a physical possession). Comparing Swale against generalizations of Swale that are also specializations of Physical Property, we see that an unusual feature of Swale is his high monetary value. Indexed under Destruction with High Monetary Value we find Insurance-Fraud, an XP that we can return to the Accepter. Starting the search with the top-level notion of a property-destruction rather than a death will result in a different set of features being selected, and a correspondingly different set of XPs being found.

3. Deciding When an XP fits

Once an XP has been found, the Accepter must check it to see if it applies to the current anomaly. The Accepter verifies an XP by seeing if it can believe the *Applicability Checks* packaged in the XP. Each check becomes a question to memory to verify a certain condition. Some of the necessary information can be obtained using the abstraction hierarchy. This is primarily useful for answering questions like "what was Swale's physical condition?" Since Swale was a successful racehorse, we know that it was probably excellent.

As we try to apply XPs, we are often interested in attributes which can't be verified in such a straightforward way. Questions like "could Swale be a jogger?" or "was Swale having a lot of sex?" cannot be answered merely by looking in a particular slot. In order to deal with the range of possible questions, the Accepter has four basic strategies for finding information:

property inheritance

normative-filler information

basic-action decomposition

direct indexing from sets of concepts

Property inheritance

The program's memory is organized in an abstraction net. For example, abstractions of Swale include successful-racehorse (which has abstractions race-horse, horse, living-thing, etc.) and possession. Each abstraction on the hierarchy can provide default attributes for its fillers. For example, a successful-race-horse is assumed to be in good physical condition. When the value of a slot-filler must be determined, the Accepter moves up the abstraction net until it finds a filler for the current slot.

Normative-filler information

Each node in SWALE's memory has information on the normative fillers of its slots. Jogging, for example, usually has a human actor, although we can imagine that a monkey could be trained to jog. Given a hypothesized action, the normative-filler information is a rapid filter on whether it is likely. (The knowledge that horses aren't joggers is why the Jim Fixx XP is initially rejected as an explanation of Swale's death).

Basic-action decomposition

As we observed about jogging, an unusual role-filler doesn't preclude an action or state from occurring. In order to analyse whether an unusual action is possible, the Accepter decomposes it into its constituents, and locates the ones where problems arise. In a MOP, it looks at the individual scenes. For example, we might want to know if Swale could be actor in the MOP M-do-recreational-drugs. M-do-recreational-drugs is decomposable into scenes like buying drugs and administering them. Since Swale doesn't have hands, it would be impossible for him to grasp the drugs to administer them. Thus Swale is ruled out as a possible actor.

Direct indexing from sets of concepts

The strategies described above involve using information that is accessible via a straightforward path from a given concept. To see whether the folk explanation "too much sex will kill you" could apply to Swale, we need to know if he was having too much sex, but here the above strategies fail. We need to be able to ask "what do you know about horses and sex?" and locate a node in memory. It is clear that people can do this easily: To someone familiar with horse racing, a question like "what do you know about horses and sex?" is answered immediately with "horses go to the stud farm at the end of their careers."

One of the program's strategies for verifying facts is intended to study the use of information indexed by concept sets. In SWALE, memory nodes can be indexed by sets of concepts. The immediate issue which arises from using this type of indexing is how, given a question and a concept related to it in some way, can you extract useful information? Once this has been studied further, we will try to analyse what must be the process which underlies retrieval of an item in memory related to a set of indices.

When dealing with the folk XP, the Accepter first tries to use property inheritance to see if Swale is having a lot of sex. When this fails, it gives the indexer "race-horse" and "sex," which pulls up the MOP M-stud-farm. To use this, the Accepter connects it both to Swale (as an expected event in his future) and to sex (the main action in M-stud-farm), to see that it can support that Swale was having a lot of sex. Although sex is a component of the stud farm, that doesn't explain Swale having a lot of sex now, so the Accepter fails to believe the folk XP.

4. Tweaking XPs to Make them Fit

When the Accepter rejects an XP as a near miss it passes the XP, along with the reason for rejection, to the Tweaker. The goal of the tweaker is to generate a new XP (or set of XPs) that might fit better. The tweaker is more of a synthesizer than an analyzer; its job is to come up with new hypotheses (which might prove to be directly useful, totally useless, or candidates for further tweaking). It is left until later for the Accepter to pass judgements on how reasonable the hypotheses are; the Tweaker is designed to come up with good ideas, not to avoid bad ones.

The high level control structure of the tweaker is very simple. There are only two steps:

4.1 Retrieve appropriate **XP-REPAIR-STRATEGIES,** from a library of such strategies maintained by the tweaker. Each strategy is a program designed to map an XP that suffers from some problem to a set of modified XPs that don't suffer from the problem.

4.2 Apply each retrieved strategy in turn collecting and returning any resulting XPs. Of course, the details of what goes on during this phase of processing are completely determined by the nature of the **XP-REPAIR-STRATEGY.**

This process is modeled loosely on the process used in Hammond's CHEF program (Hammond, 1984), to repair plan failures. Where CHEF uses goal-failure configurations to index plan-repair strategies, SWALE uses **XP-FAILURE-TYPES** to index **XP-REPAIR-STRATEGIES.** Beyond this level, the issues involved diverge since explanations are different from plans; they go wrong for different reasons and require different sorts of repair. However, the idea of using failure characterization to index repair programs traces back to this work.

Retrieval of an appropriate set of **XP-REPAIR-STRATEGIES** relies on using the **XP-FAILURE-TYPE,** developed during step 3, as an index into the **REPAIR-STRATEGY** library. In future implementations, aspects of the XP to be repaired might be used as an index as well, but currently the program only uses the **XP-FAILURE-TYPE.** Each **REPAIR-STRATEGY** is stored in the library along with a failure-type pattern. Step 4.1 essentially involves matching the **XP-FAILURE-TYPES** created in step 3 against these patterns and collecting the strategies associated with patterns that successfully match. These are the strategies that will be applied in step 4.2 Some of the actual **XP-FAILURE-TYPES** generated in the current version of the program are as follows:

```
; A routine explanation for animal death is that it was run over
; by a car. When the program attempts to apply this explana-
; tion to Swale's death it returns the following failure, indicating
; that the XP failed because it called for a small animal and was
; being applied to the death of a large one.
[XP-FAILURE
        PROBLEM - DESCRIPTION - [ATTRIBUTE - VALUE -
        CONTRADICTED
            ATTRIBUTE- SIZE
            BELIEVED-VALUE- LARGE]
        BELIEF-LABEL- SMALL-ANIMAL]
```

```
; When attempting to apply the Jim Fixx explanation the sys-
; tem returns this failure description:
```

```
; The XP failed because the jog belief called for a human actor
; but got something that didn't fit that description
[XP-FAILURE
TYPE-INAPPLICABLE-THEME
PROBLEM-DESCRIPTION-[TYPE-MISMATCH
        DESIRED-ATTRIBUTE-#(TYPE-NODE 140—HUMAN)]
        BELIEF-LABEL- JOG]
```

```
; This next failure indicates why the explanation that Swale
; died from having too much sex failed.
```

```
; An action that the XP expected to occur at a certain time wasn't
; actually scheduled to occur until much later. (Swale was an
; active racehorse and racehorses don't have sex until they retire.)
[XP-FAILURE
        TYPE-INAPPLICABLE-THEME
        BELIEF-LABEL-SEX
        PROBLEM - DESCRIPTION - [SCRIPT - SCHEDULING
                                        - FAULT
```

```
POSITIONING-PROBLEM-[ACTION-TOO-EARLY]
    SCRIPT-NAME- RACE-HORSE-LIFE
    LAST-SUCCESSFULLY-PROCESSED-LINE- 4
    MATCHING-LINE- 3]]
```

; In response to the idea that Swale died from thinking about
; sex too much, a different sort of failure is reported. No
; particular belief failed but the connecting links supporting a
; particular belief were found to be unconvincing.

```
[XP-FAILURE
  TYPE- UNCONVINCED-OF-ACTION
  BELIEF-LABEL- DEATH
  PROBLEM-DESCRIPTION- [UNCONVINCING-SUPPORT]]
```

In order to do their jobs, most **XP-REPAIR-STRATEGIES** have to make a lot of use of the internal structure of an XP. If XPs were only used for straightforward explanations, in which they applied directly, their internal structure could be quite simple. All that would be needed would be the set of indices required to retrieve the XP and the features that need to be present for the XP to apply. When doing straightforward explanation the relationships between the features in an XP is of no interest.

But if the XP is going to be modifiable, if it's going to serve as a starting point for the creation of new, original XPs that the system makes up, then the representation of the relationships between the elements of the XP becomes a much more crucial issue. The question is this: When a belief in an XP fails to hold, how can the XP be patched up? Can the belief be generalized, deleted, replaced? What are the constraints on a suitable replacement? If a system is to answer these questions it must know why the belief was important in the original XP and how it supports and is supported by the other beliefs in the XP.

The Structure of an XP

An XP is a fossilized explanation schema, much the way scripts are fossilized plan schemas. XPs are variablized, so that the application of an XP simply involves binding the variables to produce an instantiated explanation.

The design of XPs takes into account several operations in which they take part. The Accepter wants to be able to make a quick and easy decision about whether a standard explanation can be directly applied. Therefore, the XP contains a section called **Applicability Checks.** If an XPs applicability checks are passed then the Accepter applies the XP without any more involved investigation.

When some of the **Applicability Checks** fail the Accepter must decide whether the XP should be completely disregarded or if it is a good candidate for Tweaking. For this reason, the XP also has a **Relevance Checks** section. These are used by the Accepter to determine how relevant the XP is likely to be. The more of these that match the more likely it is to be relevant enough to make Tweaking worthwhile. The amount of matching that the Accepter will require will depend on what its goals are.

The remaining beliefs that form the explanation are not normally examined by the Accepter. However, they are needed to complete the explanation. They are called the **Internals.** The **Internals** are used by the system when it needs to present its explanation to the user and when it needs to Tweak the explanation. These beliefs are also adopted by the system when it decides to adopt the explanation.

The vocabulary used in the belief sections of XPs is not surprising; it follows along the same lines as most schemes that have been proposed for representing facts (such as Conceptual Dependency theory). Current XPs include the following belief types:

ACTION–DESCRIPTION: The belief that some action was performed. Specifies the usual information, such as the actor, action and object. Example: Mary hit John.

THEME–DESCRIPTION: Like an action description but describes a belief in a regularly repeated action. Example: Jim Fixx had the Jogging theme.

STATE–DESCRIPTION: Describes some state that was believed to be true. Example: Janis Joplin owned some drugs.

VALUE–DESCRIPTION: Describes the value of some attribute for an Actor. Swale's success value was high.

PACKAGING–DESCRIPTION: Describes some class that an object belongs to, and therefore inherits inferences from. Examples: Racehorses are horses and also athletes.

GOAL-DESCRIPTION: A goal that an actor has. Example: Racehorse owners have the goal of having their horses win races.

A final section of the XP is called the **Belief Support Network.** This section describes the belief support relationships between the beliefs in the first three sections. The **Belief Support Network** tells why adopting some of the beliefs in the XP leads the system to adopt other beliefs.

A belief-support node in the XP's network contains pointers to the supporting belief (or beliefs if it is a conjunctive node) and to the supported belief. It also contains an indication of the type of support involved and a pointer to the general knowledge that licenses the inference. The type of general knowledge pointed to depends on the type of belief support that the support node represents. For example, if an explainer believes that John is taking part in the restaurant script then it will also believe that he will pay the bill. This would be represented in the XP as a **Scriptal** support node. The supporting belief is that John was performing the restaurant script and the supported was that he payed the bill. The general knowledge would be a pointer to the restaurant script in memory along with the line number of the bill-paying scene. As another example, if the explainer believes that Jill lifts weights regularly it will also believe that she has big muscles. In this case the type of support will be **Physical-Causation** and general knowledge will be a pointer to the causal rule in memory which indicates that heavy exercise builds muscles.

Some of the belief-support types employed by the system are listed below:

Physical-Causation	Example: Drug overdose leads to death.
Emotional-Causation	Example: People get stressed out when they're pushing themselves very hard.
Social-Causation	Matters of law or custom. Example: Rock stars have drug addict friends.
Economic-Causation	Example: Owners want their horses to win so they'll make money.
Scriptal	Example: Restaurant-goers eat a meal.
Specification	Examples: people who are both performers and successful are stars (and therefore, it is valid to make star-related inferences about them).
P-Goal-Activation:	Example: When people get stressed out they attempt to bring their stress level back to normal.
A-Goal-Satisfaction:	Example: Politicians want to get elected.

XP-Repair-Strategies

The ideas behind **XP-REPAIR-STRATEGIES** can be best explained by discussing actual examples: Four of the strategies currently residing in the program's library are as follows:

Abandon Belief

This is the simplest strategy. Sometimes a belief in an XP is not strictly needed. It may be that the XP has more than enough support for its conclusion, and that parts of the XP can therefore be pruned away without making the XP unconvincing. This strategy eliminates the problematic belief and puts in question all other beliefs in the XP that depend on it. Depending on queries to the **Accepter,** it may abandon these as well. This strategy gets used a lot modifying the Joplin XP to fit Swale because many of the beliefs aren't relevant, although there is a core that is.

Substitute Alternate Theme

This strategy is useful when the failed belief is a theme (a script that the XP posits that the actor engaged in regularly), which was rejected because the actor in the current scenario was somehow unsuitable. The notion here is to find out which line (or lines) in the inappropriate theme was actually important in the XP (ie. which one supports other beliefs in the XP), and to search for another theme. The new theme must be one that *is* appropriate for the current actor, and one which has the necessary lines in it. In other words, the XP carries within it the knowledge of why a particular belief is important to the XP, and this strategy uses this information to find another theme that can fit in in an analogous way. Some sample output from this **REPAIR-STRATEGY,** substituting horse racing for jogging, is included at the end of this section.

Substitute Anticipation

This is a more specialized repair strategy than those mentioned above. It is applied when the problem is one of event scheduling. This strategy gets invoked when the XP has failed because it called for an action to be performed at a time earlier than when it was actually scheduled to occur. When this happens it is reasonable to entertain the notion that thinking about the future event might play a role in the explanation. Thus this strategy substitutes the belief that the actor was thinking about the event for the belief that the event actually occurred. An example of when this strategy gets used is when it is realized that the explanation that Swale was having too much sex cannot be right because he was too young for the stud farm. The strategy substitutes the idea that Swale was thinking about sex too much.

Find Connecting XP

Sometimes, an XP is unconvincing to the Accepter, not because any single belief is unacceptable, but because the connections between some beliefs are unconvincing. For example, if I said that perhaps Swale died because the moon was full, you might reject that explanation, not because you disbelieve Swale's death or the fullness of the moon, but because you don't see the connection. This strategy attempts to repair such a problem by finding another XP that will connect the two beliefs in question. It works by calling the **XP SEARCHER.** If no XP can be found to connect the beliefs directly it will try a limited amount of causal chaining. After each chaining step it will call itself recursively, using the newly inferred belief. This is used to find connections between thinking about sex and death.

Below is a trace of one of the strategies in action to give a more concrete feel for how the system works:

Attempting to apply a modification strategy:
'Substitute another theme which is more appropriate for the actor'
to XP: FIXX–XP

The faulty theme: [THEME
                ACTOR– SWALE
                SCRIPT– $JOG
                ROLE– ACTOR]

The belief labeled JOG is a support in the following way(s):

It supports the belief—RUN: [ACTION–DESCRIPTION
                ACTOR– SWALE
                ACTION– MOVE–BODY–PART
                    PART– FEET
                    SPEED–FAST]

via support type SCRIPT–LINE.

Asking memory for other life-themes for SWALE

Associated themes:

SWALE often has the ACTOR role in the HORSE–RACE theme.

SWALE often has the ACTOR role in the EAT-OATS theme.

Seeing whether any of these themes can substitute . . .

Trying to establish alternate support link.
Support type is SCRIPT–LINE, script name is HORSE-RACE.

Trying to find a line in the script that matches the RUN belief.

Found a match: [ACTION–DESCRIPTION
                        ACTION–MOVE–BODY–PART
                            SPEED– FAST
                            PART– FEET]

; The HORSE–RACE theme produces a successful tweak! Now it
; goes on to try EAT–OATS

Trying to establish alternate support link.
Support type is SCRIPT-LINE, script name is EAT-OATS.
Trying to find a line in the script that matches the RUN belief.

Failed. This script is not appropriate.

; EAT–OATS doesn't provide support for the XP so only the HORSE–
; RACE theme is returned.

5. Integrating New Explanations into Memory

After the Tweaker produces a new XP and the Accepter accepts it, the explanation is installed in memory for future use. If possible, the old and new XPs will be generalized, and the generalization installed. SWALE tries to generalize a tweaked XP by looking at the applicability checks of the old and new XPs, and selecting new applicability checks (and corresponding conditions in the underlying belief-support chains) which subsume the original ones. The original Fixx XP has the applicability check that the deceased jog, while the tweaked XP requires that he race in horse races. For the new XP, we would like to find a generalization of these two themes.

Without a way to guide this generalization, a knowledge-rich system would have to choose between an enormous number of possible generalizations. But because the causal structure of the two explanations is known, the Accepter can apply a strong constraint on which generalizations to consider: any generalized condition must support the same causal chains as the conditions it subsumes. In the abstraction hierarchy, jogging and running in horse races both have the generalization of doing physical exertion, and doing physical exertion supports the same causal reasoning as the original conditions. Consequently, that generalization is the one selected, as opposed to generalizations like "the actor spends time at racetracks." The output from the generalization step follows:

Looking at possible generalization of original and tweaked XPs

Looking for generalization of $JOG and HORSE–RACE which
        will support the same causal chains.

The theme of actor in PHYSICAL–EXERTION accounts for all necessary facts

In order to apply the new XP, predictive features of the new XP must be chosen. From the checks in the new XP, which are based on the underlying causal structure of the explanation, the Accepter selects those which were observable in the current case. In the Fixx example, there was no reason initially to suspect that Swale had a heart defect, but it would have been trivial to confirm that he did physical exertion. Hence having a theme of physical exertion is selected as a predictive feature of the new XP, as shown in the following output.

Looking at XP prechecks to see which were observable

The precondition
        [THEME
                ROLE–ACTOR
                SCRIPT–PHYSICAL–EXERTION
                ACTOR–SWALE]
        was observable, and will be retained as a predictive feature.

Since the precondition

        [PACKAGING–DESCRIPTION
                OBJECT–[SLOT–DESCRIPTION
                                VIRTUAL–SLOT– HEART–OF]
                ROLE– HEART
                MOP– HEREDITARY–DEFECTIVE–HEART]

        is not observable in the current anomaly.
        It will not be retained as a predictive feature.

When a new XP is installed, it becomes a specification of the type of event which was first anomalous, with the predictive features used to determine when it is appropriate to specify to the class of events organized by the XP. Thus a subcategory of death, using the explanation to categorize the deaths of apparently healthy people, is created and installed as a specialization of the memory-node for DEATH.

    In addition to this straightforward indexing, XPs must also be indexed using feature selection strategies compatible with the search methods used by the Exploratory Searcher. Several classes of features can be used to provide indices for XPs. The most obvious category is to pick features of the original episode that participate in the causal explanation and use those for indexing. These are more important to the explanation process than features which are not included in the causal reasoning. The fact that Jim Fixx was a jogger, for example, is more important to an explanation of

Swale's death than the fact that he was an author, because being a jogger fits into the causal reasoning about his death. The explanation process never has to look at the fact that he was an author, because that knowledge is not part of the causal reasoning chain contained in the Jim Fixx XP.

The determination of feature salience is unique to the XP, and makes no claim about the episode itself in memory. There are conceivably other explanation patterns involving the death of Jim Fixx in which the fact that he was an author would be highly relevant. For example if an explainer were trying to come up with some pattern involving ironic deaths, it might compare Jim Fixx, who died as a consequence of an activity he strongly advocated, with Euell Gibbons, who advocated the health benefits of eating pine cones and died of stomach cancer. For this generalization to be made, there would have to be an XP involving Jim Fixx in which his authorship of books about jogging would play a relevant part.

A second and very important source of indexing features involves using the anomaly that an XP is trying to explain. The Jim Fixx XP, for example, is indexed under Good Physical Condition because the anomaly implicit in this XP is that people in good physical condition do not normally drop dead. Jim Fixx's good physical condition does not causally participate in the explanation of his death, nor is it a primary characterization of the event. It is, however, an important index because it is what allows the program to find the explanation given Swale's story. The program does not yet know how to initially choose this final category of indices when storing an XP but it can use them to find an XP that has been indexed manually.

USING A NEW XP

Once a new XP is installed, it can be used in future processing. For example, when we give the program a story similar to Swale's death, it applies the XP learned from the Swale story:

Input:
>   Last Chance Louie was a racehorse.
>   He won the Kentucky Derby.
>   He died a week later.

Output from processing that Last Chance Louie died a week after his victory:

Integrating LAST–CHANCE–LOUIE's DEATH into memory

Trying to link LAST–CHANCE–LOUIE's DEATH to LAST–CHANCE–LOUIE's active scripts.

The fact LAST–CHANCE–LOUIE's DEATH will be stored as the DEATH line in LAST–CHANCE–LOUIE's RACE–HORSE–LIFE

Temporal anomaly detected:
LAST–CHANCE–LOUIE's DEATH occurs abnormally early in RACE–HORSE–LIFE

Trying to pull up XPs indexed by the anomaly
Pulled up FIXX–XP-1, XP–EARLY–DEATH–FROM–RUN–OVER, XP–EARLY–DEATH–FROM–ILLNESS

Seeing if one of these XPs is relevant

FIXX–XP-1 is accepted

EXAMPLE OF THE EXPLANATION PROCESS

The following section traces how the program explains Swale's untimely death.

- Use routine search to find XPs concerning premature death in animals.
- Find *death from illness* and *hit by a car.*
- These XPs can't apply, since Swale wasn't sick, and wasn't a small animal. The failures are severe enough to abandon these XPs without trying to tweak.
- Look for XPs indexed by unusual features of Swale. Racehorses are in excellent physical condition; death + excellent condition pulls up the Jim Fixx XP.
- Swale wasn't a jogger, so the Fixx XP can't apply. Try to tweak.
- Since the problem was invalid-theme, try the repair strategy *substitute alternative theme.* Swale's known themes are horse-race and eat-oats.
- The horse-race theme is selected because it supports his running, and the tweaked XP is *Since Swale had a heart defect, the exertion from running overtaxed his heart.*
- Check whether the XP is believable. It's reasonable, but since the heart defect can't be confirmed, continue looking for other XPs.
- No more regular XPs are found, so try folkloric explanations of death. Pull up the old wives' tale *too much sex will kill you.*
- Racehorses aren't allowed to have sex while racing. But they do have a lot of sex when they retire to the stud farm. Try to tweak.

- Since the problem was that the death happened too early, try the tweaking strategy *substitute anticipation.* Could Swale have died just from thinking about life on the stud farm?
- The new XP is unconvincing. Try tweaking to strengthen support.
- To strengthen, use the strategy *find connecting XP.* Effects of thinking about sex are distraction, excitement, and depression (if you're thinking about not having it). Distraction can be linked to death by the XP *death from stepping in front of a bus.* Excitement can cause *death by heart-attack.* Depression can cause *death from suicide.*
- The three XPs are possible, but still not convincing. Search continues.
- No more XPs are found.
- Each of the new explanations depends on conditions which can't be confirmed. Since the Fixx XP was the possibility located most directly by the searcher, the tweaked version of Fixx is accepted as the most likely explanation.
- The causally-significant feature Fixx and Swale shared was that they did physical exertion. The XP is generalized to apply to people who have an exertion theme.
- The generalized XP is installed in memory for future use.

CONCLUSIONS

In this chapter we have described a program that creates explanations for an unusual event by referring back to previous experiences and adapting the explanations that worked in the past to the new situation. The program proceeds by detecting anomalies, searching for relevant explanation patterns in memory, applying those patterns if they fit, fixing them if they don't fit, and installing the results back in memory for processing future stories. The SWALE program has addressed, in a concrete way, the issues that arise at each of these stages.

SWALE is a program still in its infancy. It currently works on one input story and produces a handful of new explanations. Its library of explanation patterns is tiny, as are its library of repair strategies, its library of search strategies, and its rule database. Because of this small knowledge base the program's behavior is quite predictable. Nevertheless, we are quite excited about the preliminary results. We believe that the basic structure for the program is sound; we think we know now what form the knowledge representation will take. The next step is to develop a much larger knowledge base, so that the program will be more flexible and can produce surprises. We have already seen glimpses of this behavior; at one point the program did not represent the difference between running and walking and unexpectedly conjectured that SWALE might have died from the exertion of walking over to his oats trough. Although we considered this explanation a bug, which we fixed by making the representation more detailed, it is not completely incomprehensible. Once the program has more old explanations and knowledge to play with, we hope that it will often go beyond producing explanations we designed it to produce. Our goal is to develop a program that can produce interesting, creative explanations that none of us have ever thought of before.

References

Abelson, R., Carroll, J. (1965). Computer Simulation of Individual Belief Systems, *American Behavioral Scientist, 8,* pp. 24–30.

Carbonell, J. (1979). *Subjective Understanding: Computer Models of Belief Systems,* Ph.D. Thesis, Yale University.

Colby, K. M. (1973). The Structure of Belief Systems, Schank, R.C., and Colby, K.M. eds., *Computer Models of Thought and Language,* W.H. Freeman and Company, San Francisco, pages 251–286.

Colby, K.M., & Smith, D.C. (1969). Dialogues between Humans and an Artificial Belief System, Walker, D.E. and Norton, L.M. eds., *Proceedings of the International Joint Conference on Artificial Intelligence,* IJCAI, Boston.

Cullingford, R. (1978). *Script Application: Computer Understanding of Newspaper Stories,* Ph.D. Thesis, Yale University. Research Report #116.

DeJong, G. (1979). *Skimming Stories in Real Time: An Experiment in Integrated Understanding,* Ph.D. Thesis, Yale University.

Dreyfuss, H.L. (1972). *What Computers Can't Do: A Critique of Artificial Reason,* Harper & Row, New York.

Hammond, K. (1984). *Indexing and Causality: The organization of plans and strategies in memory.* Technical Report 351, Yale University Department of Computer Science.

Kogos, F. (1970). *Book of Yiddish Proverbs,* Poplar Books, Secaucus, NJ.

Lebowitz, M. (1980). *Generalization and Memory in an Integrated Understanding System,* Ph.D. Thesis, Yale University.

Lytinen, S. (1984). *The Organization of Knowledge In a Multi-lingual, Integrated Parser,* Ph.D. Thesis, Yale University. Research Report #340.

Newell, A., & Simon, H. (1972). *Human Problem Solving,* Prentice-Hall, Englewood Cliffs, NJ.

Restak, R.M. (1979). *The Brain: The Last Frontier,* Doubleday, Garden City, NY.

Rieger, C. (1975). Conceptual Memory and Inference, *Conceptual Information Processing,* North-Holland, Amsterdam.

Schank, R.C. (1972). *Conceptual Dependency: A Theory of Natural Language-Understanding, Cognitive Psychology, 3/4,* pp. 552–631.

Schank, R.C. (1975). *Fundamental Studies in Computer Science,* Volume 3: *Conceptual Information Processing,* North-Holland, Amsterdam.

Schank, R.C. (1982). *Dynamic Memory: A Theory of Learning in Computers and People,* Cambridge University Press.

Schank, R.C., & Abelson, R. (1977). *Scripts, Plans, Goals and Understanding,* Lawrence Erlbaum Associates, Hillsdale, New Jersey.

Schank, R.C., & Riesbeck, C. (1981). *Inside Computer Understanding: Five Programs with Miniatures,* Lawrence Erlbaum Associates, Hillsdale, New Jersey.

Searle, J.R. (1980). Minds, Brains and Programs, *The Behavioral and Brain Sciences, 3,* pp. 417–424.

Shortliffe, E.H., Axline, S.G., Buchanan, B.G., Merigan, T.C., & Cohen, N.S. (1973). An Artificial Intelligence Program to Advise Physicians Regarding Antimicrobal Therapy, *Computers and Biomedical Research, 6,* pp. 544–560.

Turing, A.M. (1963). Computing Machinery and Intelligence, Feigenbaum, E.A., and Feldman, J. eds., *Computers and Thought,* McGraw-Hill, New York.

Weizenbaum, J. (1976). *Computer Power and Human Reason: From Judgement to Calculation,* Freeman, San Francisco.

Wilensky, R. (1978). *Understanding Goal-Based Stories,* Ph.D. Thesis, Yale University. Research Report #140.

Winograd, T. (1972). *Understanding Natural Language,* Academic Press, New York.